LOOKING FOR APHRODITE

by

David Price Williams

Paperback: ISBN 978-1-909276-51-2
Hardback: ISBN 978-1-909276-59-8
eBook: ISBN 978-1-909276-60-4

Book design by: Ian Sharman

COVER PICTURE:
Ludovisi Aphrodite.
Roman copy after a Greek original of the Knidian Aphrodite.
National Museum of Rome

www.markosia.com

First Edition

CONTENTS

There have been several notable moments in the history of mankind where some single event, usually catastrophic, has come to symbolize what was subsequently realized to be a paradigm shift in human culture – perhaps the burning of the Parthenon by the Persians in 480 BC, a disaster which ushered in the Golden Age of Athens and the world's first democracy; maybe the sacking of Rome by the Visigoths in 410 AD, seen by many to be the end of civilization and the start of the Dark Ages; or the Battle of Manzikert in 1071, heralding the arrival of the Turks in Anatolia and the beginning of the end for the Christian Byzantine Empire; or 1815, the defeat of Napoleon at Waterloo presaging the dawn of modern Europe.

But, with one remarkable exception, there has never been anything as iconic as an individual statue, let alone a female statue, which can aptly be said to personify the birth of a whole revolution in human imagination and universal ambition. That exception is the Aphrodite of Knidos. Sculpted by the gifted Greek artist Praxiteles in his studio in Athens somewhere about 350 BC, the Aphrodite came to personify the emancipation of society from prudery, prejudice and parochialism, to herald the ending of the ancient world and to chart the birth of the new all-embracing philosophies and ideals of Hellenism, many of which are with us to this day, though this event is more usually characterized by the military exploits of that world-bestriding hero Alexander the Great and the spread of a new vision of freedom of thought and commerce. The Praxiteles Aphrodite, commonly known as the *Knidia*, was so radical and innovative not only because she was said to be the most beautiful and natural representation of the female form ever created, but especially because she was sculpted undraped. For the first time a female deity had been carved totally unclothed, revealed in all her astounding beauty.

The Knidians had bought her to commemorate the relocation of their own citizenry to a brand new city which they had built at a spectacular site on the coast of south western Caria, in what today is southern Turkey. She was to make a radical statement in celebration of their entry into that brave new world of Hellenism and the consequent opening of a new epoch of internationalism. Maybe initially they had intended her to be exclusively a new patron goddess for their city; perhaps they had hoped to revere and worship her modestly and privately as their own cultic manifestation. But she didn't remain like that. She became one of the most famous statues of all time, if not THE most famous, and to this day there is none that has achieved anywhere near that same universal acclaim.

Pliny the Elder, the Roman encyclopaedist, who famously expired in the eruption of Vesuvius in AD 79, wrote:-

> *(It was through Praxiteles') fame as a worker of marble that he surpassed even himself. Superior to all his works, and indeed those of the whole world, is the Aphrodite, which many people have sailed to Knidos in order to see. For with that statue Praxiteles made Knidos famous. Her shrine is completely open, so that it is possible to observe the image of the goddess from every side; she herself, it is believed, favored its being made that way.*
>
> Pliny: *Naturalis Historia*

A further description of the actual statue comes from Lucian of Samosata, writing in the following century:-

> *When we had exhausted the charms of the gardens we passed on into the temple itself. The goddess stands in the middle of it, her beautiful form made of Parian marble. Her lips are slightly parted in a smile of proud contempt. Nothing hides her beauty, which is entirely exposed, other than a furtive hand veiling her modesty. The art of the sculptor has succeeded so well that it seems the solid nature of the marble has shed its hardness to mold the grace of her limbs.*
>
> Pseudo-Lucian: *Erotes*

Apparently people travelled from everywhere in the Mediterranean to gaze at this remarkable representation of the Aphrodite of Knidos, Goddess of Love.

But that was not all. Innumerable copies were made of the Knidian Aphrodite by a phalanx of sculptors from Spain to Syria and in that way she became the most celebrated version of the feminine figure ever crafted. The original was said to be slightly larger than life size, but there are unmistakable copies of her, in all sizes, found from one end of the Old World to the other, some as the original in the totally nude form, others with a drape around her midriff, perhaps the most well-known of which is of course the Venus de Milo, in the Louvre museum in Paris.

But what of Knidos, this city whose forward-thinking Hellenistic inhabitants bought the original of the Aphrodite from Athens over 2,300 years ago? What happened to that? And what happened to the famed sculpture itself which changed the whole perception of art and the female form for ever? And is there any evidence remaining of the temple in which the statue had once been openly exhibited, as described by Pliny, so that, as he said, her beauty could be observed on every side?

This narrative seeks to answer those questions. It charts the exploration of ancient Knidos, conducted during an archaeological excavation almost fifty years ago. And at the same time it's an exploration that launched the author, who was present at the dig, on a trajectory along which he too experienced a revolution in his own way of life, just as the Knidians had done all that time ago, rejoicing in their famed statue.

PRONUNCIATION

The Turkish words in the text are written with the Turkish phonetic alphabet used commonly in Turkish orthography. The individual letters have the following values:-

C is pronounced J, as in Cengis = Jengis or Cumhur = Jumhur

Ç is pronounced Ch, as in Çayhane = Chayhane

I without a dot is pronounced Er as in Yazıköy = Yazerkoy

Ğ in the middle of a word is pronounced silently as in olacağım =olaja'erm

Ş is pronounced Sh, as in Şerefe = Sherefe

Ü is pronounced Oo, as in Gün = Goon

David is transcribed in Turkish as Deyvit

I have used the Turkish spelling of Knidos rather than the Anglicised version Cnidus except where it is used directly or indirectly from quotations. Actually, the local Turks, not liking two consonants together, pronounce the name as 'Kinidos'.

CHAPTER ONE

YAZID GOES TO CHURCH

The sea is a boundless expanse whereon great ships look like minute specks; naught but the heavens above and the waters beneath. Trust it little. Fear it much.

'Amru bin al-'As, the Arab conqueror of Egypt

It is a cold, winter's afternoon in the Eastern Mediterranean. The low-angled sun catches the broad lateen sails of a mighty fleet of dhows sailing north-west of the Island of Cyprus from Syria towards the coast of Asia Minor, driven across a heavy sea by a spirited southeast wind. The year is 52 in the New Calendar. The landfall of this gargantuan armada will signal plunder, destruction and death.

Half a century earlier, way to the south among the deserts of Arabia, Islam had made its first appearance at the time-honoured polytheistic cult centre of Mecca which was focussed on an ancient Nabatean temple known as the Ka'ba. One thousand Arab gods were said to inhabit the life-giving waters of the nearby sacred spring of Zamzam, among them the great mother goddess Allat. The well at Mecca had been administered from time immemorial by the Quraysh tribe, yet it was from the clan of these cultic guardians that a theological luminary was to emerge who was to transform not just Mecca but the whole World. His name was Muhammad, The Praiseworthy One, of the family of Hashim.

Muhammad's visions of the One God Allah caused consternation among the Quraysh, in particular those who profited from administering the Ka'ban faction at Mecca. They forced Muhammad and his followers to flee in fear of their lives from Mecca to the small northern town of Yathrib, later to be named Medinat un-Nabi, the City of the Prophet, in honour of Mohammad.

1

The date was 622 AD, the date traditionally ascribed by Moslems to the foundation of Islam - the 'surrendering' to the One God. Allowing for adjustments for lunar months, fifty or so years from that date in the Christian calendar makes the date the fleet of ships with the lateen sails were sailing to the coast of Asia Minor as 672 AD.

The deadly armada is manned by Arabs. The ships belong to Mu'awiyah, one time Islamic military governor of Syria, now one of the first Caliphs and the founder of the Umayyad Dynasty and scourge of the Byzantine Emperors in Constantinople. Some twenty or more years earlier, in 649, Mu'awiyah himself had already led a successful 1,700-ship invasion fleet against the Island of Cyprus. Its Byzantine capital, Constantia, had been sacked and its population massacred to a man. Five years later, he did the same thing to the Christians on the island of Rhodes. Now he was sending his son, Yazid ibn Sufyan, named for his grandfather, as commander of a naval force raiding even further west towards the Aegean Sea, against the Byzantine settlements on the Island of Chios and the mainland city of Smyrna, today's Izmir. This is where our story begins, or perhaps it should it be, ends.

To reach the Aegean, Yazid's fleet must first pass through the treacherous seas off Cape Crio, the south western tip of Asia Minor where an elongated rocky peninsula protrudes abrasively into the sea lanes between the Christian Islands of Rhodes and Kos. As it attempts to round the point, the fleet, like so many before it, will probably have to heave-to for a short while to await favourable winds in the ancient harbour at Cape Crio itself, a temporary safe haven which had once served the mighty classical city of Knidos.

Let us imagine the twenty-seven year old Yazid that day in 672 AD. Yazid's fleet, built of cedar wood from the snowy mountains of the Lebanon, their planking stitched together with leather thongs and covered with pitch from the banks of the Euphrates, has arrived in the old commercial harbour of Knidos. Since the time of Alexander the Great one thousand years earlier,

Knidos had been a well-known and prosperous city, but the last one hundred years or so had witnessed the buildings of this once wealthy *entrepôt* smashed into rubble by a whole rash of earthquakes, its inhabitants ravaged by bubonic plague and its great monuments left abandoned in ruins on the hillside. News of the devastating assaults led by Yazid's father had already sent the population of Knidos plummeting further as its maritime economy collapsed, its eastern trading prospects terminally blighted and then dashed by the depredations of these Arab raids. And now the feared Arabs had come west again, like the ultimate curse of God. This must have been the last straw. By the time Yazid arrived the people living at Knidos must have dwindled to almost nothing.

Let us follow Yazid as he climbs, for climb he surely did, up from the ancient marble quayside to view what remained of what had been a great metropolis. He must have looked out across an urban wilderness, a once thriving city in terminal decay, its temples supplanted with churches which themselves have been torn apart and tumbled in the tectonic upheavals that had recently shaken and shivered the whole region. Classical pillars lie scattered about on the ground like so many groves of felled trees. The huge terrace walls, once retained by rows of marble blocks, have burst with such ferocity that their surmounting monumental buildings have debouched onto the terraces below in a cataclysm of destruction. Houses and villas lie burnt and already overgrown, their contents long since pillaged and picked over. Its civic buildings have collapsed and been plundered decades ago. And on this day, the day of Yazid's arrival, the very last inhabitants who had been eking out a pauper's existence in temporary rubble hovels have already fled over the mountains the moment they saw the lateen sails on the horizon near Rhodes. They will never return. No-one ever will, not to live.

Walking up the stepped streets of this ghost town, the paving stones worn with hundreds of years of use, Yazid arrives at the Christian Cathedral of Knidos. The roof has collapsed, but the sturdy hemi-domes of the triple apses remain. He clambers over the rubble and enters what is left of the chancel, the church's Holy of Holies. There, among those sacred stones, remembering the eternal efficacy of that consecrated sanctuary, the thin odour of incense perhaps still lingering in the coolness, he bends down and scratches his name on the floor, asking Almighty God to have mercy on him. The once illustrious city – with over one thousand years of celebrated history - lies dead beneath his feet. His graffiti completed, he walks down the ancient terraces from the church back to his ship to weigh anchor and sail away into ignominy. Indeed ignominy was assuredly to be his lot for it was this same Yazid who a few short years later participated in the martyrdom of Hussein ibn Ali, grandson of the Prophet, at the Battle of Karbala and in so doing initiated the deadly schism between Shia and Sunni Muslims which still ferociously tears Islam asunder today. But that's another story.

Yazid's act of troubled piety graphically illuminates what was probably the very last day in the life of ancient Knidos, in that late winter of 672 AD. We know that Yazid climbed those steps up to the ruined cathedral, and we know he wrote his name there, because almost 1,300 years later we uncovered his graffiti on the chancel floor, scratched in an arcane, kufic script:

Allahum ghufur Yazid ibn Sufyan

"O God pardon Yazid ibn Sufyan!"

At Knidos, there is nothing later; the city drew its last breath that day.

CHAPTER TWO

IN THE BEGINNING

Hippodamus, son of Euryphon, a native of Miletus, invented the art of planning and laid out the street plan of many cities.

Aristotle

If Yazid presided over the final days of Knidos, how and when had it all begun? How did such an illustrious city come to be built on this isolated, wild and wind-swept promontory? To discover the answer to that, we have to go back in time, beyond the turn of the millennia into the bright day and murky night of ancient history, back beyond Imperial Rome to the time when the Greeks were paramount in this part of the Mediterranean.

At the beginning of the 4th century BC, the original community of Knidos was a small, undefended agricultural settlement some distance to the east. It lay on the edge of the only agriculturally suitable plain in the middle of a finger of land in south western Asia Minor. It had probably been established there for hundreds of years, since the Bronze Age in fact, peopled by a mixed population of Carians, the indigenous peoples of the region, and Dorians, Greeks from across the Aegean with whom Knidians had by now long since intermarried. But, around about the mid 300's BC, the good burghers of Knidos resolved to reposition their city. Taking a conscious decision to decamp, the *boulé* (council) of Knidos chose to move their new metropolis 35 kilometres west, to the tip of the long, rugged peninsula sticking out into the Aegean Sea around which all ships in the East Mediterranean must navigate. Here they were going to connect an adjacent offshore island to the mainland, thus creating two harbours, one either side of the newly built isthmus. The reason why they were doing this was because a new era was dawning, an era of maritime trade, and they wanted to be in the mainstream of this change, to be part of the new world of Hellenism and part of the new financial order it brought with it. Some of the cities they knew had already made similar moves - Rhodes for example, and Halicarnassus not very far away on the other side of the Ceramic Gulf. At the proposed new site Knidos would have sheltered harbours, a haven from the dreaded Boreas, the North wind, which brought cold and rain from as far as the Black Sea and the steppes of Southern Russia. And it was going to be protected by huge monumental walls which would encompass the hills overlooking the sea. And with a civic flourish, they adopted a new style of city planning too which was to make Knidos one of the finest city-scapes in the Mediterranean. The tip of the peninsula, also known as Cape Crio, was going to be invested with a Hippodamian Grid.

The plan the Knidian masons adopted was invented by one Hippodamus who hailed from the Ionian city of Miletus. He was born around 500 BC and came to be certainly the greatest, if not the very first, urban planner of his day. He is also credited with being an architect, physician, mathematician, meteorologist and *penseur extraordinaire*, but town planning seems to have been his real forte. Aristotle, who never met the man, believed him to be an eccentric if talented fop.

"Some people thought he carried things too far," wrote the metaphysical philosopher, "with his long hair, expensive ornaments, and the same cheap, warm clothing worn winter and summer."

Whoever gave him that idea we shall never know, since Aristotle was born over one hundred years after Hippodamus. Nevertheless, Hippodamus had excelled himself by redesigning the Piraeus, the harbour out-port of Athens, which he had done at the request of no less a politico than Pericles. His concept of urban philosophy was to create a city which was a grid iron in plan, with straight streets running parallel to each other at even intervals, and cross streets, also at even intervals, running perpendicular to them. This might seem relatively simple, a sort of Manhattan of the ancient east, except

6

that there had been absolutely no town planning anywhere up to this point, and anyway his urban oeuvre was well over two thousand years earlier than New York. It's true that he is credited with more plans than he was possibly able to execute, in the sense that some, like Rhodes, happened after he had died. But there is no doubting that he was a major influence on the way new cities should be laid out, and more than a century after his birth, Knidos implemented Hippodamus' basic idea for their new metropolis. But as we shall see, the Knidians set about the 'Hippodamus thing' with even more panache than their classical neighbours.

Looking at Cape Crio today, the chosen site for their new city, it is not difficult to see why they selected it sitting as it does on this corner of the Mediterranean. But in its day it was an audacious notion and required a considerable imagination and courage to design. The site consists of an island of unusual ruggedness. On its south side, the side facing away from the city, the island, called by some Triopium, is a succession of sheer, forbidding cliffs rising straight out of the sea, with the great volcano of Nisyros not ten nautical miles distant, and the long rocky island of Tilos a bit further to the south. The sea is deep just off the island and the contrary winds that gust around the point nearly always cause the surface of the sea to boil in a squally spindrift. To the landward side, the island slopes, steeply at first, then at a shallower angle towards what was once a deep race between the island and the promontory.

The mainland, meanwhile, is a continuation of the mountain range that begins west of present-day Datça, rising to over three thousand feet and then diminishing in a series of precipitous hills to the tip of the peninsula. Today, the site has largely returned to its former uninhabited state, and to some the place has assumed its original barren and forbidding appearance.

The concept in the mind of the engineers who opted for this location was to join the middle of the island to the mainland with a man-made isthmus across the centre of the intervening straits, a distance across the narrows of about one hundred and fifty metres. By extending moles from the mainland and from the island at either end of the channel, it would thus be possible to create two deep water harbours, the one on the west rather smaller, with a narrower entrance, more susceptible to storm swells, and the one on the east slightly more open and considerably larger, with a central entrance facing towards the island of Rhodes. The thinking was that shipping from the east would pass north of the point of Rhodes, or setting sail from Rhodes itself, bear under the Isle of Symi, across the Gulf of Doris between Nisyros and Knidos, passing very close to Cape Crio before turning north into the Gulf of Kos and the Ceramic Gulf to Halicarnassus and thence into the Aegean. Not for nothing can it be said that Knidos was to be built for maritime protection exactly at the junction of the Aegean Sea and the Mediterranean proper. Incidentally, to sail the alternative route into the central Aegean, passing the southern tip of Rhodes and towards Carpathos and Crete is to court disaster. The Carpathian Sea is one of the worst I have ever had the misfortune to sail in. Like Halicarnassus, only more so, Knidos is difficult to get to by land, but very much more easily reached reach by sea.

The designers of the new city took every advantage of the spectacular local topography. With the Hippodamian grid very much in vogue, they decided to apply it here. However, unlike the Piraeus, or Rhodes, or Miletus, which were on a level plane, the Knidian grid-iron was to be elevated to around twenty degrees. In a truly remarkable feat of engineering, huge artificial ashlar-blocked stone terraces were erected, one above another, filled in behind with the spoil created by cutting into the slope at the back of each terrace, row by row, up the hillsides on the mainland and facing them on the island, set out like two gigantic opposing straight rows of stadium seats, one on either side of the newly built harbours. Along these terraces were built horizontal roadways, linked at regular intervals by stepped streets, to create a series of regular, tiered city blocks. At the crucial position on the mainland just above the western Commercial Harbour, a three-width block was planned as the focus of the city.

Incredibly, the whole site was to be defended by a massive stone wall, probably twelve to twenty metres in height, running down the side of the island from near the present lighthouse, across the mouth of the western harbour, along the mole and up the precipitous slope of the ridge behind the site to an acropolis at the top of the mountain where the planners conceived to build a huge block-walled fortress, a redoubt of monumental proportions, from where the city wall ran down the slope to the city's eastern gate, around the commercial harbour and up the eastern slope of the island. The wall was punctuated with no fewer than sixty one protruding towers. When one considers the vast numbers of masonry blocks required both for the defensive wall and the city terraces, and their immense weight and the physical difficulties of parts of the site, this was an extraordinary accomplishment for the 4th century BC. And all this was to be done before any buildings were to be erected inside the city proper. The terrace wall blocks were to be laid in pseudo-isodomic, orthogonal courses (variously sized but neatly horizontal), but left with a *rustica* outer finish, a rough 'countrified' facing which when complete created the appearance of a series of 'natural' rock outcrops, each one above and behind the other. On these artificial scarps the formal, often pillared, buildings were to be laid out tier upon tier, giving the whole as seen by an approaching vessel a deliberately dramatic, ascending perspective of classic facades. Also, for the inhabitants of the mainland, the view over the sea and the adjacent islands would be idyllic.

All that was envisaged was accomplished. The mighty terrace walls were erected, the blocks being hewn from immense quarries on the eastern side of the city. The protective breakwaters were thrown up in the sea across the narrows. To see the one leading from the island defending the eastern harbour is to appreciate the scale of the work. Some of the blocks are the size of small trucks and must weigh many tons. The blocks are truly massive, especially in the moles and the upper theatre. It was as if they had been placed there by giants, which in a way they had …cultural giants, at least.

Thus was the city planned and completed, and, like Halicarnassus, the people of Knidos, the demes and the clans and the families of the peninsula, moved into their new mercantile home. The age of intercontinental sea traffic had begun. The date – around 350 BC; Knidos was to enjoy just over one thousand years of sometimes palpable and sometimes precarious prosperity, an ebb and flow of security and distress as the centuries unfolded, until that fateful day in the 7th century AD when Yazid ibn Sufyan finally signed its death certificate on the marble stones of the chancel floor of the Byzantine Cathedral.

The investigation of those one thousand years was to lead to my own personal exploration. The expedition which I joined in 1969 as a surveyor, planning trenches, drawing sections, and laying out areas for the teams to dig, for me ushered in a whole new way of life.

CHAPTER THREE

GETTING THERE

*Your lost friends are not dead, but gone before; advanced a stage
or two upon that road which you must travel in the steps they trod.*

Aristophanes

I had been invited to join the excavations at Knidos by Mark, the Expedition's assistant director, in the basement coffee lounge of the Institute of Archaeology in London one showery afternoon during the previous winter. They needed a field surveyor, he said, someone who could make plans and sections of the excavated areas ready for publication. I was at that time making a living by drawing book illustrations for archaeological publications to get me through my PhD so I suppose it made some sense. But I had no idea about the site; in fact I didn't have much experience of field survey either but I was sure I could pick it up as I went along; at least, that's what I suggested at the time.

So that was why, the following June, I was negotiating my way to Knidos at the beginning of the dig, on my own. I had not expected it to be all that easy either, Knidos being so far off the beaten track, but I followed Mark's advice on how to get there. I spoke not a word of Turkish, so the notion of trying to make my destination understood locally had caused me some anxiety, to say the least. But I did fly, for the very first time as it transpired, from London to Athens and buoyed up by that excitement next evening I took a ferry from Piraeus to Rhodes, sharing a cabin with a rather disagreeable gnome of a mathematics teacher from Kos. He disembarked there at dawn amid a clangour of dockside paraphernalia. The ship had then throbbed out of the harbour again and south across the Ceramic Gulf. At eight o'clock in the morning I went on deck. The sun was already quite high in a cloudless sky and for the first time in my life I beheld the azure blue of the Aegean Sea in all its beauty. What had I been doing in cold, rainy Britain all this time, I thought?

As the ship approached the end of the Reşadiye Peninsula I saw the forbidding mountain landscape of Turkey for the first time, tier behind tier of grey silhouetted peaks reaching skyward from the sea. The air was fresh, with a light breeze, and the white waves danced away from the prow. The open foredeck was cluttered with students in sleeping bags, surrounded by a jumble of back-packs. The bright sunlight had woken them, but they had not yet risen. One or two were idly smoking. The ship passed very close to Cape Crio and Knidos as it rounded the Peninsula on its final leg to Rhodes. I could even see the tents on the beach which were to be my home, and just make out the outline of the lower theatre. But of course we could not stop; I had to cross into Turkey through a port of entry, and that would have to be Marmaris via Rhodes. I remember a song that was playing on a tinny tape recorder. I had never heard it before and it was some time before I discovered what it was. But it was to become the talisman of my new life, my 'Knidos music' - Judy Collins singing 'Both Sides Now'. Every time I hear it I am transported back to that morning passing Knidos to Rhodes. And every time I make the journey the words still haunt me – "It's life's illusions I recall, I really don't know life at all!"

So I had arrived in Rhodes that same mid-morning. There was someone touting hotel rooms on the quayside and I accepted. In fact, he was the owner of a recently-built, small hotel in the new part of the city, in Kolokotroni Street, very close to St. John's Gate through which I had to pass into the Old Crusader town that afternoon to organise my ferry from Rhodes to Marmaris for the following day, a task which turned out to be far more difficult than I had imagined. At this time in the 20th century, with the calamitous rule of the Colonels in full swing in Greece promoting a rife and morose anti-Anatolian jingoism, Turkey as a country, and by definition Marmaris as a port, seemed not to exist in the minds of most Rhodians, so that theoretically it could not even be a topic of conversation, let alone be reached by sea. They had collectively blotted it out of their imagination, despite the huge land mass across the water that could clearly be seen from the northern end of the city.

For some time, the only answer I got to my questions about a ferry, assuming anyone was willing to talk about it, was:

"Is'a no possible!"

Many were not even prepared to go that far, preferring to purse their lips, narrow their eyes, grimace and to raise their stubble-laden chins in an ultimate gesture of silent and defiant negativity.

This geographical charade went on for most of the afternoon with every travel agent I went into. Finally, when I was near my wit's end, a man sitting at the back in one of the agencies beckoned me to follow him outside and motioning forwards we walked together briskly up one of the old Crusader streets passed shops selling hundreds of miniature Greek windmills, acres of lace work and ceramic versions of Greek theatrical masks for the tourists from the big cruise ships to buy who came to visit. We ended up in a shop which sold wines and spirituous liqueurs in lurid coloured bottles. It turned out that the family which ran this emporium, of which it seems he was the son, were originally Turkish Greeks that had left Smyrna in 1923 during the exchange of population following the Treaty of Lausanne. Anyway, almost fifty years later they still had relatives in Turkey and crossed over regularly. A couple of phone calls later and a sea captain appeared and said he was crossing early the next day. Some crumpled drachmae changed hands and he told me where to be in the harbour at seven the next morning.

I duly appeared at his boat, which turned out to be a small converted naval vessel, and after he had cast off we set out across the Gulf to Marmaris. It was a fine day with clear skies and a deep sapphire sea, the spray breaking into a bright white spume at the prow. The Greek flag, with its white cross and stripes on a pale blue background, flew jauntily from the flag staff. After an hour or so the mainland of Turkey loomed out of the morning sea mist, becoming more and more rugged and daunting as we came close in to the shore. So rocky and threateningly forbidding were its cliffs and peaks that I could not imagine who could possibly live in this wild country. The captain broke out the Turkish flag on the stay, a sinister blood red with white crescent moon and star. I really began to wonder where I was going; it seemed so far from any kind of civilisation, and so alien. But finally the less inhospitable harbour of Marmaris hove into view at the far end of a narrow inlet surrounded by towering mountains and we moored near the tiny customs house on the quayside. In those days, before mass tourism and endless hotels along the sea front, Marmaris was a small fishing village with only a couple of streets opening off the *maydan*, the village square, overlooked by the unkempt ruins of a 16th century castle.

The captain showed me into the customs building where I at once began to ask nervously about transport to Knidos. The port police there were very helpful and as they stamped my passport, they pointed to a row of Ford Transit mini-buses on the corner of the square. I walked over and started mouthing my final destination. After a very short time, in fact what felt like almost immediately, some dollars changed hands and I was ushered into the back of the nearest of these minibuses, the doors were closed, and off we went without further delay; it was as though they had been waiting half the morning for me to arrive. This, I learnt, was a *dolmuş*, a shared taxi, and it was already full of passengers who, I reasoned later, must have embarked maybe an hour or more earlier and had sat patiently for the bus to fill up. I happened to be the last. Occupying all the main seats in front were leathery faced men with flat caps, rather rotund apple-cheeked women with head scarves, and a number of small children. I was given a wooden stool by the back door which as I soon found out rocked and rolled each time we went round a bend so I had to wedge myself in such a way that I didn't fall forwards every couple of minutes. I just hoped that the back doors had been properly closed otherwise I would be propelled unceremoniously into the street.

We left the village behind and started to climb slowly up a winding dirt road, higher and higher above the harbour, until Marmaris eventually disappeared from view and we were travelling in rough mountain country ever westwards – at least I hoped it was ever westwards as I had no idea where we were going or how we were going to get there. It was clearly no use asking my fellow travellers as no-one spoke any English. I tried to work out where the sun was to discover the direction, but the sun was high overhead and the twists and turns in the road made it impossible. I had to trust that the assembled villagers, I assumed that's who they were, were hoping to go the same route as me and that my initial description of the destination had been fully understood.

Periodically the mini-bus would come to a stop and one or two of the occupants would disembark. This seemed to me to be in the middle of absolutely nowhere, amid trees and scrub along the road-side. There was no sign of any habitation, no village, no farm or house – just what appeared to be an empty and craggy landscape. Other times we would be waved down and other travellers would join the party, again from what seemed equally uninhabited country, some of them carrying chickens in baskets which they kept in their laps. Now and again there was what appeared to be a field, in one case with a lone camel standing amid the stubble which gave the scene a mildly oriental flavour, but otherwise everywhere appeared to be entirely wild nature.

After about two hours of this bumpy, uncomfortable journey the road came down to the sea's edge for a short while and ran among groves of Aleppo pine trees. My spirits rose that we were arriving somewhere, but then it dived back into the hills soon afterwards and the discomfort continued. It was not until about four hours into the drive that the road straightened out and we speeded up and curved into the first village I had seen since Marmaris. This turned out to be Datça, a collection of old houses along the sea-side surrounding a small harbour filled with little fishing boats. And Datça, it transpired, was to be the end of the line for our mini-bus. Everyone got out, chickens and all, the back doors were opened and I was motioned to climb down. I didn't know where Datça was but I had arrived there in the centre of a dried out mud patch which served as the village bus station. Several other conveyances, mainly horses and carts, were lined up in the middle of this bus park. Otherwise, there was nothing. I stood with my holdall by the Transit in the middle of that warm afternoon totally unsure of what was to happen next. I quizzed the driver – Knidos? Knidos? He beckoned me over to a higgledy-piggledy clutter of small chairs and illustrated that I should take a seat. After a few minutes a glass of tea was brought to me on a little plastic saucer with two lumps of sugar. I sipped nervously and watched what was happening, trying to make some sense of the scene. I was offered a tiny cigarette from a paper packet – 'Birinci' it said on the front of the packet; "First class!"

The driver of the Transit was talking to a gaggle of men, pointing to me, and then pointing westwards. Heads nodded sagely. A small boy arrived with a brass tray which he held shoulder high by a tripod; more tea was handed around. I rose to remonstrate with the men, but the Transit driver nodded to me to sit down. It was all under control, as he seemed to understand it. After an hour or so had passed, the sun noticeably getting lower in the sky, and several more glasses of tea having been brought to me I was just becoming really anxious to know that I wouldn't be spending the night in the Datça municipal bus park when an aged light green Willys Jeep puttered into view and stopped. Smiles were exchanged all round and I was motioned into the front of this ancient conveyance. As I did so, the driver alighted and went over to drink a glass of tea. I too was brought yet more tea such that I wondered if the jeep was perhaps the first tea-driven vehicle I had come across. More time passed. More tea was drunk until the jeep driver, as though suddenly remembering why he was there, jumped into the somewhat patched driving seat and we rattled off out of Datça and into the mountains again.

The dirt road became narrower and more rutted as we climbed the slopes, with jagged peaks lacerating a sky blushing pink in the slowly setting sun. We clattered ever westwards – I was sure of that now with the sun going down in front of us – until we reached the cobbled street of a little village crowded with stone houses which I learned was Yazıköy, later to become my very own village. The driver stopped the jeep outside a miniscule café-style building and glasses of tea were handed out again and a couple of cigarettes smoked before we lurched onwards. It was getting dark by this time and the shadows of trees crowded in along what had now become a very rough single track. The jeep vibrated its slow, winding way into the dusk. I was speculating where on earth we were heading when abruptly in the headlights a classical polygonal marble wall appeared and fell behind, then another and another, with pieces of fallen, carved stonework lying about in the undergrowth. This, I later learned, was the necropolis of Knidos and my spirits rose that we were arriving at an archaeological focus of some description out here in the wilderness. The driver pointed in front and shouted 'Kinidos' over the noise and way in the distance I could make out the dark reflection of the sea and some small points of light. A few bumpy minutes later we arrived in a cloud of dust and I found a group of men seated watching a film being projected onto the back of what was to be my drawing office. No-one looked at us. They were too intent on the film. But in no time a couple of Brits arrived out of the gloaming and I was welcomed with open arms. My Knidian experience was about to begin.

* * * *

There were few if any permanent buildings at Knidos when I arrived apart from the dig house, our drawing office and the police post. The lower orders of our own Expedition staff, of which I of course was one, were billeted under canvas, three or four to a tent, pitched on the open space of the isthmus half way between the island and the mainland. We had little if any mod cons. But the workers had even less, and spent each night sleeping among the field walls in the midst of the ruins, with their donkeys tethered nearby.

That first night I arrived at Knidos I was assigned to a tent and I was immediately warned about scorpions. 'Never mind the big ones, it's the little flesh coloured ones you have to worry about', I was told. I imagined being infested with these predatory arthropods. Unfailingly every morning I banged my desert boots on the ground to see if one had inadvertently climbed in during the night. They never had. I also made sure that I didn't turn over rocks inadvertently either; I pushed them first before putting my fingers underneath, though it has to be said that throughout the whole time I was there I never saw a scorpion alive.

But we did have some scorpion visitations. I remember one morning a young lad from the village was brought to the dig house by his father. He was in intense pain, having been bitten on the neck by one of these dreaded arachnids. He had been sleeping alongside the field walls with all the other men when a scorpion had fallen onto him and he had inadvertently swatted it in his sleep, and bang! It had inflicted the bite. The boy had the remains of this arachnid in a screw of newspaper to show anyone who might be interested. But there was nothing we could do, and indeed his dad was quite happy to leave him sitting at the house. He said it was good that the poor chap was getting the experience; it would harden him for later life! This seemed a bit harsh to me, but what could I do. So the lad sat there silently holding a cold compress to his neck all day long without a murmur until in the evening he got up and calmly walked away, apparently none the worse for his experience.

However, on one occasion, in the pitch dark in the middle of the night, one of our dig staff did get bitten and all hell was let loose. It was our very own English rose, Harriet, very well bred and very public school. Our tents were equipped with camp beds and sleeping bags, which incidentally, whenever there was a high wind, which there was every three or four days or so, would fill up with sand blown in from around the Trireme Harbour. It got into every nook and cranny and made sleeping very uncomfortable if you had not swept and shaken everything out before you collapsed into bed.

Anyway this particular night there was a vocal protest from Harriet. One of these little scorpions had got into her sleeping bag some time during the previous day and finding that it couldn't get out, had stung Harriet on the thigh.

"Oh my God," screamed one of her tent mates, "Oh my God what are we going to do. Oh you poor thing!"

Others joined in and a full-scale, high-decibel chorus of "Oh my God" developed from the interior of the tent which, of course, woke everyone else up as well.

"No! No! Please don't worry," Harriet remonstrated, "Don't let anyone worry. I'm perfectly alright."

"Oh my God," shrieked the girls from the next tent. "Oh Harriet are you OK?"

"Yes, yes! Please don't concern yourselves. I am fine, really!"

"We should do something. Why can't we do something? Someone do something. It's just awful! Truly awful!"

A collective wailing, wringing of hands and gnashing of teeth developed among the troops, except for Harriet herself who lapsed into a stalwart silence the more the brouhaha grew. In the end everyone else except Harriet was genuinely distressed by this untoward turn of events until slowly the commotion subsided and we all went back to sleep.

The next morning, Harriet was her normal restrained self. True English phlegm had won through.

* * * *

I quickly discovered that swimming was the one great fun feature that was to make my stay at Knidos more enjoyable. For the really keen, there was always the opportunity of a quick dip even before starting work at 6.00 am, though few ever took that opportunity that I know of. It was the swim in the middle of the day that I looked forward to. Lunch, such as it was after a hot and gruelling six hours in the sun, was at 12 o'clock. Then we were free until three, so a couple of hours could be whiled away with a dip or two. For some, the over-keen, this meant just a quick leap into the ancient Commercial Harbour and back to the dig house for a spot of extemporary cataloguing or recreational pottery conservation. But for me the best, and to a great extent, most private time was to be had at one of the beaches facing the Aegean, north west of the site. Here, sheltered below high cliffs, there were two or three tiny coves where, provided there was no wind or heavy swell, a relaxing and contemplative swim could be enjoyed, soothing away the tensions of the daily round.

From the dig house you could walk across the isthmus and then round the north side of the Trireme Harbour and west across the ancient wall below the main part of the site. From here, a track scrambled down to the first of the three coves, then round the point to the second and third. The middle one was my favourite. There was even a small amount of sand to lie on, albeit mixed with sea weed and eroded potsherds. It was a very private little beach, out of sight of the city and used by almost no-one.

It was here that I learned a most liberating experience - to snorkel. What an extraordinary activity that turned out to be. Within a few days I could dive from the surface and swim along the sandy bottom observing the wild-life for what felt like minutes at a time. There were fish moving in and out of the rhythmically oscillating sea-weed, not very big ones its true, but with strikingly variegated colours, and they seemed not to be afraid of me at all. But the thing which really gave me a thrill were the different tints and hues cast in the calm water by the sun – pale turquoises, pastel blues and light pinks reflecting from my outstretched hands as I swam. That, with the silent, twisting wave shadows on the sea floor was truly psychedelic, or at least as psychedelic as I had ever seen. I couldn't get enough of it, but all too soon the time would come to go back to the dig. By three o'clock we had to be back on site until six. My snorkel-induced out-of-body happening was over for another day.

There were some days of course when the wind blew too hard, the 'büyük rüzgar' the 'big wind' as the locals called it, and the breakers were pushed relentlessly into the little coves on this north west side of the peninsula. This is a wind I learned more about as time went on, a mischievous wind very well known to those who live in the Aegean, called the 'meltem', a summer wind that starts around ten in the morning and which by mid-day can become intolerably strong and dangerous. This wind funnels south and eastwards down the eastern side of the island of Kos during the late morning and hurls itself with a notable fury at the coast on this corner of the Mediterranean. At these times the sea turned a murky brown colour, breaking roughly on the sand and making swimming if not totally impossible then certainly desperately unpleasant. But at this remove I only remember the calm days, when the sea surface was flat and I could enjoy that other-worldly psychedelia.

Once during my stay we made a lunch-time boat trip. We had a volunteer on the dig, Alf, who was the son of the vice-chancellor or some such worthy at one of the universities notionally sponsoring the dig. Alf thus carried more clout with the High Command than any one of the rest of us. He was a large and fearless character and reckoned that since 'his' university was helping support the dig he had rights to things we could never have aspired to. Thus one lunch time he persuaded the High Command that he wanted to borrow the zodiac dinghy, ostensibly for a survey of the coast to the east of Knidos. I happened to be passing when he called out,

"Wanna trip to Mycenean Beach?"

Why not, I thought, and hopped into the waiting boat with another two or three of the staff. Alf gunned the outboard motor and we set off at speed across the Commercial Harbour. It was a powerful outboard; one or two of the Management liked to water-ski round and round any new yacht that came into the bay, which incidentally was a source of great irritation to us lower orders because they were wont to do this at mid-day and we had to wait for lunch until they had finished. Anyway, this meant the outboard was large and hence fast. We crossed between the two moles and bounced out across the open sea to one of the headlands in the eastern distance.

After perhaps five minutes or so Alf yanked the tiller and slewed the dinghy very competently into a quiet and very secluded cove with a light shingle beach. He cut the engine and we leapt out and pulled the dinghy onto the shore.

"Welcome to Mycenean Beach," he cried.

It was idyllic, a totally private beach with a slightly shelving profile and the sea this side of the peninsula so quiet, a gentle susurrus of wavelets running along the water's edge. Apparently a sherd of Mycenean pottery had once been found here, hence the name of the beach, which implied there had once been a Bronze Age presence near Knidos, but a very cursory look at the shore showed no further sign of any ancient merchant venturers from the Argolid that day, so we lay on the beach and dozed in the heat punctuated by the occasional dip in the warm, pristine sea. After an hour or so we all jumped in the dinghy and roared back to camp. That 'survey' was over, at least.

CHAPTER FOUR

ONE PROMISCUOUS MASS OF RUINS

*The Society of the Dilettante is a club, for which the nominal
qualification is having been in Italy, and the real one, being drunk:
the two chiefs are Lord Middlesex and Sir Francis Dashwood who
were seldom sober the whole time they were in Italy.*

Horace Walpole 1743

Various savants and august bodies have conducted archaeological
investigations at Knidos in recent centuries. The first to identify the site as
that of the ancient city and to encourage archaeological exploration here was
the Society of the Dilettante in 1812. This organisation, originally founded
in 1732 by Francis Dashwood, began life as a group of wealthy if somewhat
disreputable rakes who created a drinking club for gentlemen under the
guise of purportedly studying the Classical world. They had all been on the
Grand Tour and felt a corporate association with the ethereal past, though
their main interests were rather more inclined to the debauched present.
But by the early 19th century the Society was in fact supporting more serious
antiquarian pursuits in the Mediterranean, and the discovery of Knidos was
at least one of their successes.

It is obvious from their description of the site that rather more of the city's
remains were visible the year of the Society's visit. A certain William Leake,
a military man who visited Knidos at more or less the same time and wrote
about his experiences in 1824 in a book about his travels in Asia Minor
describes the remains of several temples, stoas, artificial terraces and three
theatres, of which certainly only one and a bit now remain. A huge amount
of stone-work had clearly been robbed soon after his time. Indeed, we have
records that only a few years later, Muhammad Ali Pasha, the ambitious
Ottoman governor of Egypt, organised several ship-loads of blocks to be

taken from Knidos and transported to Alexandria in order to build his new palace at Ras el-Tin, which he began in 1834. This is the very same building which is shown in a lithograph by the famous artist David Roberts where he features himself at an audience with 'the Viceroy of Egypt' in 1839; when you think about it, Roberts is actually sitting among the block-work from Knidos! Meanwhile, back at Cape Crio, robbing the terraces, theatre and other buildings of their stone-work to construct such a palace would seriously have depleted the already damaged ancient city and would have left it in a much more ruined state than the passage of time and sundry earthquakes must have previously wrought.

The next researches at Knidos were conducted in the late 1830's by the Royal Navy. The then hydrographer to the British Navy, Captain (later Admiral) Francis Beaufort, the one who invented the wind scale, had some twenty or so years previously sailed around the coast of Asia Minor in a captured Dutch frigate called the *Frederickssteen* and in 1817 he published a memoir of his journeys which he called the *Karamania,* an old name for southern Anatolia. In this memoir he discusses some of the ancient sites which he had examined and identified using classical texts like Strabo's 'Geographies' which he carried with him for reference. These cities of the past had of course been 'lost' to the world for over a millennium and one can feel in his narrative Beaufort's excitement at rediscovering them. It was in the early stages of his voyage that he called in briefly at Knidos, which he described in the *Karamania* as 'one promiscuous mass of ruins'. Though he said he had no time to investigate Knidos itself, after his experiences in other parts of Turkey he was considered to be a bit of a self-taught archaeologist and indeed he later successfully described a somewhat more extensive study he made of some of the Classical cities in Lycia further east.

When Beaufort was later made responsible for sending surveyors to the Eastern Mediterranean to make charts of the seas around Asia Minor for the Admiralty, to be used in case of Russian naval expansion from the Black Sea, he urged his men to locate and to map as many of the ancient sites near the coast as they could, "against the day," he rather far-sightedly wrote, "that the local people awake to their importance." The naval surveyor who actually mapped Cape Crio and Knidos on Beaufort's behalf was Lieutenant Thomas Graves, Captain of a decommissioned warship 'Meteor', a leaky 378 ton tub which had been re-named HMS Beacon. His survey, in 1838, included the whole city – the mainland, the island, the harbours, the walls, the streets, the acropolis and some of the ancillary buildings as well. It's a masterly work, with the physical features beautifully stippled to show the rugged nature of the coastline.

Twenty or so years later, between 1857 and 1859, the site was looked at again, this time in some detail, by C. T. Newton, later Sir Charles Newton, of the British Museum. He carried out excavations in various parts of ancient Knidos, and especially, he exposed a sanctuary dedicated to Demeter and Persephone high up in the north-eastern part of the city where he discovered a seated statue of what is presumed to be Demeter herself as well as a head which he interpreted as that of her daughter Persephone, more of which later. Meanwhile, in the lower part of the city he cleared part of the theatre and a Temple to Dionysus.

But his most well-known discovery was made a couple of miles east of the city, on a headland overlooking the sea. There he found a sculpture of a huge marble lion half buried in the ground which had once surmounted the roof of a monumental tomb nearby, a building which he maintained had been a victory cenotaph to the mariners who perished in a sea battle off Knidos in 394 BC. After a huge amount of effort he managed to transport this stone lion by ship to London and place it in the British Museum. It now sits in a commanding location in Norman Foster's recently built Great Court right in the centre of the building.

* * * *

Since Newton's day, there had been no further explorations at ancient Knidos until our present expedition in the late 1960's. These new investigations had perhaps from their inception been conceived with a somewhat more ethereal goal in mind, a slant towards art history rather than dirt archaeology. Those who conceived, financed and managed the whole affair were basically art historians from the USA, and maybe that characterized their aim at Knidos. I learned that previously there had been some involvement with art objects from other excavations in Greece. Perhaps for obvious reasons a focal interest in archaeology and in the people of ancient Knidos seems to have been secondary to the search for its art treasures, especially its sculpture. The choice of Knidos was of course made because of the city's association with the *Knidia*, one of the greatest sculptures ever created, by one of the greatest Classical artists who ever lived, namely Praxiteles. That in the end was undoubtedly one of the ambitions, to rediscover the lost statue of Aphrodite, and if not that, then the temple in which the statue had been displayed. Could the new excavations succeed where Beaufort, Graves, Newton and others had failed – "Knidos reveals the art discovery of the century"; that kind of thing? And remarkably as far as I am able to judge the expedition came very close to achieving this ambition.

It was suggested, no doubt conceitedly among us ignorant foot soldiers, that the excavation permit had been obtained from the Ankara Department of Antiquities only by bringing in 'trained field archaeologists' from Great Britain like the Assistant Director, Mark, who then recruited other established field workers to act as site supervisors, small finds and pottery experts, cataloguers and conservators and architects. That would include a field surveyor like me, though I openly have to admit that my own field experience at that time was extremely limited. To this so-called professional team were added all manner of flotsam and jetsam – friends, acquaintances, students and hangers-on who were brought along for politically expediency or simply personal attachment. As for the sponsors, I heard of various East Coast institutions being mentioned, but I was not involved very far up the chain of command so I really didn't know very much. As a result I tended to stick with the British contingent who without doubt rather pompously felt that they were there to give archaeological respectability to the whole affair.

The actual digging at Knidos, such as it was, was conducted by a varying number of between seventy and one hundred local men from the nearby villages on the Peninsula who, of course, lacked even the simplest understanding of what they were supposed to be doing. It was the site supervisors who kept the men in order and the assistant director who oversaw the site supervisors in what I suppose might better be classed with one or two exceptions as controlled clearance rather than forensic excavation. But labour relations were always a bit strained between the workers and the Management, not helped by the Management's apparent lack of empathy with what might be considered to be uncouth Turkish villagers, and the fact that they were overseen by a rather effete Turk, and man called Ümit. He tended to behave rather imperiously towards the diggers, hiring and firing them at will. Ümit notwithstanding, the villagers for their part, ignoring the hardships involved, saw the expedition more as a means of gaining a little cash during the slack summer months, when from the fields the wheat crop had already been harvested and in the orchards the olive crop was yet to be gathered. It was also perceived by them to be something of a lark and from my own observation they all played around relentlessly much of the time and on the whole thoroughly enjoyed themselves.

I personally had very little to do with the High Command. Being one of the two surveyors, I didn't have to report the discoveries in any trench and I didn't have to get on with any of the other eccentrics on the excavation. But it did mean that I got to know all the trenches being excavated throughout the site. It was Mark, the Assistant Director, to whom I reported and otherwise I could watch the whole social jamboree taking place without getting involved in any intricate personal politics and its proponents and opponents. In this regard I counted myself very fortunate!

Actually, one of the Inner Cabinet was a rather approachable lady called Mary. Mary was like the 'aunty' to the team, a rather laconic, unflappable lady of older years. She acted like a guardian, protector, and mother figure to the Commissariat, all rolled into one. I think I remember once someone telling me she might have been somehow related. Whatever the association, Mary prevented the over-enthusiastic Management from becoming involved with any kind of imbroglio and being battered senseless by irate creditors, workers, staff and friends alike. Mary could recognised the tell-tale signs of anyone becoming agitated - any slight involuntary quivering of the head, a combative positioning of the feet, any knotting of the brows or clenching of the fingers – which preceded an all-out show of belligerence. At the critical moment she would physically interpose herself between whoever it was and their tormentor and gently push them away from the seat of the fracas, and quietly say, like a prayer, "Don't lose your cool. I'll take care of it. OK? Just don't lose your cool."

And amazingly calm would be restored, and whatever the problem was, it would recede under Mary's soft voice and gentle persuasion. Those involved lived to fight another day.

Mary tried valiantly to supervise a trench or two as well, and approached the workers in the same casual way, speaking to them in a kind of pidgin Turkish but with a full East Coast New England accent.

"Oh, say, Moo-stafa, would you just *kaldir* the *taş* over *buraya*. *Çok mersi*," (would you lift the stone over here? Many thanks!).

"Oh Fewsi, would you just *temiz* the *toprak* from around that pillar?" (would you clean the earth from around that pillar?).

Somehow, her temperate approach worked, and the toprak would get temized. If any of us had a domestic problem, it was to Mary we would go and ask her advice rather than to The High Command, who tended to float above the melee.

Over the years since I was at Knidos, I have listened to some very unkind things spoken about those in charge of the dig. Several local Turkish archaeologists have more recently totally pooh-poohed their ideas quite publically, along with their methods and their results. A number of other American archaeologists have recounted outrageous stories which they say were circulating, of dynamite being used to remove difficult objects from the excavation, of not grasping the elements of basic techniques, and of riding rough-shod over the local people. I have to say I saw none of these things, and always have thought of such stories as more a case of them venting generalised academic spleen than anything at all realistic. Relations on the dig might have been a touch brittle now and again, as they so often are in such unfamiliar circumstances, but they were not impossible; certainly the Director of the whole operation was really encouraging to the underlings on the staff, me included. And, consciously or otherwise, the excavation gave me the opportunity to soak up all there was to learn about this beautiful site, on my own, without interference. For that I will always express my heartfelt thanks, though some over-serious Classicists have sometimes suggested that there were plenty of other sites that would have been more educational. I have to say that I don't think so!

* * * *

But I read that one or two of the Management were nothing if not controversial with other contemporary scholars. One incident, widely reported at the time, stands out amongst several contretemps that came about; this one relates to the British Museum and the material that had been brought back there in the 1850's by C. T. Newton. Some time during excavation at Knidos it was decided to look at Newton's discoveries stored in the Museum's vaults in London to see if there was anything which might relate to the current researches. There among the finds was a small head, the sculpture of a female which Newton had discovered during his excavation in the Temenos of Demeter and which I mentioned earlier. This was immediately seized upon and it was publically suggested that it was the head of Aphrodite, and if not THE Praxiteles head then one very similar to it, and it was implied that the Museum had neglected this masterpiece and left it to gather dust in a store room. A huge song and dance was made about the said sculpture, and somehow the newspapers got hold of the story and inflated it into a full-blown scandal – this all-important piece of art history which the British Museum had ignored for over a century, unrecognised and unpublished, which had been consigned to the bowels of the basement – that kind of thing.

Well, all hell broke loose. Classical scholars waded in demanding to know what was happening. But the art historians stuck to their guns. It had been carved, they said, in the same fine-grained white Parian marble favoured by Praxiteles, just like the Aphrodite would have been, and the quality of workmanship, a late classical variety, the styling of the hair and the delicate folds in the neck, all indicated that it came from the hand of the master. The experts in the Graeco-Roman Department of the Museum were embarrassed, exasperated and angry by turns, accusing all and sundry of impugning their custodianship of their international collections, not to mention their own scholarship. They pointed out that the head had come from a very specific part of the site, the Temenos of Demeter, a shrine which was well known to them, and that this location precluded the sculpture from being anything to do with the famous statue of Aphrodite.

Actually, you will remember that at the time when it was first found, Newton had tentatively identified the head as that of Persephone, the daughter to Demeter, and most contemporary specialists tended to agree with this diagnosis. Far from being ignored, as was being suggesting, the head had actually been mentioned by Newton in his excavation reports and alas, the

Museum experts intimated, their present detractors appeared not to have done the homework on the original discovery. It represented a considerable fracas while it lasted. And as for me, I was rather pleased that Knidos, which I had just had a hand in excavating, and the temple which I had just surveyed, had come to attract such public attention. I was able to bask in the warm glow of the media spotlight, albeit caused by an academic furore, which, of course, was in any case far beyond my own competence, a point I was only too eager to admit.

Alas, apart from the occasional newsy notes in the early 1970's in some annual American journals, as far as I know no-one ever went on to publish fully any of the discoveries that were made at Knidos. In a way I suppose this behaviour might be construed as a kind of archaeological inattention, since the full details of the new discoveries were never to be subjected to legitimate academic scrutiny nor were scholars able to use the findings to compare with other sites in the region. So I never did get to see my surveys, plans and sections of Knidos, of which I for one was rather proud, in print. It represented for me at least a rather damp squib, a somewhat ignominious outcome to what was otherwise undoubtedly a magnificent expedition.

CHAPTER FIVE

PEOPLING THE PAST

*There the centurion found an Alexandrian vessel bound for Italy
and put us aboard. For a good many days we made little headway,
and we were hard put to it to reach Cnidus. There the wind
continued against us.*

Book of Acts 27:7

I must have heard this verse many times when I was young, read from the
pulpit in church. Little notice did I take of it at the time, and little did the
name 'Cnidus' mean to me, at an age when an hour in a pew seemed like a
geological epoch to a small boy, a boy who preferred fishing in mountain
streams, or later, to a teenager who spent many a hapless time pondering the
incomprehensible mysteries of curvilinear country girls. Little did I know or
care then where or what 'Cnidus' was, as St Paul sailed his way westward two
thousand years ago across the eastern Mediterranean and into the pages of
theological history.

And yet, some years later, I was to experience a similar life-changing
transition as Paul had done on the road to Damascus, a conversion which
had brought him on this voyage to Rome and his destiny. But mine was not
on the road to Damascus, but at the very Knidos that Paul was passing in
'Acts'. I was to go where Paul had never gone, though he meant to, to moor in
the ancient commercial harbour and to marvel at the city-scape of this once
thriving metropolis.

Knidos of course was essentially a Greek city, designed and built with all
the panache of the many *poleis* of the Greek mainland, though probably the
inhabitants were a mixture of Greeks and indigenous Anatolian races. Now,

before I arrived in Knidos, when it came to the Classical Greeks there was nothing you could tell me about them that I didn't already know. I knew them through book learning as a priest knows his bible. I had studied Greek since I was thirteen years old, sitting in a hard pitch-pine desk in Form 3A. I'd conjugated the verb λυω in all its moods, and those tricky third declension nouns were my constant companions.

I had gone on to study more and yet more Greek at University, being introduced to Alexandrian Greek and *koine* Greek, the Greek of the New Testament. I knew everything about the ancient Greeks – Greek language, Greek grammar, Greek syntax, Homeric poems, the philosophy of Aristotle, the plays of Sophocles and Aristophanes, the debating style of Socrates, the botanical observations of Theophrastus and the cynicism of Diogenes. Of particular fascination was Xenophon's Anabasis, a history of the march through eastern Anatolia to the Black Sea after the Battle of Cunaxa, with that famous tearful moment at the end of Book Four when the ten thousand reach the sea – *Thalassa! Thalassa!* they cried. Marvellous! Also, R.E. Wytcherley, who wrote the famous book, 'How the Greeks Built Cities', was one of my professors, so I knew the architecture, the triglyphs, the metopes, the gymnasia and the Greek political institutions too. Yes, I knew it all. Everything!

I knew it all, that is, until I arrived at Knidos. Here, walking the stepped streets, looking up at the terraces, seeing the mason's initials on the walls, a bolt mark on a threshold block in the Hellenistic houses on the Island, a worn tread on a stair, or gazing out to sea, across to the Dodecanese, I suddenly became aware that I had missed one crucial, all-important ingredient in my Hellenic education, namely, the people. I had omitted to relate any of the academic elements I had amassed to anything actual, things like men and women, life and death, the marble you walk on, the water you drink, seed time and harvest, in short, everything that makes human existence tangible. I knew the theory, but none, absolutely nothing, of the practice. Although I had become educated it was an artificial world I had studied.

My book learning was totally theoretical and, I now realised, completely sterile, lacking in that essential vitality that makes studying other people, past or present, in any way worthwhile. A well head, a game carved on a paving slab, an oil lamp, a broken amphora, a fragment of graffiti, these were evidences of daily life, of a living people, infinitely more than could be found in the pages of Abbott and Mansfield's Primer of Greek Grammar. The austerity of the Aorist tense and the idiosyncrasy of the iota subscript suddenly transposed themselves into the veracity of a people going about their daily round, speaking to one another in authentic situations. The experience struck me like a lightening bolt. I was at once smitten.

* * * *

To understand Knidos in its full geographical context, the best and most spectacular views of the city are from the Acropolis, high above the north east of the site.

"Say, David, would you like to lead us in a hike up to the Acropolis tomorrow?"

This is many years later, and speaking is the leader of one of our visiting Transatlantic groups who had invited me to show them the ancient world.

"I realise David that you are probably totally unfit, not playing tennis, going to the gym or jogging and all, but, Hell, we'd really like to do it, and we'll even let you rest, and we'll wait for you half way. OK?"

"Well, if you really want to, then I'll take you. But be warned, it's a tricky ascent, very prickly, very steep, with lots of scree, and it will be hot."

"Oh that's OK. We can go real early. How about six tomorrow morning? You up by then, David?"

"The only problem with that, on a summer day like today, is that there is no wind and the heat can be extremely enervating until the breeze comes up around eight. Still, we'll go."

Next morning the expedition assembles, dressed in heavy climbing boots, woollen socks, drill trousers, safari jackets, large hats and huge back-packs full of juice, sun cream, medications, camera gear, compasses, walking poles and enough rations for a week. I appear in sandals and T shirt, carry a small bottle of water.

"We need to hike! hike! hike!" says their leader, making alternate motions upwards with her index fingers. Looking at me, dressed simply as I was, she asked:

"Are you not coming with us, David?"

Ignoring this jibe, I set off. We climb slowly up the well-known paths, past the lower theatre, the Corinthian temple and the Byzantine houses. Skirting the upper terrace walls the snake of people reaches the upper theatre, its huge ashlar blocks of the auditorium wings, the only ones left, dwarfing the party. Everyone looks keenly upwards at the great backbone of the ridge leading onwards and upwards to the Acropolis. So far so good!

I mention the loose rocks and sharp tree branches to come and we set off again. In Classical times there used to be a zigzag pack-way to the fort at the top, up which donkeys would no doubt take supplies. The roadway has long since been washed away, but the massive retaining blocks point the way to the summit and this ascent skirts around the dangerous cliffs lower down.

We get into the harder pathways, where balance and stamina are needed to negotiate the boulders, the thickets of pistachio bushes and the spiny broom which make the going tough. We get to the second turn, higher up the mountain.

"Say, David, could we stop for just a moment. You know, the younger ones may need the rest."

Ten minutes go by. I start up the mountain again. The group is lagging behind, talking constantly.

"Oh, David, we can't see you, David. Where are you? We're lost."

They are a few metres below me. I stop again, and again, all the way up to the top. It has taken well over an hour to do a half hour climb, but it's been worth it. As we breast the last rise the Hellenistic fort of Knidos comes into view, its block-built walls festooned over the three summits of the mountain, and in places still standing an impressive five meters high, punctuated with eleven square towers. From the top there is the view, one of the finest in the classical world.

From the Acropolis we can look north across the Ceramic Gulf to the dark outline of the Bodrum Peninsula. Somewhere at the foot of those hills are the relics of the city of Halicarnassus and the remains of the Mausoleum, the tomb of Mausolus, one of the Seven Wonders of the Ancient World. The intervening sea stretches out like a luminous plastic sheet, lightly corrugated by the early summer breeze, shimmering silver in the reflected sunlight. To the west lies the whole extent of the Island of Kos, its northern half a mass of brooding mountain tops. On the other side of those mountains lies the Aesclepeion, the centre of healing were Hippocrates challenged the non-rational, animistic approach to medicine – dominated by superstitions, spirits and sympathetic magic – and ushered in a new understanding of the human body and of medical practice.

To the south, beyond the tranquil, turquoise water of the Commercial and the Trireme Harbours of Knidos, way in the distance behind the crenulated rocks at the top of the Island site recline the southern Dodecanese. To the east is the huge whale of Rhodes, one of the largest of the Greek islands. In

Classical times the citizens of Rhodes built the famous Colossus overlooking the harbour – another of the Seven Wonders - to celebrate the liberation of their city in 305 BC. Many centuries later the Island became the fiefdom of the Crusader Knights.

Due south in the distance is the spine of Tilos, once home to pygmy elephants, long since extinct. Extinct too is the volcano of Nisyros to the south west, with its associated islets of volcanic ash forming a vast collapsed caldera which must once have dominated the southern Aegean. It exploded catastrophically some 25,000 years ago, when huge flaming clouds of ash must have blown many miles into the Stone Age sky, flinging pulverised ash and debris over a vast area. Nisyrian pumice can be found all over the northern tip of Tilos, the southern part of Kos and even on the mainland in the eastern part of Knidos.

Above the crater of Nisyros, wispy fumaroles are now and again still to be seen. From the Knidian Acropolis on a clear day you can just make out the tiny white houses of the village of Nikia set dramatically on the rim of the crater. The last major eruption was in 1888, but according to legend continuing rumblings are the groans of the giant Polyvotis, who was crushed when Poseidon threw a huge lump of rock wrenched from the island of Kos at him, a comforting tale for the olive farmers of the island.

And here atop the Knidian Acropolis the garrison of the demes of the city had once fortified their walls and towers with tens of thousands of local marble and conglomerate blocks, each one weighing up to a ton or more. Laboriously drilled and chiselled from the unyielding rock faces of the quarries overlooking the city's eastern gateway, they must have been dragged in an endless procession, one by one, for perhaps a decade. Arduously lifted in place they were formed into a last redoubt against an enemy who seemingly never arrived. We lie back in the sunshine on the springing turf and muse at the folly of Man.

Coming down from the mountain seems even more precipitous than the ascent. The scree is loose and assists the general downward movement of the group, to the accompaniment of miscellaneous screams and thuds. I don't look round until the intrepid acropolids have emerged at sea level again and trudged towards the landing stage where the tender is waiting. Each hiker passes me wearing the badges of their achievement - various cuts and bruises on their arms and legs and rips in their clothing. They look as though they've been through a small war, which in a way they have. But everyone looks victorious and, looking back at the Acropolis from the rail of the yacht as we glide past the outer moles of the harbour into the open sea, everyone feels they have skirmished with untamed nature up there on the mountain.

"Wow! That was some climb. That's really steep up there you know. I bet hardly anyone has ever gotten up to that fort."

I forbore to mention that it was probably part of everyday life in Knidos two thousand years ago.

CHAPTER SIX

TIME AND TIME AGAIN

I saw from out the wave her structures rise
As from the stroke on the enchanter's wand;
A thousand years their cloudy wings expand
Around me, and a dying Glory smiles
O'er the far times.

Byron Childe Harold Canto IV

A millennium of human time lies buried at Knidos. One thousand years of living and dying, of loving and lying, of heydays and holidays, of ancient lore and sacred ritual, of daily routine and wearying toil, of imperious power and slovenly insolence, year by year, decade by decade, life by life, epoch by epoch. I suppose those one thousand years could be measured in a catalogue of architectural achievement, in the monumental buildings that began the great city, in the theatres and temples which speak of civic pride and man-made genius. Or we could see it era by era, in the broad brush strokes of re-constituted history - Hellenistic; Roman; Byzantine – each segment coupled to significant players in the ancient world. Here was Alexander, or Hadrian, or Justinian, none of whom as far as I know had ever been to Knidos but whose lives have intellectually been used to punctuate, stage by stage, the city's chronological pageant.

Or we can see it in a different light, through the protracted ephemera that make up the life of an individual resident, hour by hour; the tranquil radiance of each new day contrasted in slanting shadows between street walls, the defining sharp shades of noon day, or the chromatic softening of the westering sun, the warm half-light of a summer's evening and the myriad pin-pricks of starry light over the dark pan-tiles of the houses, asleep. A dog barks hollow among the ancient stones, and the moon rises over the shimmering, darkling sea. Each man and woman subsists, counting or not counting their daily round, through monotonous days or momentous catastrophes, living their collective life in their own city, the senator and the slave, the poet and the peasant, the merchant and the malformed, drawn together by the unseen threads of common existence. Together they lived, generation by generation, in their particular parenthesis of united time until for them history itself ran out, the day by day process faltered to its close, the final inhabitants breathed their last and the once beloved city fell in ruins, blown by the uncaring winter wind, prey to the onset of wild-flowered interment and ultimate earthy decay.

What schemes and hopes, what fears and failures, what sexual exhilaration and bitter rejection, what expectations and adversities, once so real in their contemporary mental constructs, lie vanquished and vanished among the dusty goat paths and dry-stalked thistles of the melon fields of Knidos today? The once proud, seemingly everlasting families have been erased forever. The wealthy and wanting alike have faded utterly from the scene. The ruined houses that were once theirs and the everyday streets which they trod mutely trace a coarse outline of the once great metropolis. But the human animation which gave it its meaning, its relevance, has not only ceased, it has disappeared and left no footfall, no sound, no trace.

* * * *

I am standing in the dark, panelled foyer of the majestic meeting rooms of the Society of Antiquaries opening off the courtyard of the Royal Academy in Piccadilly, central London. The year is 1967, two years before my translation to Knidos. A murmur of voices rises from the soberly suited diplomats and their less severely dressed wives who have come to hear a lecture about new discoveries in the Eastern Mediterranean. Many have served out distinguished careers in the British Foreign Service. Some among them will remember their time sipping Earl Grey tea on the balcony of the British

School of Archaeology overlooking the Tigris in Baghdad, or standing in the heat of the Jordan Valley visiting Dame Kathleen Kenyon's excavations at Jericho. British archaeology has in many ways led the world in technique and discovery over the previous half century and there is an air of both pride and expectation among the guests here today.

For me, everything is new and intimidating – the august assembly, the hallowed location and the ill-defined philosophy of archaeology. One can imagine the 'Antiquaries' still dominated by the Olympian 19th century founding fathers of British archaeology. Here might be General Pitt-Rivers, considered to be its initiator through his excavations at Cranborne Chase in Wiltshire. There is John Evans, whose work on the hand axes of the Somme gravels in northern France set the seal on World Prehistory. These Patriarchs of the Past defined the catechism of archaeology. As a student, new to the subject, I was not only in awe of the whole affair, but I was also desperately unsure of the nomenclature and the parameters, the finds and the artefacts.

Before us, in the flesh, stood one of the contemporary icons of world archaeology, Sir Mortimer Wheeler, who almost single-handedly through the newer medium of television had raised the subject to its now popular status. His white hair flowed in waves and curls behind his distinguished head, offset by his small moustache and shrewd, twinkling eyes. He was then at the peak of his illustrious career, a colossus among pygmies, in my case at least.

"And never forget," he encouraged us that afternoon, in his stentorian, commanding voice. "You young students here, never forget, archaeology is about people. People, not things, d'you hear? Not pottery, or brooches, or villas or hill forts. It's about people; the people of the past; the people of our past. Our own predecessors! Never lose sight of that truth!"

And with that he turned to glad-hand some aging knight of the realm who had been 'Our Man' in India or Iran, and merging with him, arm around his shoulder, he disappeared into the admiring crowd. The pronouncement was over. God had spoken.

* * * *

Two years later, resting on an upturned marble frieze which protruded from the scrub oak and pistachio bushes high above the excavations at Knidos I was confronted with that very dilemma – the people of the past. It was a fine summer morning and the sun was already high, the Mediterranean a silvered, reflective calmness to the far horizon, its symmetry disturbed only by the dark masses of the islands of the southern Dodecanese. Below me, lower down the slope, I could see puffs of dust rising from the various diggings - shovelfuls of earth being thrown into wheel barrows. One hundred men, like insects, were picking and scraping their way into the entrails of the long dead city. The remains of the temple facades and the street junctions they were uncovering were real enough. But where were Wheeler's people? Surely they had faded into oblivion long since. I squinted into the distance, but no Hector or Lysander, no Helen or Herodotus, no Hadrian in greaves or Socrates deep in thought walked up through the prickly undergrowth to where I sat. This was my first overseas appointment as an archaeologist and here I was unable to connect the ancient rubble with any ancient reality. I was failing at the first hurdle.

But though it didn't happen quite as I expected that day, or for many days and maybe months to come, it did happen. Not in the way or at the time I thought it might. But happen it did, on many occasions, so that in a moment of time I was able to touch the past, ever so briefly, ever so fleetingly, and in so doing I was able to feel a part of the great warp and weft of humanity rather than being isolated in my own cubical of twentieth century existence.

* * * *

It is now years later - I don't know, maybe twenty, maybe thirty years later. I am sitting at the back of the lower theatre at Knidos. On the seats directly in front and below me is a small party staring attentively downwards to where the orchestra, the place of dancing, once had been. We've had a long day on the site, reconstructing the various monuments in our mind's eye, raising the pillars and the fallen architraves in our imagination. At the end of the visit people are always grateful for a real seat, albeit of weathered marble. To lift the mood a little I mention that in ancient times there would have been cushion sellers at the entrance. Several unvarying hours in the best-made theatre seat would have taxed the rear ends of even the most culturally advanced peoples.

And so we sit contemplating the structural architecture of the past. After a while, I pull out a folded paper from my pocket. On it is typed a piece from Aeschylus' Persae, 'The Persians', written almost 2,500 years ago. The play describes the story of how Xerxes, the Great King of Persia, with five million men, had attacked and burnt the city of Athens only to see his own fleet destroyed at the sea battle of Salamis. It was the classic dramatic construction of the *hubris, catharsis* and *nemesis*, the essence of tragedy, the over-weaning pride followed by the inevitable fall. In the play, as in the historical fact, Xerxes had pitted himself against the immortal gods and the people of Greece and had failed.

When news of the burning of Athens had reached the Persian court at Susa, in south western Persia, there has been widespread rejoicing. But now a messenger had followed there with the news of this catastrophic defeat.

I begin to read.

> *The King himself, escaping by weary, winter journeys with his bare life across the plains of Thrace.*

Nemesis indeed! Xerxes' Queen Atossa was told the awful news of Salamis.

> *On that fateful day,* continued the messenger, *the whole sea was one din of shrieks and dying groans, till night and darkness hid the scene. If I should speak for ten days and ten nights, I could not tell you all that day's agony. But know this: never before in one day died so vast a company of men.*

It is believed that the playwright either saw or may even have participated in the battle, so moving was his description of this wholly factual account. In the theatre the audience would be totally engrossed with the emotion of the plot.

I read the last lines of the play, describing the aftermath of the battle and the resulting horror in Persia.

> *There, threshed by currents' eddying motion,*
> *Unsightly lie those well-loved forms,*
> *Now feasted on by voiceless swarms,*
> *The children of the untainted ocean.*
> *Here, every house bewails a man,*
> *And parents, childless now, lament*
> *The troubles that the gods have sent*
> *To end in grief their life's long span.*
>
> *Now fear no more shall bridle speech;*
> *Uncurbed, the common tongue shall prate*
> *Of freedom; for the yoke of State*
> *Lies broken on the bloody beach*
> *And fields of Salamis, which hide*
> *The ruins of our Persian pride.*

(Trans: *The Persians* Penguin Classics)

As I read the last few lines, I can hardly bring myself to finish, so sudden is the sensation, so immediate is the passion. For the others sitting there, I can sense that they feel the same. We have reached the very heart of Greek tragedy, where the audience automatically sympathises with the core of the calamity and the nexus of the people involved. That play would have been performed in this very theatre, here at Knidos, maybe many, many times. And the audience, like us today, would have been drawn into the same emotional climax.

Then two things strike me most forcibly. This play is about actual people. It is a real tragedy. Parents in Susa that long time ago did become childless in their old age. But more astoundingly, it was a Greek audience who, like us, would have cried, lamenting the tragedy of a people, the Persians, who had so recently been their sworn enemies.

In that moment I touch the past, not only in a physical way by being in that theatre among those ancient stones which had witnessed the same play long ago, but in a spiritual way too, empathising with peoples who have throughout time sought to cope with impending doom and actual disaster.

CHAPTER SEVEN

THE TEA HOUSE

Around the world, the term "tea house" may be used to refer to a restaurant or Salon de Thé. They are present in the Middle East, notably in Turkey. Such tea-houses may be referred to as 'Chaee-Khaneh' - literally, the 'house of tea'. These tea houses usually serve several beverages.

Wikipaedia

In every sense of the word, Cengis's Çayhane, Cengis' tea house, to me could be construed, somewhat I felt to High Command disapproval, as the nucleus of the whole excavation. It had not much to commend it architecturally, made as it was of a few reed screens and a reed roof, but for me it became the human interface between the various disparate elements of the excavation – the site supervisors, the workers, the dig house staff, Mehmet the light house keeper, the Jandarma (militia), the musicians, the *bekçiler* (site guardians) and any other visitors, hangers on, sea captains, passers by and ne'er do well's who were part of the ebb and flow of the life of this incongruent, isolated community.

The Çayhane was strategically placed on the site. It was quite close to the theatre where the sinuous dirt road from Datça and Yazıköy finally petered out, and it lay at one end of the isthmus which linked the mainland, where all the workers slept in the fields, to the island where The Trans-Atlantic contingent kept court at the dig house, some one hundred and fifty meters away. Like the classical theatre, the Çayhane had its own conventions – approaching from the road – outside news; approach from the dig house - home news. Cengis had erected it on a small, slightly prominent knoll overlooking the Commercial harbour, actually a knoll supported by the original block-work of the harbour isthmus and adjacent to what was now the only jetty, where the little fishing boats tied up, convenient for the daily catch – foreign news from the sea. This was important, because food, especially fish, was one of the main attractions of the Çayhane. The other, the real glue which cemented the diverse elements of the Çayhane together, was alcohol. Cengis sold booze!

It was to the Çayhane that the field staff would repair at the end of the day, to sink an Efes – the appropriately named Ephesus beer. It was to the Çayhane that the villagers would gather to drink tea, or later in the evening, if they felt flush, *aslan sütü*, lion's milk, the local sobriquet for rakı, the equivalent of the Arabic arak or the Greek ouzo, that milky-looking fiery liquid that turns a young man into a…well, stumbling wreck! And it was to the Çayhane that I would go to eat with the men each night, on the principle that the Reşadiye Peninsula was a veritable cornucopia of comestible resource, something of which the Expedition's frugal budgeting had never made use.

On a tiny gas ring, and a small tin tray which acted as a charcoal barbecue, Cengis could produce the most remarkable dishes – kebabed fresh grouper, lamb *köfte* and a variety of egg recipes. He brought from the village a colossal array of fruits – sweet grapes, huge peaches, green and black figs, mandarins, apples, oranges, apricots and cherries - and olives, which grew in super-abundance, and nuts, especially new-season's almonds, for which the area around Yazıköy, his own village, was famously and justly renowned. The Çayhane offered an absolute profusion of comestibles for a growing lad like me, and Cengis also had wine - not very good wine, admittedly, but there were suggestive elements of Keats' 'Ode to a Nightingale' about it, you know, the one about 'A drowsy numbness pains my senses' etcetera. Well, it didn't really classify as quite like Keat's blushful Hippocrene, but the purple stained mouth was right, and the beaded bubbles winking at the brim, and the drowsy numbness did indeed pain my senses, especially the next morning.

One of my favourite dishes which Cengis made in the Çayhane was, and still is, *menemen*, a singularly Turkish dish made with tomatoes, onions and green peppers which are sweated in butter until soft, and then into which an egg is scrambled. With fresh village bread and a glass of Efes, this was nirvana to a budding field surveyor like me. Another collation I made my own was a plate of two fried eggs, with the dark yolks bursting, dipped with fresh crusts. My Turkish at that stage didn't stretch to the full *kizartilmış yumurtası*, 'eggs that are fried', so I would order with my abbreviated version, *yumurta pfssss*, to indicate the process. Many a dish did I order of 'yumurta pfssss' over the months. But in the end it somewhat backfired on me. One particular evening, near the end of the excavation, a night when for some reason I was especially popular – I must have bought a round of drinks or something – the recipient villagers, without consulting me or Cengis, each ordered plates of 'yumurta pfssss' and then donated them to me, so that I ended up with seven plates-worth, a total of fourteen eggs, all of which out of politeness I had to eat. Never again!

It was in the Çayhane that I learnt most of my Turkish, and much more importantly, my great admiration of and my love for the Turkish people, something which has become more profound as the years have rolled by. Haltingly, in my case anyway, we discussed major topics and characters of the day. Recurrent themes were:

Amerikanlar fena. 'Americans are bad', on the basis that the bosses were American and responsible for the wages, and therefore were always fair game.

Ümit fena 'Ümit is bad', not unnaturally I suppose, in that he was the Management's right-hand Turk who was also the hire and fire merchant.

Ruzgar fena 'the wind is bad.'

This needs slightly more explanation. Knidos, being at the end of the long peninsula and surrounded by open sea, was prone to terrific winds whistling round the headlands and blowing at strength across the isthmus. Every few days, these strong winds blew, picking up sand from the beaches and dust from the excavations which then insinuated itself into everything, especially into our tents and our bedding. It really was most uncomfortable. Knidos, ancient and modern, must be considered the 'windy city', the Chicago of the Eastern Mediterranean.

But then there were good things too.

'*Sonny iyi*' - Sonny is good

'*Deyvit iyi*' - well, I wouldn't argue with that.

'*Olga güzel*' - 'Olga is beautiful', which was a bit of an over-statement perhaps, but was probably meant in a more spiritual than physical sense.

The Çayhane also doubled as our music hall, and it was there of an evening that sundry members would bring their musical instruments and play. There was Birol who played the *saz*, a four-stringed, long-necked lute, sometimes accompanied by his brother Mehmet, the *fenerci*, (light-house keeper), who played the *keman*, the violin. Cengis kept a *dümbelek*, a narrow-bodied tubular drum, on the shelf with the soft drinks which someone would take and pick up a tintinnabulating rhythm. And we also had Ömer, the flute player, who played the *zurna*, an ancient wooden pipe, the kind one sees in cartoons of snake charmers, which emitted a coarse, reedy oboe-like sound. And the rest of the assembled rakı drinkers would begin to sing. I can remember the songs to this day, largely because they tended always to be the same ones, night after night. They were old folk songs of the region, of unrequited love, or of a man about to go on a long journey, who would forget his sweet-heart back in the village. They were sung in the minor key and became more poignant as the evening wore on. The arty lot in the dig house, who were all fond of grand opera, ridiculed them. The raucous singing drifted across the water of the Commercial Harbour, disturbing their enjoyment of the record player. But for me they were among some of the unforgettable sounds of Knidos. And with the music, the men would dance, often with a slow, balanced, twirling motion which as a genre went back hundreds of years. For me, it was magical.

* * * *

It was while I was at Knidos in that summer of 1969, in July of that year to be precise, that we heard that man had landed on the moon. We were so cut off where we were that world news rarely penetrated as far as the outer edges of our consciousness, and being none the wiser, we were happy not to know about floods in India and the progress, or lack of it, of the war in Vietnam. But one of the High Command kept a radio and could tune in to the 'Voice of America', and this was the chink in our otherwise hermetically sealed, news-free armour. We had been blissfully unaware of moon probes, Saturn V rockets or Apollo missions. The nearest we got to Apollo was that we had a temple dedicated to the same god half way up the mountain - the real Apollo, that is, if there is such a thing!

One evening, with the Çayhane extravaganza approaching full swing, complete with terpsichorean twirling and unrestrained musical accompaniment, someone came out of the shadows from the Dig House and bawled a few words above the din. This was an event so alien that the party took a while to wind down to a halt, musicians slowly stopping one by one in mid phrase and dancers being caught, literally, on the hop. It was like a wheezing bagpipe slowly expelling air and eventually falling silent. In the ensuing uncharacteristic quiet and to our surprised and questioning faces the messenger spoke. The message was delivered.

"Man has landed on the moon," we were told.

From the Çayhane inmates the response was an uncomprehending silence.

"The Americans have landed a man on the moon. It's just been announced on 'Voice of America.' One small step for man, one giant step for mankind! That kind of thing?"

In that we must have all looked suitably blank, the messenger continued.

"Isn't that kinda great? Man on the moon, I mean. We've done it. The US has done it."

Still nothing. The disillusioned alien turned on their heel and went back to their own universe.

"Ne diyor, Deyvit?" "What are they saying?" was the puzzled question.

I did my best to explain.

"Ayda adam var!" "There's a man on the moon."

"Ne?" "What?" came the disbelieving response.

"Ayda bir Amerikan oturuyor …şimdilik." "There's an American sitting on the moon … right now."

"Ne? Sen dangalaksin, Deyvit?" "What? Are you some kind of idiot David?"

I went outside the Çayhane onto the beach and, pointing up at the moon, I said in a loud, rather exasperated voice:

"Bak! Ayda adam duruyor." "Look, there's a man standing on the moon."

51

Only afterwards did I realise how foolish that sounded.

A number of men had come outside into the darkness to see what the fuss was about. They peered up at the luminous orb, and then looked at me, and with growing scepticism said:

"Ne yapıyor, Deyvit? Rakımı içiyor?" "What's he doing Deyvit? Is he drinking rakı?"

When I said nothing, they turned and went back into the Çayhane, calling over their shoulders.

"Çünkü şu anda biz rakı içiyoruz! Tamammı? Haydi Deyvit!"

"Because right now we're drinking rakı. Is that OK? Come on Deyvit!"

So we all trooped back inside, opened another bottle and continued the party.

I have thought many times about that night, and about the reaction of the villagers in the Çayhane at Knidos and I think there is something deeply philosophic in their reaction to the astounding news that man had landed on the moon, namely, total indifference. Here was the bouncing balloon Neil Armstrong, self importantly announcing to the world about one small step for man, one giant leap for mankind, or words to that effect, when for the people I was with it had no appreciable impact on their lives whatsoever, in 1969 or at any time since. Thinking about it, that would probably be true of the wider population of the Earth as well. To hunters in the Amazon rain forest, or to cattle keepers on the Nqutu plateau of Central Zululand, or to sheep farmers in the Nant Ffrancon Valley of Snowdonia, or bullock-cart drivers in the Araveli Hills of Rajasthan, it has made no appreciable change to them at all, no giant step in any direction, for good or bad. In fact, so bored have people become with the non-eventfulness of man landing on the moon that even the Americans have stopped sending people there.

And for me, was I ever touched by it? Well, I was once given a frying pan of some ceramic substance which I was assured by the label was totally heat resistant and absolutely non-stick, because the material had been developed for the nose cone of the rocket that took man to the moon. It was totally resistant to anything adhering to it, it said. Well, let me tell you, the NASA space team which sent those astronauts to the moon that July night should be very grateful that the Earth's outer atmosphere is not made up of hen's eggs, because an egg fried in this extra-terrestrial wonder pan, with or without oil, instantly welds itself to the pan's surface with such tenacious permanence that at one time I might even have considered marketing the product as a super-bond adhesive. But in the end I threw the pan away.

One giant step bollocks! Pass the rakı!

* * * *

Cengis was of course from the Village, from Yazıköy, of which more later. His hair was already turning grey, which with his marked Asiatic features gave him a distinguished appearance, not unlike a latter day but slimmed down Confucius. This singular oriental mien enabled him to stand slightly aloof from the cut and thrust of day to day Çayhane life, ever the servant but ever above the fray. It turned out that his father was the local *hodja*, the person who presided over the mosque at Yazıköy, the equivalent I suppose of the village priest, since it was Cengis' dad who officiated, amongst other things, at most of the marriages and funerals.

By and large, we had all taken this information about Cengis' dad fairly matter-of-factly, so that when, one morning, it was announced that the holy father was about to come to see his son in Knidos that afternoon, no-one at first realised the implications of the intended visit. It was only at lunch time when the alarm bells began to ring, as the crates of beer and boxes of rakı were being moved by human chain from the Çayhane to a special store near the Trireme Harbour where they were covered with a tarpaulin, out of sight. Cengis motioned to us all, finger to his lips, as every trace of wine and other alcoholic beverage was expunged from the menu, to be replaced by tea, and Mindos, a locally made, saccharine-sweet, fizzy orange drink. It then dawned on us that of course Cengis' dad was by definition a full on, practicing Muslim and therefore, eschewing alcohol as he did, would expect his son to do the same, especially in his place of business. Cengis could hardly be seen actually to be selling the forbidden liquor, could he?

We went about our afternoon work as usual, and as the sun began to climb down the sky, we trudged back along the dusty pathways of the ancient site to converge on the Çayhane. Instead of the normal happy throng of beer drinkers we found sundry people loitering about in the open air, while there, in pride of place in the front of the Çayhane, sat Cengis' dad, wearing a faded grey-green tweed hacking jacket and collarless shirt. He was flanked by a couple of similarly attired worthies who had accompanied the old gentleman from the Village. All three wore grey woolly hats with a stalk on the top. They were drinking Mindos from small rakı glasses – our rakı glasses - with a plate of peanuts and sunflower seeds in front of them. They looked very set, as Cengis came in and out of the Çayhane to minister to their every need – cigarettes, matches, more Mindos, ash trays, melon seeds, more peanuts. To add verisimilitude to the scene, Cengis surreptitiously motioned some of the workers to come and sit in the Çayhane, offering free glasses of tea for those willing to act as extras. Others, who would have preferred something a little more astringent were sent away with a flea in their ear – 'tea or nothing' was the message.

At this stage we were not unduly worried. I mean, how much fizzy orange juice can one old man drink without getting bloated, especially on Mindos?

Well, it turned out that Cengis' dad was a world class Mindos drinker and after we had come back to the Çayhane, having showered, the old chap was still there pouring it in. By this time a dozen or more of our men were standing furtively about, shuffling their feet behind the Çayhane, most of them hidden by the reed screens. From time to time, a representative would be sent to peer round the corner of the Çayhane only to confirm that the religious trio were still firmly ensconced by the entrance. Half an hour later the news came that they had now moved on to drinking tea. This was considered a good sign, like the parting glass before they hit the road back to Yazıköy. Alas this was a false dawn. A second glass was soon poured, and a plate of biscuits had appeared.

Speaking of false dawns, behind the Trireme harbour the opposite was happening. The sun was sinking low in the western sky, silhouetting the mountains of Kos across the straits. Still there was no movement from the holy trinity. By this time the Çayhane regulars were like men gathered outside an occupied gent's toilet, crossing their legs and fidgeting with unlit cigarettes in the hope that any moment the door would miraculously open and they could be let inside. It was almost twilight before someone came up with a brainwave. Recognising the car in which Cengis' dad had come from the Village, and praying there wasn't another one around the corner somewhere, he sidled up to Cengis and whispered a few words in his ear. Cengis' eyes widened and you could see the bulb of recognition switching on. With a less servile demeanour, Cengis strode out from behind the reed screens and standing in front of his Dad, the palms of his hands twisting together, made a suggestion which had an instant result. Abruptly, the old man and his friends shot up and leaving half finished glasses of tea almost raced to the car, jumped in and at high speed, well, sort of, the car was off in a cloud of dust back up the dirt road to Yazıköy. The visitation was at an end.

Instantly a human chain was formed and all the concealed supplies were restored to the Çayhane in no time. The evening's festivities could begin again, which they did, allegro con brio. It was some time later that someone thought to ask how this miracle evacuation had been achieved. I vaguely overheard the reply of something '*Yok.*' Something was 'not in being.' It was later still that I caught the full story.

"*Arabada lamba yok!*"

The car had no lights. There was no way they could have driven the rocky bends back to Yazıköy in the dark, and also there was no way the old man wanted to spend the night in the discomfort of sleeping among the ancient walls with his parishioners, so they had shot off up the road before the last rays faded.

We breathed a sigh of relief and raised a glass – *Allah şükür* – God be thanked!

* * * *

It was some thirty years later, sailing into the ancient harbour of Knidos from Bodrum one afternoon en route to Palamut Buku further along the coast, that Birol, Fenerci Mehmet's (the light-house keeper's) brother, greeted me and told me that Cengis was here, at Knidos. The Çayhane was long since gone and forgotten, cleared away and burnt many years ago, I shouldn't wonder. Nearby, in its place, was a rather extravagant stone-built, terraced restaurant that catered for the passing young yachties from France, Germany and Holland. In front there were strings of fairy lights and a small statuesque fountain resembling the Knidian Aphrodite, surrounded by encrusted bits of amphorae and razor clam shells. It didn't look a bit like the humble tea house that we had known so well.

I didn't see Cengis at first, until Birol led me round the back of the restaurant and there was Cengis and a couple of friends, seated in the open by a wall, a small table in front of them with a plate of peanuts and sunflower seeds. He had aged quite a lot, and taken on the identical visage of his long-deceased father. In fact, the whole scene was reminiscent of that afternoon many years before. The son had become the father, with the one exception, that instead of Mindos, Cengis and his friends were drinking the *aslan sütü*, the fearsome Lion's milk and already, by this time in the afternoon, they were well into their alcoholic safari.

"Selamünaleyküm, Cengis Bey. Nasılsınız? İyiysınız?"

"Greetings Cengis Bey! How are you? Are you well?"

"Oh ho! Deyvit Bey. Aleyküm Selam. Bende iyiyim. Nereden geldiniz?"

"I am well. Where have you come from?"

Then immediately

"Rakı buyrunmaz mısınız, Deyvit Bey?"

"Won't you take some rakı, David? Bring a chair for David. And another glass. Please, do sit and join us."

I explained that I had a party of very important guests with me and I had to take them around Knidos and introduce them to the site, and that afterwards I was going to cruise on to Palamut Buku the same evening.

Cengis wouldn't hear of it. How many years had it been, he computed, since we had last drunk rakı together. Then, he wanted to know how everyone he remembered from the dig was faring.

"How is Rudy? How is Sonny? How is Olga?"

I forbore to tell him that I hadn't seen hide or hair of any of them for more than three decades, but he continued as though reading a passenger list - Coral, Mitt, Amanda, Hugh, Mary - including some I had totally forgotten about. Even with the rakı and his advancing years, his mind was still sharp. I had learnt some time before that Cengis had become a VIP in Yazıköy. Both his father and his mother's family had owned many lands among the olive and almond orchards of the peninsula, and he had inherited the lot. He was now an *ağa*, a major land owner. But apparently he and his wife were unable to have children, so that he was without an heir, something that must have saddened him greatly. As someone had said, 'he has become rich to become poor'.

I looked into his familiar Asiatic eyes, now rheumy with age, or was it the rakı, and felt I couldn't let him down. I agreed that after the visit I would let the boat continue down the coast, and I would go with him by car to Yazıköy, and that later he would get someone to drive me to the coast at Palamut to rejoin my ship. And so, after the site visit, I instructed the crew to weigh anchor and, temporarily taking my leave of my guests, I told them I had to meet my old friends from the excavation. Then I turned back and sat with Cenghis. He was in no hurry to leave, and another bottle of rakı was ordered, with more ice, water, nuts, cucumbers, cheese and olives. We talked over old times, about the Çayhane, about the excavations, about the stories from our shared past. Still there was no sign of movement. Time was passing. I had quite a long way to go and already the sun was sinking behind the Trireme harbour, low in the western sky, silhouetting the mountains of Kos across the straits. It was then I remembered the ruse that we had used on his Dad.

"Arabada lamba varmı, Cengis Bey?"

"Are there lights on the car?"

That did the trick – not the same car, but the same problem. We rose immediately, jumped into the waiting vehicle and set off up the dusty road to Yazıköy. We drove passed the theatre, the stepped streets and the Eastern Gateway and wound our way towards the tombs of the Necropolis. How very nostalgic, I thought. Like old times. But as we turned another bend, out of sight of the harbour, Cengis abruptly stopped the car and leapt out. From underneath a nearby bush he drew a double- barrelled shot gun, something prohibited in Knidos, where there were Jandarma to ask questions. He took a box of cartridges from under his seat and loaded the gun. We continued our bumpy ride, with the difference that every few hundred meters or so a covey of red-legged partridge would whirr up from the scrub, at which Cengis would stamp on the brake pedal and shoot wildly out of the car window – Boff! … Boff! – violently waving the barrel skywards.

Another few meters, another whirr of partridge– Boff! … Boff!

And so on - Boff! … Boff! - as we lurched on into the gloaming. Needless to say, the partridge had nothing to fear. The rakı had seen to that, that and the gathering darkness. Thus the *Ağa* of Yazıköy reached his estates, unsteady but unscathed. And after a little more suckling on the Lion's Milk in the village, I was driven somewhat thick-headed down to Palamut to join the others on board.

"Have a good time with your excavation friends, David?" they asked politely. "I'm sure there was so much to catch up on, what with the new biographies of Alexander the Great, eh? I'm sure they keep up to date with the literature, don't they?"

"Oh yes," I replied sheepishly. "Bang up to date!"

CHAPTER EIGHT

IN THE PINK

Some of the ancient architects said that the Doric order ought not to be used for temples, because faults and incongruities were caused by the laws of its symmetry.

Marcus Vitruvius, Ten Books on Architecture

Surely, only someone of an uncertain classical education would ever name the remains of an original, classically proportioned Doric shrine - most austere of the orders; a miniature of the Athenian Parthenon - the 'Pink Temple'. But that's what the Temple of Apollo was referred to when I arrived - The Pink Temple. The origin of this rather saccharine sobriquet lay in the fact that, when new, the building had been clad in a sort of pinkish stone. It wasn't what the Turks would call *'pez pembe'*, I mean, 'really pink', a bright shocking pink, but rather that in the right light the marble blocks assumed a slight cerise tinge. Ask a geologist and he would tell you that the pale rose staining in the blocks was on account of iron being mixed in with the limey ooze on the sea bed some eighty million years ago which, when it had been metamorphosed and cooked into stone, created a lightly tinted, marble raspberry ripple. Ask him where the oxidised iron had come from, and what was it doing far under the ocean when the limestone was forming and he'd talk about detrital clays brought down by primeval rivers which flowed into the Tethys Sea, the proto-Mediterranean. But maybe that's a story for another time. Suffice it to say that some architectural arriviste in the Hellenistic era had specified this particular stone-work, on the basis that 'You don't want it like that, you want it like this!', and some marble quarry somewhere, probably among the Aegean Islands, had made a fortune shipping the blocks to Knidos. Ah, *Plus ca change!*

By the time we got to it, there wasn't much left of the original temple. Time, wind, rain, earthquakes, thieves, theological bigots, stone robbers, scrap metal merchants and Anatolian peasants had all contributed to its demise. There was not a lot to look at now; in fact there wasn't anything much above ground to see at all, only the shadow of a once great building, but it still had its points of interest for those who looked at it with imagination. And that was just the way I had to look at it, because I was detailed to survey its remains, drawing out the salient elements so that it could be reconstructed, not for real of course, there was too much missing, but in the mind's eye and the architect's drawing office. To do this I was using what in those days passed for the absolute state of the art in small-scale survey instruments, an RKI Self-Reducing Tacheometric Telescopic Alidade made by Wild Heerbrugg AG, originally Heinrich Wild, Werkstätte für Feinmechanik und Optik, Switzerland. Wild made, and in fact still make, the very best survey instruments in the world, proving if it were needed that the Swiss aren't just good at cuckoo clocks.

Anyway, we had acquired this superb piece of equipment by virtue of the fact that Sonny, our topographic surveyor, had first persuaded the Americans that we needed one and then had travelled in person to the Wild factory in Heerbrugg, at the southern end of Lake Constance, and actually bought it direct from the factory. The only snag from Sonny's point of view was that having been bought in Switzerland the instructions for the use of this all singing, all dancing Anzeigeinstrument were written in French and German only (it used to be like that in those days) and he was competent in neither. That was the moment when I arrived, and I at least had an 'O' level in French, the second time of asking admittedly. But, as the old saw goes, in the country of the blind, the one eyed man is King, and so I got to use the alidade. I have to say that once I had mastered how to conjugate the present subjunctive of the French regular verb, and thus could read the 'shoulds' and 'should nots', there was no stopping me. It was up with the lark, or rather, with the donkey, and straight to 'les fouilles de Cnidus', my knapsack on my back. And the knapsack was the only drawback. The metal case for the instrument was indeed worn like a knapsack, but it weighed a ton, and with the huge tripod and plane table needed to keep the plotting steady and horizontal, it was one of the most cumbersome bits of equipment I have ever had to use. After a few moans and even more groans, I was allocated one of the diggers, Mümtaz, as my bearer, at least for the Pink Temple survey.

Imagine a smaller version of the Parthenon without the roof, which isn't too difficult because the roof of the Parthenon had been blown off by the Venetians when they accidentally hit an arms dump while bombarding Ottoman-held Athens in 1687. Then imagine the building without the frieze, which isn't too difficult either. The Parthenon frieze had been somewhat cavalierly removed by Lord Elgin in 1806. Then take away the pediments and the walls, then all the pillars, leaving only the floor. Then strip the floor away too, leaving, well, not very much really. Then cover whatever is left with earth, potsherds, bits of unidentifiable broken masonry, pistachio bushes and a carpet of dried out spring flowers and you get the sense of what the Pink Temple looked like when I first saw it – not really 'saw', because you couldn't see it. It just wasn't visible. Enter the diggers to uncover the remains, and me to put the building back together again, artistically at least.

I have often watched visitors to Knidos peering down the excavated holes at the ruins of the Pink Temple and wondered what they make of this disembodied sanctuary. Actually, there's quite a lot of it there if you know where to look, though what now still exists is very much in kit form. Think of the Parthenon again, and note that the base is made up of three large steps known architecturally as the 'crepidoma' which forms a podium on which the building proper sits. These are the archetypal 'three steps of the Doric', each one slightly too high for a comfortable approach – the proper access stairs are on the east side only. The 'three steps' are still there around a part of the Pink Temple, it's just that most of the facing blocks have long since been stripped away. You can recognise the characteristic pink slabs in other later buildings in the city, to where they had been taken away and re-used. The underpinning to the 'three steps' is still there, but made of such poor quality local stone that it isn't monumentally imposing and is easily overlooked. But a closer examination reveals that the 'three steps' were once very beautifully finished, and the few of the original facings which are still in situ show that although the shape of the platform was formed with rough local conglomerate it had been clad with perfectly cut and highly polished marble, the part that would have been seen. There was no mortar at that time – it hadn't been invented yet – so the blocks were held together with iron ties set in molten lead to keep the foundations firm, but these were located in such a way that they were cunningly concealed by the next layer of step blocks.

If we now replace all the step blocks in our mind's eye, even the platform takes on a beauty of its own. First we see a marble curbing at the base, on top of which, and set in from it, is the first of the three steps, about knee high, and with an outward curving moulding at the top. That is followed by the next, again knee high and again set in from the last. On top of that is the third layer of step blocks similar in size and position, reaching the level on which the pillars are going to rise, the so-called stylobate. From a distance, the highly polished steps might have looked like three weakly developed horizontal lines, merging into one another in the bright light. But this horizontality is enhanced by a clever architectural ruse whereby at the base of each block, where it sits on the step below, two insets are cut, like tiny inverted steps, and in the high-angled sun's light these would create a delicate double shadow, one faintly deeper than the other, which would act to the distant observer like two pencil lines, accentuating and separating each of the steps and in consequence ever so slightly lifting the profile of the podium. It's a small feature, but it brings us into direct contact with the aesthetic sensitivity of the designer, and thus for a brief moment allows us to touch the past. As I have said, I was once told by that great exponent of archaeology, Sir Mortimer Wheeler, 'Archaeology is not about objects, it's about people'. Well, here from two thousand years ago, and for a brief moment, is the visual concept of a real person.

$* * * *$

Back to the present, or at least, to 1969. I was standing by the side of my RK1 Tacheometric Alidade plotting and measuring what remained of the Pink Temple during the early stages of its excavation when along the dusty track leading from the harbour I saw one of the High Command toiling up the hill with a rather aged couple in tow. I could see by their demeanour that there was about to be an exposition of the Pink Temple, and that lacking any architectural magnificence I was to be the star attraction. The couple was composed of a superannuated and rather rotund tycoon-like figure with masses of curly white hair, wearing what appeared to be McAlpine tartan Bermuda shorts and chewing on the end of a large cigar. He was accompanied by an overdressed, flagging wife who, wilting in the heat, was wont to punctuate her participation in the proceedings with a regular, breathy exhalation of 'Oh my God!'

As the guests were led onto what had been the temple podium, I was rather pointedly introduced to them.

"Oh David, this is Mr and Mrs Aaron Liebowitz from Atlantic City, New Jersey, who have very graciously made a donation to our important research here. Would you care to show Mr Liebowitz your survey instrument which we have bought with his money?" The 'donation', 'research' and the 'his' were heavily accentuated.

"Good morning Mr Liebowitz, Mrs Liebowitz," I began.

"Oh my God!" intoned Mrs Liebowitz, sotto voce, by way of an acknowledgement.

"This is an RK1 Tacheometric Alidade, made in Switzerland, which I am using to measure the dimensions of the Hellenistic temple we are currently excavating."

I waved expansively with my arm at sundry workmen smoking in a corner. It was a cigarette break at just the wrong moment.

"This is a very exact way of plotting the various features of the temple on the plane table here."

I showed Mr Liebowitz the plot, which consisted of a few radiating lines and some unpromising pencil squiggles. It was the beginning of the plot, after all. He harrumphed unsympathetically, echoed in falsetto by Mrs Liebowitz with a quietly dismissive and, I detected, a somewhat crabby rendition of "Oh my God!"

"Perhaps you would care to look through the eye piece, Mr Liebowitz."

Now this was a mistake. As the translated instructions for the instrument say:

"The RK1 has a 25x magnification, internally-focusing telescope, with a routable eyepiece inclined at 45° to the optical axis, allowing the observer to work comfortably and without bodily strain."

All very well, but the observer has to understand what he is looking at in the first place. The aperture through which Mr Liebowitz was craning over to see comprised a prism in which were reflected a mass of rotating figures, graticules, and cross hairs, incomprehensible to anyone without a knowledge of tacheometry. Also, the 25x telescope was trained on a red and white ranging rod not three meters away, which totally filled the image with a scarlet blob.

"I can't see a damned thing through this. D'you mean to tell me we paid all this money for something that doesn't work? Hear that, Evie?"

"Oh my God!" concurred Mrs Liebowitz, supportively adopting what I considered to be an unhelpfully peevish tone.

I had to think quickly. I was burying my audience in a blizzard of science. Then, remembering the description in the manual about the x 25 magnification, I had an idea. It just might work. I unscrewed the prism on the eyepiece, making the barrel into a clear, powerful telescope, with none of the normal scientific interruptions. This I focussed on the lighthouse on the point of the Island over a kilometre away. Mehmet the Lighthouse keeper's wife Fatma had just hung out her laundry on the line and her capacious bloomers were blowing friskily in the wind, crisply in the centre of vision. Mr Liebowitz applied his eye again to the eyepiece.

"Say, is that … is that the lighthouse over yonder? Oh My!"

He bent down to the eyepiece and looked again then rose, beaming at me.

"Hell, that's some kind of an instrument you've got yourself there! That's real great, eh Evie?"

"Oh my God!" intoned Mrs Liebowitz, encouragingly.

* * * *

"We need to establish the limits of the temple, David." This was Mark, the Assistant Director speaking.

"We need you to tell us where the other two corners are, somewhere . . . over there."

He gestured languidly at a featureless expanse of waste ground that had recently been a melon field.

"What do you think I am?" I was minded to ask. "A bleeding clairvoyant?"

But I stopped myself in time, realising that this was supposed to be part of my job, to work out where things were so that the excavators could uncover them. Thinking quickly I guessed that the ratios of all these classical buildings were more or less the same, and since I already knew the width between the two western corners, six columns wide according to the marks on the stylobate, and I knew the inter-columnar spacing, and that the temple was likely to be a six by 11 – six columns on the short sides and 11 on the long – I should be able to calculate and then plot the probable position of both the eastern corners. That was the theory.

"Don't tell them how you do it Dave," said Sonny, my partner in survey, when I discussed it with him. "Just do it, you know. They'll think, 'Its magic; this guy's magic', and that's what it is, see – magic! OK?"

So I did it. Creating a hostage to fortune, I laid out two square trenches and said, somewhat pretentiously:

"I think you'll find what you're looking for there."

The new excavations, in which I now had a much deeper interest because they were going to prove my logic right or wrong, were to begin on the following Monday. But that night in the Çayhane there were serious murmurings against the Management.

"*Amerikanlar fena.*" "Americans are bad," seemed to be the text that evening.

We tried to ascertain why, and were referred to a young, fresh-faced man incongruously dressed in a laundered white shirt, pressed trousers and polished shoes – polished shoes no less, in all this dust - sitting in a corner and answering to the name of Mahmut. It turned out that he had declared himself to be the owner of the melon field where I had just laid out the two new trenches at the Pink Temple, and if we were going to sink holes in his

Knidian estancia then he was here to claim compensation for the loss of his property. He was not part of the excavation team, but had been alerted by what must have been an undercover agent from Belenköy, his own village, that his extensive holding, all one hundred square meters of austere hillside of it, was about to come under the archaeologist's shovel. The irritating thing was that in principle he had right on his side. It was a condition of the excavation permit issued by the Department of Antiquities in Ankara that any land that was to be investigated had to be expropriated on behalf of the Turkish Government from the owners, to whom financial restitution must be made.

This was far too deep for us, so members of the High Command were summoned. A debate ensued, which developed into an argument and thence escalated into a full scale shouting match. Voices were raised, fingers were pointed, tables were banged and sizeable sums of money were talked about. The High Ups kept threatening to leave, to fetch the Jandarma (who actually were already there, saying nothing), to take the case to the Provincial Governor in Muğla, or the Prime Minister, or the United Nations. Cengis was consulted, and in the end, calm was restored, with the High Command leaving the proceedings and Ümit, the Management hit man, who handed out the agreed sum of money. The excavation could begin on schedule.

First thing on Monday morning we trooped up to the melon field to wait for the diggers to arrive, which they duly did. They went over to the trenches already excavated and brought their picks, mattocks and shovels to the new area. The first spade had barely touched the ground when from behind the nearby bushes a huddle of women from the village appeared and started to harangue the workers, screaming like banshees. They were dressed in black, with black head coverings, and though some were young, the main antagonists were elderly ladies we'd never seen before. It was like a scene from the blasted heath. They were not interested in the site supervisor, or me thankfully, only in the diggers. Some of the diggers tried to ignore them and started picking away at the ground, at which point the women rushed forward, wrestled with the men and, taking away their tools, disappeared back into the bushes.

After a while, the complex truth emerged and we learnt what had happened. This field did not belong to the sartorial Mahmut alone, but to senior members of Mahmut's extended family, the rest of whom had not received a single *kuruş* of the cash that had been handed over and these women were representatives of the dispossessed and they were naturally not willing to allow work to begin until they had received their portion. The problem we now faced was that as we had no access to the female lineage, even though they were clearly the key to the decision-making process, we had reached an impasse. Not only that, but the wily Mahmut had naturally enough leapt on the nearest *dolmuş* (minibus) and buggered off hot foot to Marmaris with the loot to spend it no doubt in riotous living.

The root of the crisis that we now faced was to do with the way in which Ottoman land transactions had been formulated. If a man owned three fields and had three sons, then upon his demise, each son was entitled to one third of each of the three fields. Do this often enough, and of course they'd had four hundred years' worth of it, and you wind up with a piece of land only three meters wide being owed by thirty six people from eighteen families scattered across ten different villages.

We finally resolved the problem with recourse to Mehmet Bora, the Lighthouse Keeper, who always seemed to be the fount of all local knowledge and the person before whom all immediate ownership disputes were laid. He pronounced that the ladies in black, to whom he was able through some local village alchemy to speak but which we were not, should be paid the same sum again as the scheming Mahmut, and that at the next *meclis,* the mayoral meeting at Yazıköy, this matter would be extensively discussed and hopefully one half of the money would be restored. Fat chance! After that, it was decreed that all land expropriations were to be handled by Government land surveyors from Datça, a process which took forever and so was seldom requested.

The excavation of the new trenches proceeded, and sure enough, dead on target, there in the centre of each trench appeared the two eastern corners of the Pink Temple. My logic had been flawless.

"Very good," said Mark. "Glad you know your business."

"It's this new instrument," I replied, then quickly added, "it's magic."

Mark walked away with a puzzled look.

"Don't tell 'em, Dave!" Sonny would have said.

＊ ＊ ＊ ＊

Now that the edges of the Pink Temple had been defined, it was time to investigate its centre. A minimal amount of clearance revealed, not the marble flooring of the inside of the building, but a series of rubble and mortar walls, reused threshold blocks and a small quadrangle paved with terra cotta tiles. The rubble and mortar walls gave the date. It was early Byzantine. In fact, it was a miniature Byzantine chapel built right on top of the centre of the Pink Temple, replete with terra cotta tiled atrium, the outer courtyard, leading to a small transverse narthex, the vestibule, which gave onto the single nave, at the far end of which was a tiny semi-circular apse and an eastward facing window. The reasoning behind the location of the chapel, slap on top of the Temple foundations, was to ensure that there was no apostasy, no theological uncertainty about who was going to be worshipped here.

There had been loose talk among those in the excavational know that the original Doric temple had been dedicated to Apollo Karneios, the patron deity of the Dorian league, of which Knidos was one of the six members, along with Halicarnassus, Kos, Ialyssos, Kameiros and Lindos, the last three being on the Island of Rhodes. But Apollo or no, this chapel, probably erected seven hundred years later than the Temple, was here to declare that the more recent incumbent was the Lord God of Hosts, Christ Pantokrator, Ruler of the World. But that reign hadn't lasted either and eventually the chapel had fallen into disrepair, probably as early as the 7th century AD. And that would have been the end of the story had it not been for something which I mentioned earlier – the iron ties that held the original pink marble blocks together, or rather, not the iron ties alone, but the lead which held them firm. Once guns appeared in the late Middle Ages, circular lead bullets – rounds as they were called – were in great demand. Why bother to go to all the expense and the hazardous business of mining lead when there was tons of it at every ancient classical site, by that time owned by no-one. All you needed was a crow bar, a maul and a chisel and the lead was yours for the taking. And it was that piece of thievery which led to the eventual annihilation of what was left of the Pink Temple. At the back of the site a row of pink stylobate blocks lay stacked on end like paving stones ready to be laid, but in fact they had come to rest where they had been uprooted, one by one, to get at the lead and the iron underneath, a sad end to a once great building.

* * * *

I was on my own one lunchtime drawing the blocks at the Pink Temple when across the mountain came Mustafa, one of the older workers we had on the site. His back was bent and his leathery face was deeply lined with age. He wore the characteristic village uniform - broad-brimmed flat cap, trousers with bracers, an old collarless shirt and shoes without laces. He waved and gave me a rather one toothed smile as he passed. By his side was his grand-daughter, Dürşen, a lithesome, tom-boyish little girl of six, leading their majestic family pet, Beyaz, a billy-goat with a luxuriant cream-coloured coat and an imposing pair of twisted horns. This was a daily event; they were taking Beyaz down to the sea. Dürşen leaped athletically, bare foot, from the top of each upturned slab to the next and then hand in hand with her granddad, Beyaz prancing behind, they left the site and walked down the rugged path to the beach. There, fully clothed, they paddled into the waves with Beyaz, as though swimming with him. Mustafa lovingly washed the goat's shaggy hair while Dürşen squeezed out the excess water. Beyaz put his head down and drank – there was fresh water upwelling in the sea at this point. I used to watch this bucolic ritual day after day and found it so simple and so touching, the old man, the little girl and the goat, alive in the ruins of this once great but now dead city. The Pink Temple had come and gone, ancient Greeks, Roman imperialists, Byzantine monks and mediaeval robbers had all done their stuff, and now it was the turn of this little family and their beautiful goat from the village.

I walked down to the dig house for a late lunch. Miracle of miracles, we were having meat stew today.

"What's the meat, Halil?"

"*Keçi, Deyvit Bey.*"

Goat!

I wish I hadn't asked.

CHAPTER NINE

LEARNING TO SPEAK

And the blind fate of language, whose tun'd chime
More charms the outward sense; yet thou mayst claim
From so great disadvantage greater fame,
Since to the awe of thy imperious wit
Our stubborn language bends, made only fit
With her tough thick-ribb'd hoops to gird about
Thy giant fancy, which had prov'd too stout
For their soft melting phrases.

Thomas Carew

Singularly, apart from among the British and American dig staff, English as a means of communication was non-existent at Knidos. The late 1960's was a time before Turkey had suffered the onslaught of mass tourism, charter flights, box-inspired high rise hotels, factory-made ice creams, 'I love Sandra' tattoos and livid, vermillion, sunburnt families from Smethwick eating kebab and chips and quaffing krugs of Efes beer. Few inhabitants from the peninsula villages like Belenköy and Çeşmeköy had ever seen a European before, let alone heard them speak.

There were few radios and certainly no televisions to intrude into the unperturbed, pastoral existence which had persisted here more or less uninterrupted for centuries. The villagers lived in an immutable world whose rhythms were naturally governed - by sunrise and sunset, seed time and harvest, birth and death. Europe and the United States and all their self-absorbed consumerism were only barely perceptible if at all in this remote Resadiyeh Peninsula.

There were some exceptions, of course. There was a large, ostensibly NATO naval base at Izmir, though from reports of those that had been there, it seemed wholly peopled with Americans. There was even a phrase book knocking about the dig house which some local supernumerary at the base had strung together and had published, to help Turks at the base to communicate with their foreign visitors. 'Teach Yourself Amerikan', the title read. It was divided up into groups of sentences to be used in particular situations – *Postanede* 'At the Post Office', or, *Lokantada* 'At the restaurant'. Perhaps the most useful was *Bankada* 'At the bank'. A flavour of the linguistic competence of this practical oeuvre can be gained by the following entry:

"Afferdersiniz, Bey Effendi, kaç para sizinde?" which should translate simply as:

"Excuse me, Sir, how much money do you have."

This was rendered into 'Amerikan' as:

"Say, Mac, how many greens you got?"

∗ ∗ ∗ ∗

For an English speaker, Turkish is a really difficult language to master. It bears no structural relationship to any European language. Most linguists classify it as an Altaic language, part of the Uyghur, Kazakh and Uzbek group, from the heartland of the Turkic tribes in the Altai Mountains, on the borders of the Gobi Desert of Mongolia and the extreme western part of China. Even Japanese and Korean are said to be part of a similar overarching group. As such it has a noble origin indeed. Its westward spread was associated with historical characters such as Alp Arslan, second sultan of the Seljuk Turks, or later, Genghis Khan and that great sweep of Mongol power in China. Genghis (Cengis), or Temüjin (Temucin) the Khan's own birth name, are common fore names in Turkey today. And they do say that you can speak modern Turkish from Bademli to Bukhara and as far as Samarkand and beyond, thousands of miles east along the ancient Silk Road, and still be understood.

But in the twilight years of the Ottoman Empire, during the last few decades of the 19th century, Turkish as a language was disparaged, as was Turkey itself. The sick man of Europe was in terminal decline. In 1907, that somewhat self-opinionated yet extraordinarily adventurous traveller Gertrude Bell, passing through Syria, then part of the Ottoman Empire, wrote in her estimable book, *The Desert and the Sown*:

> *There is not such a country as Turkey (which there wasn't then, in name at any rate) … the upper grades of the Ottoman Empire have proved so defective, [that they are] filled with Greeks, Armenians, Syrians and personages of various nationalities generally esteemed in the East, not without reason, untrustworthy. The Greeks and Armenians have become the bankers, the Syrians merchants and landowners.*

Even as visualised by their own Ottoman government in Istanbul, Turks in the vast agricultural swaths of the Anatolian hinterland were perceived to be servile peasants, and thus the term 'Turkish', and with it their language, was considered rather churlish.

Some years ago I entertained an American professor of Ottoman history to dinner on a yacht in the harbour of Knidos, and he spoke to our Turkish crew in an extraordinary tongue, a sort of High Turkish, that I for one totally failed to follow. The crew nodding knowingly at what this luminary had to say, adding the occasional *evet* (yes) and *tamam* (OK), but I was completely demoralised, thinking that my grasp of the finer points of the language was sadly lacking. After he had left, I asked the captain Bekir,

"What did he say?"

"Hiç bir şey anlamadım, Deyvit!" "I didn't understand a single thing!" he replied laconically.

75

We worked it out later. The good professor had been speaking in Osmanlı dili – Ottoman Turkish – a mixture of arcane Turkic, Arabic and Persian. It was as if Geoffrey Chaucer had been speaking to 19th farm labourers in the Devon or Dorset countryside – individual words would be vaguely recognisable but their combined meaning would have been totally incomprehensible.

Turkish as presently spoken, especially among the villagers, was anathema to the 19th century Ottoman upper crust. They considered their own peasantry coarse, unlettered and culturally illiterate. It was once again Mustafa Kemal who raised the language to a national treasure, and who in the 1920's gave Turkish its current status, throwing out the Arabic script and Persian phraseology in favour of the rich language we have today.

* * * *

But two European languages had made their presence felt in late Ottoman Turkey. The first was French. Searching for greater world influence, the French Government took great interest in the Christian populations of what were to become Lebanon and Syria, then still part of the Ottoman Empire. Also, French lawyers, as far as the Ottoman administration was concerned, influenced the latter-day legal system in Constantinople. I remember that in a particular land dispute at Knidos we were referred to an aristocratic old gentleman whose family hailed from Datça, home of the heaviest topers on the Peninsula, of which, it must be said, he was certainly not one. He was an *ağa*, a local land-owner from an old family, with extensive orange and mandarin orchards. When asked in Turkish about his interest in certain property at Knidos, he refused to reply in his native tongue, and would only speak in French, despite the passage of more than forty years since the establishment of the Turkish Republic. It was explained to me that he did not wish to be identified, in speech at least, with what he still considered his own serfs.

The other European influence was, at least temporarily, German. The war-mongering Kaiser Wilhelm, late-comer to the scramble for empire, was eager to get his Teutonic fingers on all or part of the imploding Ottoman Empire, a feature that scared the wits out of the British, by the way, Suez Canal politics being at the forefront of British Foreign Policy. The Kaiser offered all sorts of novel inducements to the corrupt Sultanate of Abdul Hamid – building the Hejaz Railway to Mecca, for example, the one blown up by Lawrence of Arabia. To this day, in the old Byzantine Hippodrome of Istanbul, right next to the *Medrese* of the Blue Mosque in Sultan Ahmet, there is a rather magnificent but totally incongruous black marble fountain donated by the Kaiser, with his own insignia inter-twined with that of the Ottoman Sultan cum Caliph. I hope the Caliph enjoyed the gift. His successor Mehmed V unadvisedly joined the German side in the First World War, the price of which was to be the loss of his Empire.

So, how did these linguistic influences play out at Knidos? Even to someone like me who just scraped through 'O' level French, I could spot the French loan words in Turkish - *plaj* for beach; *büfe* for snack bar, *beton* for concrete and, rather more taxingly, *kuaför* for hairdresser, for example. But the loan words were few and far between, little god-sends in what is otherwise a truly central Asiatic language. I came across German from time to time, though spoken by very few. It was the only non-Turkish language that anyone, apart from the *ağa* and his like at Knidos, had actually heard of. However, this was not the result of the preceding bellicose ambitions of Kaiser Wilhelm. It was more to do with the later financial inducements of Daimler Benz, Siemens A.G. and Krupp Steel. The great economic miracle of post Second World War Germany was being built on the sweat of the *Gastarbeiter* toiling on the Ruhr. The Turkish guest workers, or perhaps less complimentary, the *Wanderarbeiter* – migrant labourers – were one of the keys to this industrial success. Turkish guest workers returning to Turkey on holiday from the factories of Dortmund, Duisburg and Düsseldorf drove fancy cars, albeit second hand bangers, and flashed them in rural areas, where there were no paved roads. These local-boys-made-good were objects of both envy and suspicion, talking as they did about the German Mark and about the sexual freedoms of the west. Knidos and its villages were rather too far away, at the end of an impassable, cul-de-sac of a peninsula, to feel any direct influence from the fleshly inducements of the Rhine. As a result, there was only one trace that I ever saw at Knidos of the German language. It had been typed on a single dog-eared sheet lying about on the finds room table and inexplicably was a list of military questions which had been pertinent, no doubt, at some point in the past. I remember only one of the entries:

"Ist diese unbefestigte Strasse fuer Panzertruppen angemessen?"

"Is this dirt road suitable for tanks?"

How useful would the answer to that be to someone studying the impact of Hellenism on the Eastern Mediterranean? But thinking on, had I been asked that question in relation, say, to the road from Yazıköy to Knidos, the answer at the time would have been an emphatic: *"Überhaupt Nichts!"* "Absolutely not!"

* * * *

To communicate at all at Knidos, which I for one was desperate to do, it was necessary for me to learn Turkish, with which I therefore proceeded to grapple. The effect was immediate and socially satisfying, but what I didn't consider was that I was learning a particularly local, and more especially, a distinctly rural dialect of the language. In a general way, this has stood me in very good stead in my subsequent travels around ancient Caria, from Bodrum to the Meander Valley where, despite my outward appearance, my local accent seems to suggest that I was a Turk. On several occasions, when I have answered the preliminary questions about where I live, saying 'London', I have been asked in all seriousness:

"What's it like for a Turk living in London?"

Anyway, day by day at Knidos, my Turkish expanded. My old friend Ali Karadeniz, the *Bekçi*, added greatly to my vocabulary.

"Günaydın, Ali Bey," I would say. "Good morning, Mr. Ali"

"Nasılsınız," I would continue. "How are you?"

And he would reply:

"Günaydın, Deyvit Bey. Iyiyim teşekkür ederim."

"Good morning Mr. David, I am well thank you."

So far so good! But as the days wore on, he began to sprinkle his responses with rather more idiosyncratic phrases. On being asked how he was today, he would reply:

"Günaydın, Deyvit Bey. Deyvit Bey, ben bugün beton gibi olacağım!"

"Good morning Mr. David. Mr. David, today I will be like concrete!"

As he issued this greeting, he would clench his right fist tightly and flex his arm muscles in what I assumed to be a gesture of strength for the work of the day, a sort of Charles Atlas generalised signal of personal power. Much to Ali and the other workers enjoyment, I came to copy the same phrase and gestures each morning.

"Good morning! Today I'm like concrete, thanks very much!"

I imagined an association, at least in my own mind, with the hammer and sickle and a kind of proletariat solidarity.

The phrase would alternate with:

"Ben bugün çelik gibi olacağım."

"Today I will be like steel!"

And not as I once mistakenly remembered, alternating the vowels:

"Ben bugün çilek gibi olacağım."

"Today I will be like strawberries!" which, after a moment or two of confused surprise, had everyone in hysterics.

Anyway, armed with these colourful idioms, some years later in a highly cultured environment in Istanbul, I thought I would display my greater knowledge of colloquial Turkish. Meeting my host, a Professor of Turkish history, for breakfast, and being asked how I was this bright morning, I launched forth:

"Günaydın, Cünyet Bey. Ben bugün beton gibi olacağım."

He looked puzzled and pained by turns. He obviously hadn't been to Yazıköy, I thought. I told him of my experiences at Knidos, and the muscle clenching which accompanied the greeting. Then, his face lit up with a slightly embarrassed smile.

"I think you should be careful where and to whom you reply like that," he said.

"You see, I think the speaker is referring to and graphically illustrating not so much his general feeling of well-being, but to the hoped-for conduct of his private parts. I think he is indicating that later in the day, his, how you say, 'dick', will be fully erect. It refers to his intended sexual prowess, not to whether he had a good night's sleep or not!"

Like strawberries, eh? No wonder everyone was in hysterics.

* * * *

In the nightly symposia we enjoyed, field staff and workers in Cengis' Çayhane, there arose the constant problems of communication. No amount of sign language could express the more complex issues we wanted to share together. Slowly, haltingly, we learnt the basic vocabulary. Turkish has a number of extremely useful words which articulate a world of meaning. One of the most practical is '*var*', 'in a state of being', 'in existence', 'available'. How useful!

"*Kırımızı şarap var!*" - "There is red wine."

Conversely, however, there is another catch-all in the form of '*yok*' 'not in existence', 'not available'.

"*Para yok!*" - "There's no money."

Finally, there is the word '*çok*' – 'lots of', 'many'.

"*Bira çok, ama burada yok.*" - "There are lots of beer, but not here!"

Used imaginatively, we could weave quite complicated ideas around these three words. But inevitably, there came a time when the workmen decided they would like to learn English, and who better to teach them than Paul, an English teacher on Peace Corps duty in central Anatolia who had joined us for his summer vacation.

"*Öretmen var!*" we might say. "There is a teacher."

From somewhere, one of the villagers produced an elementary school book as a basic text. The lessons were scheduled for 2.30 the following day, at the end of the long lunch break and before work resumed at 3.00 pm. Paul felt that twenty minutes a day would probably be enough.

Duly, the next day, in the ancient theatre, the lesson began. Amazingly, nearly all our one hundred and twenty workers turned up, which was a huge handful for Paul.

He began, referring to the text book.

"*Günaydın.*" "Good Morning. All say after me: Good Morning!"

"Gut murnik…Güt mörniks."

"*Günaydın.*" "Good Morning."

"Gut murnik…Güt mörniks."

By the time he'd got round the whole group, time was up. More tomorrow, he motioned with his watch.

Next day, only half the number appeared, which made it slightly easier.

"*Günaydın*". "Good Morning". "*Nasılsınız*", "How are you?"

"Güt mörniks … Hav arr ü … Hauv arr ooo. Ha….vur uo…oo"

One day later, only about 20 people showed up, but Paul persisted.

"*Günaydın! Nasılsınız? Iyiyim*"

"Good morning. How are you …I am fine."

He showed them in the book, so that they could read it as well.

"Güt mörnik! Hav arr ü? I am fayn."

And on the following day only six of the workmen bothered to appear. For some inexplicable reason, the next phrase in the book was a real odd-ball one.

"Mehmet hapishanede." "Mehmet is in jail."

Paul followed the book, but in fact this was to be the last day. After that, no-one seemed interested. Maybe it was the rather suggestive phraseology, or maybe the remaining few would rather play cards and smoke. Anyway, you could always identify the last six students. Each morning they would stop in front of you, raise their hand and with great deliberateness and at high volume say, all in one sentence, rising to a crescendo on the last word:

"GÜT MÖRNIK HAV ARR Ü I AM FAYN MEHMET IS IN **JAIL!**"

* * * *

There were some poignant moments during the time we were getting to know each other, the villagers and me. On many occasions, during a cigarette break when one by one they came to peer at my plane table, head on one side, puzzling over the pencilled doodles and figured points of reference, they then would point to my clapped out wrist watch and say:

"Lutfen Dayvit, bilek saati istiyorum." "Please David, I want a watch."

I often wondered at this request, made by villagers whose whole lives were patently governed much more strictly than mine ever was by the ebb and flow of the natural world. In such a life-style, a watch seemed to me to be a superfluous appendage.

By the same token, another request would be

"*Lutfen Dayvit, araba istiyorum.*" "Please David, I want a car."

But there were no navigable roads for normal cars. The surfaces of the cart tracks around the villages were so execrable that no car would stand up to such punishment for very long.

Perhaps it was me. Perhaps I was being too patronising, seeing what I considered an idyllically simple life being ruined by the peripheral and unnecessary trappings of modern western society. That was all to change in Turkey during the next few years, when the Japanese pick-up truck began to oust the horse and cart and the Fiat Tractor to replace the donkey.

But for now, rural life seemed to have its own innate charm, its own pulse and its simple attraction. For the Wordsworth in me, it all represented an unadulterated idyll, a tranquil and unspoiled existence, a pastoral innocence, though one which I now have no doubt that I totally misunderstood given the probable realities of life in this harsh landscape.

CHAPTER TEN

DRAMATIS PERSONAE

People have told me that when I get really stoned I babble on about shit that makes no sense. I always know what I mean, but nobody else seems to understand any of it.

Hippie Speak 1980

Maybe the very notion of pitching up in a remote country on the shores of the Mediterranean with an unfamiliar culture and strange language, sifting the alien earth from the ancient past, is bound to attract its fair share of eccentrics, adventurers, high-born flotsam and jetsam, low-grade drifters and multi-purpose misfits. If this is the case, the excavations at Knidos were no exception. And trying to mould such an extraordinarily disparate band of co-workers into a team must by definition be well nigh impossible.

Take Eddie, for example. Good looking, physique toned to perfection, highly artistic but otherwise totally off the wall. Eddie had in his day been engaged in photo-shoots for Esquire magazine, that cerebral man's essential reading matter. Either because of this, or perhaps in spite of it, he now found himself at Knidos cast in the seemingly respectable role of Expedition photographer.

But it immediately became obvious that Eddie grooved to a beat, a rhythm which more often than not didn't quite syncopate with his graphic function on the dig. Also, we all quickly formed the impression that Eddie was experiencing diverting images additional to the ones he saw through the eyepiece of his camera.

As for his function on the site, the general idea was that at each stage of the investigation of a trench Eddie would come with his photographic equipment and measuring rods and take pictures of the exposed area - from above, from the side, the right corner, the left corner, the wall detail, the section, the artefacts, in fact, whatever the site supervisor needed for the dig records. Day by day Eddie was supposed to be there to make a pictorial essay of the excavation, discovery by discovery. That was the theory. In practice, Eddie was at the very least wayward and, more usually, uncooperative and often totally incomprehensible.

"Eddie, I've just finished the next level of Trench One at the Bouleterion site. Any chance you could take photos of it before lunch?"

"Aw, Man, I mean, that's so far out. And I'm kinda, kinda…all fucked up and stuff. So fuck the friggin' photos! Hey, d'ya hear that, Man? That's, like, 'F' major!"

"But Eddie we can't continue unless you …"

"Don't give me that shit, Baby." Eddie's limbs gyrated to an unseen pulse, his eyelids closed, his fingers clicking. "If this is, like, Tuesday, I gotta groove, know what I mean?"

Quite what Eddie did mean frequently escaped us all. Aside, to me, he later observed, "Hey, you wanna know something? That fuckin' Olga, Man. You know what her problem is? You wanna know? Too much fuckin' with the Booleterioo, that's her problem. These ski chicks, Man, they're all the same. It's down hill all the way with them, know what I mean? I seen it before. Slide for me baby. Yeah!"

But somehow Eddie would do the job and the photos would get taken, and the excavations would continue. It was just that you had to go through the whole unconstructive dialogue before you arrived at the job itself.

"Hey, that dude, Soo-lay-man, he's cool Man. Scope those shades. He's real cool! I kinda vibe that guy, know what I mean?"

He made a reciprocal rocking motion on the balls of his feet, the palms of his hands describing opposing circles in front of him.

"Yeah, when it comes to ar-chae-ology, I mean, he digs, Man!"

Which particular Suleyman he was referring to was anybody's guess, since we had a number working on site, and Eddie was not about to elaborate. Each day was the same, the battle of simple logic against the forces of unfathomable Eddieobabble.

"Oh, Eddie, could you please photograph that cornicing in the theatre which Nancy uncovered yesterday so we can move it?"

"That's a bunch of jive, Man. Yesterday, that's like…like, yeah, that's like history. For me, that's like Hell-en-istic, know what I mean? It's kinda Splitsville, Man. Yesterday, huh? When the fuck did that happen?"

Mercifully I didn't have to request that any photos were taken, and the women of the team could usually get what they wanted out of him, given time, patience and a dictionary of contemporary American street idiom. During daylight hours, if you spoke to Eddie about anything, you would like as not be treated to a diatribe of invective, or even more, a mouthful of a beat-hippie fusion-speak from whatever planet he thought he was on at the time.

But in the evenings, a wondrous metamorphosis would take place. He would change from being like an unintelligible bear with piles to becoming one of the most gentle people on the dig, though you felt that just under the surface he was like a tightly wound spring. Come six o'clock, after he'd taken a shower, he would disappear into his tent – he had his very own tent, pitched well away from the rest of us, which he had brought with him from the States. Half an hour later, he would emerge, like a butterfly from a chrysalis. He had changed from his daytime short shorts, tee shirt and sneakers into a light drill all-in-one cotton jump suit, his long blond hair slicked back, and wearing a pair of lilac tinted 'easy rider' spectacles and tooled cow-boy boots.

"Hi, Dave!" he would say, slowly, while very deliberately describing a wide circle in the air with the palm of his right hand. "But, I mean, Hi! How you doin' Man? You, like, OK, or somethin'? I mean, real!"

Then he'd click his fingers and throw his pelvis forward. "Yeah, Dave, I am ready to party, Man!"

It became obvious that his daily ritual in his tent at sundown must involve some ingestion of recreational chemicals, though it was never spoken of. He would join us in the Çayhane and drink quietly, smiling beatifically at everyone. Once, he chose to drink wine, and then changed to rakı, then back to wine, something we were always advised never to do, but he started throwing the booze back in equal quantities, becoming more animated and more loquacious as the evening wore on. Finally, when we had all told him this would end in disaster, he stood up, and pointing his finger down from a great height, said to us all:

"You wanna know somethin'? You really wanna know?"

At which moment he very slowly fell backwards and passed out. The next day, he was rather more ursine and haemorrhoidal than usual, but otherwise unscathed.

But one of my most enduring memories of Eddie was on one of the last days of the season. He was in fine form that evening in the Çayhane session.

"Hey, Man, this Turkish lingo, it's real cool, you know? I'm gonna get off that plane, in New York City, that's where. And my ol' daddy, well, he's gonna be there to meet me. And he's gonna say, 'Hey Eddie, how you doin' Son? How are yuh?' And I'm gonna say, 'Hi Daddio. You wanna know how I really am?'"

He raised his arms and flexed his biceps. "Man, I'm like concrete, that's how I am!"

* * * *

To Sonny belonged a brooding, sensitive character. He was brought up by a family who had originally been from the poorer parts of Brooklyn and from whom he had inherited that well-known, New York, rapid-fire repartee, poignantly tempered by an almost self-deprecating sense of humour. He was slightly built, prone to melancholia, and yet he sang constantly as he worked in the drawing office we shared. Our duets became legendary. His delicate, sallow features and dark eyes, combined with his outward enthusiasm, made him very attractive to women, as you will hear later.

Sonny was dedicated to his topographic survey, his contour plan of the ancient city, and for this he was using a rare but fascinating system called tacheometry, an ingenious method which relies on the Reichenbach principle – you see more of an object between the two cross hairs of the eyepiece of a theodolite the further it is away, which is, with some fancy trigonometry, a known fraction of the actual distance. He taught me tacheometry, which can be totally absorbing once you understand it. He would set up over his triangulated points, zero down a given base line and then measure distance, angle of inclination, and height, from which, with the cosine of the level of inclination and a few fancy tables he could arrive at the position and height above sea level of any point at Knidos. Back in our drawing office, he would play with the readings and finally plot out the contours.

"Let me tell you something, Dave," he would say, pointing to his rows of readings. "See these figures? You've got to keep it like that. Keep it in figures as long as you can. Figures, they're magic. Someone will come along and say, 'This is Sonny. He's a genius. Just look at his figures.' See, Dave, once you draw the picture out on the paper, everyone can understand it, and they'll say 'Yes, the Corinthian temple is … here.' They forget about you altogether. So, I'm telling you, keep it in figures. Figures are magic!"

He had certainly equipped the expedition with the very best materials which he had bought with him. Not only did I have the advantage of the up-to-the-minute alidade he had bought from Switzerland, but from New York he had dragged out with him reams and rolls of the best Keuffel and Esser drafting papers, far superior to anything I had ever used before. There was a plastic coated paper called, appropriately, Herculene which we used for outdoor work.

"See, Dave, it doesn't distort with the heat and the sweat", said Sonny. "And you can use the Albanene for making the finished drawing on white!"

Sonny and me, as the surveyors, we lived a bit in a world of our own. We were not attached to a particular site, or a team, nor were we close to the Management, and this allowed us to stay to a certain extent aloof from the cut and thrust of the day to day politics, back-biting and gossip that formed the average fare of the other staff members. We had our own drawing office on the other side of the isthmus from the dig house, next to the artefact store. Here we would often spend time together of an afternoon inking in our maps and plans and it was then that we sang. We made a good duo, and harmonised everything from opera to folk and pop – 'Moon River', various Beatles numbers, that kind of thing. But there was one song which Sonny and I sang that he had brought with him from New York City. I didn't question its pedigree at the time, but it turned out to be of the oddest origin.

The words went like this:

> *Come pack your bags and trek Ferreira,*
> *Johnnie with the bandy leg.*
> *Hop, hop, hop on the right foot,*
> *Hop, hop, hop on the left foot*
> *Pack your bags and trek Ferreira,*
> *Johnnie with the bandy leg.*

Ten years later I was in South Africa whistling the tune to Sonny's 'Knidos' song when an Afrikaaner farmer stopped me and said:

"How do you know that tune? I thought only Africaaners knew it."

So I told him that I had learnt it at Knidos from Sonny, who'd learnt it from his Dad in Brooklyn, and at the time I thought it was an American song, you know, 'Pack your bags' and all that.

He was amazed, and said there was no English translation. It was purely Afrikaans. I was equally vehement that there was. We reached a stalemate. But how did Sonny, who'd never been out of the US until now, know not only the song, but a translation that didn't exist?

It was another twenty two years until I finally discovered the answer from an Afrikaaner who worked at the South African embassy in Paris. She was a second secretary there and I met her at a dinner party. When I related this odd tale, she gave me the answer. In the 1950's a popular South African singing duo, Marais and Miranda, had gone to the USA on tour, and they had translated a few of their native songs into English. Sonny's Dad must have been at one of the concerts and remembering the song, had sung it to Sonny, who sang it to me. Amazing!

91

＊ ＊ ＊ ＊

Amanda was one of those slender, languorous women who always look as though they have just walked straight out of a cinema set, never a hair out of place. And in Amanda's case it was her hair that was her defining feature - ash blonde, flowing straight and film-like from the crown of her head to the small of her back. She smoked long, Balkan Sobranie cigarettes, holding them indolently at the very tips of her elongated fingers, her hand vertical in a scouting salute, her heavy-lidded eyes focussed on a distant horizon. When she spoke, it was with a very far back English Home Counties accent, her speech slow and mannered. One had the impression her studied hauteur allowed her only obliquely to engage in conversation. As for men, from my albeit limited angle, for all the interest she displayed they might be from a different species – *la belle dame sans mercie* sprang to mind, or maybe she was a one way shopper, direct current only. Who knows? Anyway, she spent her time in the dig house, cataloguing artefacts and listening to tapes of the more abstruse Richard Strauss song cycles.

Eddie, if I understood him correctly, summed her up:

"Hey, that 'Manda chick, she is soo anticlockwise, Man, she clicks in another zone. I mean, she is so far out, she's like, out of sight."

"Yes," I agreed. At least, I think I agreed. "She is fairly typical of some of our upper class English women."

"No shit, Man! I mean, but how do you dudes pro-cree-ate? By remote fuckin' control or somethin'? I mean, how do you beget and stuff?"

I knew what he meant … I think.

At the opposite end of the cultural spectrum among the expedition's dramatis personae was the *Muhtar* (mayor) of Yazıköy, a character who had stepped

92

straight out of a violent Chinese movie about Altan and the Mongol hordes. He was a powerfully built man in his thirties, chosen as mayor no doubt for one who could bang heads together. His formidable, leather-tanned Asiatic features were preceded by cinematographically impressive, unkempt black mustachios, the ends of which he would curl slowly to add emphasis to his somewhat suspect profundity. He was accompanied by two large mastiffs who would fix their audience with a blood-shot, baleful stare, and by four 'minders' with bare chests, wearing tight swimming trunks which displayed their prominent manhood, and heavy, steel-toed boots to intimidate the opposition. Whenever the *Muhtar* of Yazıköy appeared at Knidos, everyone deferred to this local municipal war-lord, this village Mr Big.

His henchmen were constantly offering him morsels for his approval – a kebab here, a rakı there – but his favourite power gesture was to make an ostentatious refusal, with a deriding sneer and a slow, upward movement of the chin, eyes closed, followed by a disdainful back-handed wave from his chest. Here was a man who could select his own morsels. The whole performance was like a mime show, with little or no speech. When he did say anything, it was in a harsh, guttural voice with minimum converse. He preferred to sit in silence, his deeply knitted brows a picture of ill-temper and his narrowed eyes flicking sideways, this way and that. He was in his own way totally aloof, unapproachable, uncommunicative … and profoundly sinister.

It was all the more extraordinary then that these two characters, Amanda the aloof Home Counties heiress and the uncultivated *Muhtar* of Yazıköy, should somehow be attracted to each other. The *Muhtar* spoke nothing other than Turkish, and for her part, Amanda knew absolutely not a word of the local language. I would have bet money that this highly improbable couple, the one a privately schooled, untouchable English Sloane and the other an ill-educated, coarse Anatolian village superman, would never have anything to do with one another even if they were the last couple left on earth. But attract each other they did, so it seemed.

It was Hakkı Bey who pointed it out to me. Hakkı Bey was the Turkish Government commissar, the Antiquities Agent sent from Ankara to oversee the conduct of the excavation, to sort out any local liaison problems and see to it that none of the artefacts went missing, slipped into someone's pocket accidentally on purpose. Hakkı Bey was a sort of piggy-in-the-middle, highly suspected by the workers of being a management spy, and totally disparaged by the commissariat as a Departmental stooge and administrative nuisance. This bi-polar disrespect was exacerbated by the fact that he was originally from Cyprus – neither fish nor fowl, so to speak, not really Turkish and yet not European. Hakkı Bey befriended me because maybe he saw me in the same position, not really in with the High-ups, a sort of independent trench-less supernumerary.

One night in the Çayhane he confided in me. He spoke good English but with an incongruous Cockney accent. Being Cypriot he'd spent some years in Tottenham, of all places.

"'Ere, Dave, what do you know? That there village mayor is having it off with Amanda. It's not right, that isn't."

"That can't be, Hakkı Bey. That's a totally bizarre idea. It could never happen!"

"Honest to God, Dave. I'm not joking. They're at it right now. Come on, I'll show you."

With that he dragged me unthinking into the silky blackness of the Knidian dark. It was a moonless night and, once away from the reflected light of the Çayhane, it was almost impossible to see anything but indistinct shadows. We made our way by a familiar path towards the Pink Temple and the sea, the wraith-like bushes leaping out at us as we walked. I began to think. What am I doing? If Hakkı Bey was right, we were about to disturb one of the most disturbing men I had ever met in a scene from Gengis Khan and the

Angel of Death, replete with muscle-bound samurai. As a late developer I have always carried a rather feeble frame and it dawned on me that any minute now I could be seized upon by vile men in sexually explicit bathing costumes and substantially 'duffed up', as Hakkı Bey might have put it. What a tragic end to a promising archaeological career.

Suddenly, Hakkı Bey motioned to me to stop. I cowered behind a rubble wall, not daring to move. My heart was thumping against my ribs and my breathing sounded like a steam engine. He waited for the scene to settle, then, slowly extending his right arm he pointed, first to one spot, then another, then another. At each place I could just make out in the starlight what I took to be the dim frame of a semi-naked helot, and then, in the middle distance, silhouetted against the starry horizon I thought I saw the reciprocal movement of a torso, which, with a little imagination, could have been the couple in question 'on the job'. On the other hand, the all-powerful Muhtar of Yazıköy, if indeed it was he, might just as well have been shagging a piebald goat, for all the detail I could make out. I indicated to Hakkı Bey that I was returning to the relative security of the Çayhane and a stiff drink. Once back there, nursing a large rakı, I sat torn between the cloying purity of my Non-Conformist upbringing and the pornographic shadow boxing I had just seen outside. If that was truly what it was, I was terrified that I had that night passed a transgression of no return, my innocence lost for ever.

Next morning I surreptitiously side-spied Amanda in the dig house. Not a hair was out of place; she was as cold and composed as ever. She certainly didn't look as if she'd been humped senseless the night before by the hairy Man Mountain from Yazıköy among the ashlar blocks of the ancient city. Maybe I had imagined the whole thing, I told myself, my modesty restored. Nevertheless, fearing arrest, or divine retribution or worse, I kept my nocturnal voyeurism to myself. I didn't want to be labelled a peeping pervert either.

"That 'Manda chick, Man, she is a piece of work. I mean, Fuck! You know?" mused Eddie to me, one evening some time later, apropos of nothing in particular.

Mistaking his casual remark for historical observation, I gave it my full attention for once, and pausing, said:

"I don't think so, Eddie. No, on quiet reflection I really don't think so. I think it was a pair of goats; I am sure I read that they do it in the dark!"

"What the fuck do you mean, Man? You been on the happy pills or somethin'?"

It was his turn to knit his brows with incomprehension for once.

CHAPTER ELEVEN

TAKING THE PITHOS

If our designs for private houses are to be correct, we must at the outset take note of the countries and climates in which they are built. As the position of the heaven with regard to a given tract on the earth leads naturally to different characteristics, it is obvious that designs for houses ought similarly to conform to the nature of the country and to diversities of climate.

Marcus Vitruvius, Ten Books on Architecture

It turned out to be the villa to end all villas, set in what must have been one of the wealthiest residential parts of the city. But that would only become apparent after prolonged excavation and interpretation. The villa was located in a part of the city which was way off to the east, near the point where the present dirt road from Yazıköy enters the ancient site more or less through the eastern gateway, well away from the civic part of Knidos in the western quarter - the part with the temples, theatres and other monuments that would impress any excavation's backers so much. It was a miracle really that we were excavating it at all. But here we were, in one of the great residential *insulae* of the city.

You will remember that Knidos had been laid out on a Hellenistic grid iron plan, each 'island' bounded by horizontal streets running roughly east to west, and interlocking stepped streets running south to north, thus describing evenly sized city blocks about 45 by 45 meters square, a bit like a miniature Manhattan, but of course 2500 years earlier. Our site at Terrace East was one such block, and working from the bottom layers of the excavation upwards, the lowest levels were composed of a group of four quadrilateral stone-founded Hellenistic houses set on massive polygonal block terraces. The characteristic pottery shards indicated that they dated to the last three centuries BC, as one might expect.

But it was what happened next that made Terrace East archaeologically and culturally interesting, for me at least. It seems that in Roman times, Knidos had become a whole lot wealthier. The citizens of Rome had developed an insatiable appetite for costly commodities - silks from northern China, perfumes from the Persian Gulf, frankincense and myrrh from the deserts of South Arabia and Somalia, spices from the Malabar Coast, exotic animals from equatorial Africa - as well as a need for the more mundane local exports such as wine from Knidos (it was famous for its wine), timber from the Taurus Mountains, leather and wheat from the interior. All of these goods travelled by sea around the coast, from city to city, being bought and sold, bartered and stored. Financial and commercial institutions flourished and the agoras, the market places of Asia Minor, bustled to the business of making money. Knidos was ideally placed to profit from this passing commerce, and the archaeological evidence indicates that at Terrace East, a rich merchant took over the whole of the original insula and redeveloped it as his personal villa.

At the beginning of the excavation, as the earth was removed from the surface, only the stubs of walls were revealed, and Coral, who was initially in charge of the site, had great difficultly establishing which wall was 'bonded' with which.

It was the next part of the investigation which proved to be the defining excavation of Terrace East, and for this a new site supervisor had been installed, the Roman villa supremo, Mitt. Mitt had two characteristics which singled him out. He was an absolute genius at deciphering the site as a series of rebuilt and refurbished Roman houses. But he also had a very short fuse. He did not suffer fools gladly, or anyone else, come to think about it. The art historians, who were not really interested in residential Knidos, allotted all the lower orders of workmen to Terrace East, men like Ömer the flute player, the intellectually-challenged Şükrü Tunç, the ever-enigmatic Ali Kocadurmuş and an assortment of donkey boys who joined in for the fun.

The excavations were carried out under Mitt's watchful eye and lashing tongue.

"You've got to keep these chaps at it, you know. They can be real slackers, if you let them."

Every few minutes, one of the shovellers would cry out

"Sigara molası, Mitt Bey!" calling for a cigarette break to which every hour or so they were entitled - shovelling earth in the hot sun could be hard work. It was during one of these breaks that Mitt tried to disabuse me of any romantic notions about Turkish villagers which I had acquired at the beginning of the season.

"Do you know what these men talk about, all the time? Do you really know? Well, it's how long is a donkey's dick, that's what they talk about. I mean, all the time."

"Surely not?" I queried.

"Yes. It's true. By the way, do you actually know how long a donkey's penis really can be? Have you ever seen one fully erect? It's this big." He motioned a distance between his two hands. "I mean, this big!"

As if to emphasise his observations, one of the men jumped up from his trench, threw down his shovel, and shouted:

"Hayır! Hayır!" "No! No! Mitt Bey, Not that big, this big, this big!" measuring an even greater distance with his hands.

The other workers collapsed with mirth.

* * * *

Donkeys constituted one of the main sights and sounds of life at Knidos, especially sounds. Soon after first light each morning the braying would start, a kind of bucolic alarm clock – 'time to get your ass out of bed'. The sounds would ring eerily around the rocky mountains of the mainland and bounce back from the island. It always began with a single laboured hee-haw, slow and loud, reaching a quickening, final whinny. This would be the signal for serial braying, as many more donkeys joined in, creating a cacophony which echoed for a long time, reverberating around the ancient city. Many of the workers had brought this mode of transport from their villages on the Peninsula - there were few cars in those days. Cumhur, one of the diggers at Terrace East, owned a small donkey not much bigger than a foal, a rather energetic little animal of which he was inordinately proud. Looking at it, one could hardly credit that it was capable of taking his weight, and I foolishly made the mistake of saying so.

"Hayır, Deyvit Bey. Bu eşek Herkül gibi!"

"No, David, this donkey is like Hercules," the Turkish paradigm for anything big and strong.

To prove the point, I was invited to sit on the animal myself. At first I declined, but I was cajoled into it, until finally relenting, I agreed. There was no saddle, but as I was only going to sit on it for a moment, I didn't think it mattered. Unfortunately I had not yet acquired a diploma in bareback donkey riding and didn't realise that you are supposed to sit on the rump, not in the middle of the back. Anyway, the donkey was not very high, so I easily threw my leg over and sat amid ships. That was my mistake. No sooner was I astride than the proud owner whacked its rear end and the beast took off, ears erect, at a full gallop, with me astride the spine, my feet trailing the ground and the donkey's vertebrae splitting me in two at every step. This was the signal for wild merriment, as the donkey ran down the dusty road pursued at high speed by ten workmen in hysterics. It was at this point that I also discovered I didn't know how to stop. This was becoming the test drive from hell.

Cries of *"Dur! Dur Deyvit. Halat çek!"* were to no avail. "Stop! Stop! David. Pull the rope!"

Donkey and rider careered past the theatre, passed another audience of cheering diggers who were having a cigarette break. It was only near the Çayhane that a group of tea drinkers, hearing the commotion, jumped up and forming a human barrier across the road, leaping at the donkey's head, and bringing it to a standstill. I stood up and alighted, feeling as if I had been sliced in two vertically.

Cumhur, the owner of the beast caught up with us.

"See, I told you he was like Hercules!"

Rubbing what was left of my macerated private parts, I saw no reason to disagree.

Some days later I was back at Terrace East, where digging was in full swing. I say full swing because the diggers were wont, when the boss wasn't looking, to swing their long handled shovels at one another in a game of 'shower your neighbour with earth'. It was either that, or they would hurl the shovel-full high in the sky and see how the wind blew the dirt away. If not checked, they could play like that all day. Anyway, I was surveying in the middle of the site, drawing in the newly uncovered walls when I espied my bête noir, the little black donkey of the week before, tied to a bush at the edge of the excavation. It looked suspiciously restive, prancing back and forth around its halter.

Its interest had been aroused by a female donkey tethered to a stake some distance away in a field of dry stalks close to the water's edge below where we were working. She stood there, quietly grinding her teeth on some thistles whilst emitting the occasional sad braying blast. I don't speak 'Donkey', but apparently this call must have been charged with powerful reproductive imagery. Cumhur's little black conveyance began pulling violently on its halter, which highly amused the diggers, who were anthropomorphically enjoying this manifestation of sexual repression. Suddenly the whole bush to which it was tethered pulled out of the ground and, thus released, the frustrated animal was off down the road at high speed, rope and bush dragging behind in a cloud of dust. It reached the first terrace and leapt over it, going at full tilt. Cumhur was suddenly in hot pursuit, diving and grabbing at the trailing bush, but he was too late. His transportation had reached the female in the field, vaulted into place, and was pumping away vigorously, while the female in question clenched her teeth and flattened her ears with what I took to be a show of obvious enjoyment. I was told later that it was very bad form to allow your donkey to impregnate another's without the owner's consent. It's the asinine equivalent of having a car accident, so Cumhur was pulling with all his might trying to stop his donkey doing what of course came naturally. But tug as he might, the animal pumped on, firmly glued to his task until he'd finished, before finally stepping down. If it's possible for a donkey to grin, that's what it was doing, baring its teeth at Cumhur in unalloyed satisfaction. From their viewing platform in the Upper Circle, the Terrace East diggers were bent double with rustic mirth. When Cumhur came disconsolately back to the site, donkey in tow, I reminded him

"See, you always said he was like Hercules!"

* * * *

As the season progressed the villa was already revealing its form. It had been built in a classic style, but somehow its position overlooking the sea singled it out as a once magnificent building. Reconstructing a day in the life of the villa from the rubble walls, one gets the impression that, for the owner at least, this was a superb place to live. Walking back from his day at the Harbour Agora along the street which ran towards the eastern city, the owner would have risen up one of the stepped streets, past a couple of landings, and there in a blank wall was the double door into the villa. The threshold block shows that normally only one of the two doors opened, the other remained bolted down. Turning the handle, he would have immediately left the noise, the heat, the dust, the smells and the harsh light of the city and entered a cool, dark vestibule. This was a small anteroom, where he would leave his sandals. The anteroom gave access through a second door into the focal point of the villa, a large atrium, an indoor garden open to the sky but sheltered from the glare of the sun by mature trees. The atrium was rectangular, surrounded on each side by a shady veranda, its pan-tiled roof supported along all four sides on a wooden framework. A small wooden balustrade divided the tiled veranda floor from the garden itself. Aromatic shrubs and leafy foliage filled the central garden, giving a pleasing feel of light and shadow, whilst in the middle of the atrium was a shallow pool of water fed by underground pipes from the rear of the villa which would have the effect of cooling the air. It was created as a haven of peace and serenity, the antithesis of the bustling commerce of the market. This wealthy merchant had literally closed the outside world away.

Along the left side of the atrium, towards the slope, there were a series of reception rooms, each one opening separately from the veranda. They had been finished in white plaster with a dado decorated with red lined panels below, above which frescoes with dark red or dark yellow ochre surrounds were finished with vignettes of birds and goddesses. In the far corner of the veranda was a small shrine, the lararium, sacred to the personal gods which protected the household, the spirits of the family's ancestors. The remains of food and wine offerings would have been left in the alcove of the shrine.

From the corner of the atrium nearest the entrance, a passageway led down the side of the villa, along side the stepped street, into a courtyard at the rear where there was a well-head and large basins for water. This, and the area to the rear of the villa, would have been for the household slaves and servants.

On the opposite side of the atrium to the vestibule would have been the tablinum, the dinning room, with rich mosaics on the floor and reclining benches around the walls. But the room which would have attracted the most attention would have been the one along the seaward, the southern, side of the atrium. It was suspended on rafters above a series of mud-brick walls of basements down the slope. Walking in from the veranda, the two aspects of this room which would have been quite spectacular would have been the wall decoration and the views from the balcony. The walls had been covered in the richest frescoes, pictured panelling of rural scenes of animals and human figures painted with an almost impressionistic skill. The panels were topped with plaster cornices featuring *tromp d'oeil* mouldings, intricate three dimensional details painted on the curved surfaces in delicate shades of green, red and gold. Across the room, the pillared balcony opened high above the street giving a panoramic vista looking across to the breakwaters of the Commercial harbour and the Island, then beyond, across a seascape of the azure Mediterranean to the outline of the Island of Rhodes far in the distance. This was truly a vision of loveliness.

＊ ＊ ＊ ＊

So that is what the villa looked like in its first century AD heyday, but to arrive at that state of knowledge, the excavators had to dig deep. The rear of the villa was the most difficult. The digging seemed bottomless. With trench sides more than three meters high, the loose earth had to be thrown onto an interim platform, and then heaved up onto a waiting barrow on top of the baulks which divided up the trenches before being carted away and tipped over the spoil heap. The precarious nature of the baulks and the unsteady planking along which the barrows were wheeled gave rise to another illicit prank the diggers discovered – *arabası yarışçılık* – wheel-barrow racing. You first had your wheel barrow filled, waited until someone else did the same, and then you challenged them to a race. The idea was to bowl down the slope with your heavy barrow towards the spoil heap, but between where you had started and where you were to finish was a bottle-neck comprising one single plank between two deep trenches. Ostensibly, the first across the plank was the winner.

Ali Kocadurmuş created a variant of the game, especially when competing against Şükrü Tunç. Beginning slightly ahead of the starting pistol, Ali would waylay Şükrü at the plank and with a deft flick of his barrow cause him to lose his balance and pitch head first into the trench, followed by the barrow and the earth which had just been dug out. Mayhem ensued. The diggers were most unhappy at having their carefully trowelled debris showered all over them and Şükrü would climb out of the trench covered in dirt and swearing as only a country boy can. Yet he never learnt, and a short while later Ali Kocadurmuş would challenge him again, and the whole episode would be repeated. After another and another, Şükrü Tunç would emerge foaming at the mouth and vowing revenge, to which the more powerfully built Ali would simply hiss at him:

"*Siktir git!*" "Fuck off." And there the game would end.

Only once did this performance ever come near to real fisticuffs. Şükrü emerged as usual after his fifth or sixth tipping. He rushed at Ali, who dismissively said:

"*Siktir git, Hergele!*"

For some reason this so enraged the somewhat slow-witted Şükrü Tunç that he drew a knife and lunged at Ali. The other workers rushed in and restrained him, and after a few minutes things calmed down. But I always wondered what the additional insult must have been to have sent Şükrü into such a knife-wielding frenzy. I looked it up in an extensive Turkish Dictionary in the library when I got back to London. Maybe I had misheard, but the only translation I could find which sounded anywhere like it was a scientific expression – *'hergele'* (n) ornithological 'Glossy ibis'. How odd, I thought. How provoking is that meant to be? 'Fuck off, you glossy ibis!' I have since used it myself, to everyone's total puzzlement. It was years later that I discovered that the real meaning was far more infuriating. 'Hergele' means 'oaf', or 'naughty boy' and impugned Şükrü's maturity and thus his manhood.

Deeper and deeper they dug in the rear of the villa, uncovering the arched well head, beneath which was a three meter deep terracotta-lined shaft which amazingly still had water at the bottom. Around the head were plaster-lined basins for storing water. The diggers were down almost four meters now, and greater dangers presented themselves – what with flying wheel barrows and falling debris. I was discussing this with Mitt when all of a sudden a squealing cry of what I thought was Testes! Testes! came from the depths of the back trench. Not thinking, I heard this as though it was in English and running to the edge of the trench, I peered down, expecting to see Huseyn or Ahmet deprived of their reproductive equipment. There, at the bottom of the trench, they had uncovered three complete Knidian amphorae. They had been drawing attention to this fact by shouting: *"testi! testi!"* "Water jars."

* * * *

The excavation of the villa at Terrace East was in full production when Sonny approached me with what at first was a simple problem. He had been mapping out all the street junctions, where the stepped streets crossed the horizontal streets, so that he could complete his topographic map of the city and superimpose the street plan onto the contours. Where he had been able to triangulate junction positions, a small amount of scrabbling in the undergrowth, or even a modicum of digging, had revealed the exact four corners of each intersection. But he had come across a slight anomaly in the lowest main street that ran alongside the Commercial Harbour below the excavation of the Terrace East villas. Here the overburden of the land slide of debris that had accumulated over the centuries - washed down earth, broken masonry, pot sherds and rock fall rubble - had reached so great a thickness that simple skirmishing techniques would not solve the problem. A different approach was needed. He asked for and was granted four men to make a deep sounding over the assumed position of the junction and as I was spending days at Terrace East, he asked me to keep a perfunctory eye on things. There was no possibility of any archaeological damage, as they would only be digging through unstratified slippage.

The men who were assigned to the task were considered to be the poorest of all the workers, people like Musa the Drummer, Hasan the Sucu, and the toothless Baba Veli, the oldest of all the workers, who was only taken on because his son begged that he be allowed to stay for the family's sake. I laid out a 4x4 meter square, issued the team with shovels and told them to dig until I said stop. There was no sense in trying to explain about street junctions. So they dug, not very fast, in fact, incredibly slowly. Each day I would examine the hole, and each day they had made some progress, but each day there were always problems – the handle of one of the shovels had broken, or the wheel on the barrow had come off. Each day they would take extemporary cigarette breaks when they assumed no one was looking. Each day one of them would be injured, not badly, but enough that he, escorted by two others, had to go all the way to the dig house for a plaster for his finger or thumb. If I had time, I would go and examine the progress of 'the hole', looking sagely at the sections and spurring the team on to greater effort with cries of:

"Çok önemli! Çok ilginç!" and most significantly, *"Çok eski ama."*

"Very important; very interesting, and really old."

107

After such encouragements, for a while they would go at it like men possessed and showers of earth would emanate at high speed from the hole, though how much actually landed outside the square was difficult to see from where I stood. Then they would gradually slow to a standstill. But progress was made. They dug lower and lower and still the same waste debris went on down with no end in view.

Eventually, they were down low enough to be out of sight. This of course allowed for untrammelled lassitude, and all I could see were disembodied shovel-fulls of dirt from time to time being thrown into the air. Another week passed, and another, and they were now down low enough that they needed a ladder to get in and out of the trench, which led to more merry japes like one of them throwing the ladder out of the hole so that they were all stuck there and couldn't work, they said.

I calculated that by now they must now be only a meter or so above sea level, and in fact the earth was becoming damper. They thought they might soon come upon a well, like up at the villa, not connecting the nearby shore with the seepage. But they continued. Then one morning, when I was back at Terrace East, I looked up and to my astonishment I saw all four of them out of the hole, dancing and clapping around the edge of the trench like a scene from the Rite of Spring. They were skipping and throwing their arms about more animatedly than I had ever seen them. Now what was the problem, I wondered, and walked down to see.

"Bak! Devit, Bak!" Look David they said, pointing excitedly into the trench.

I looked down and saw to my dismay what they had discovered. There, in the bottom of the hole, right in the middle of the hole, was the earthenware rim of a very large pithos, a huge storage jar. The mouth must have been a meter across. These jars were not meant to be moved. They were normally placed, or even made in situ, in rows, to store dried grain, or pickled fish, or anything really. What this rim told me was that this was no street junction but the middle of a storage magazine associated with the harbour, some kind of warehousing for goods. In the whole of Knidos, this was the one horizontal road that had made a dog leg around the edge of the quayside. It was no wonder that Sonny couldn't reconcile his street plan. Dejectedly, after five weeks work, we dismissed the diggers.

But that night in the Çayhane, I was the toast of the men. Fried eggs, rakı, anything I wanted were mine for the asking. When I enquired why, Musa stood up and, shoulders back, with his hand on my head announced:

"Çok akılı, sen, çok akılı Deyvit! Bunu nasıl toprak altında bildinmi?"

"You are very clever, David, very clever. How did you know it was there underneath the ground?"

Aaargh! How could I tell them that all their efforts had been a total waste of time?

* * * *

Back to the domestic evidence. The real interest now focussed on the front of the villa, where the elaborately painted wall plaster which once graced that magnificent front room with the balconies had all collapsed into the mud brick basements two meters or more below the atrium floor. Recovering the plaster was taxing work. It had fallen into the narrow basement rooms and broken into small fragments which invariably lay face down in the dank earth. Remembering that Terrace East had the least skilled diggers, Mitt was having a nightmare of a time. The plaster was highly chromatic and the damp conditions made the colours even more vibrant and attractive. The problem was that while the binding agent kept the paint together, it didn't necessarily hold to the plaster and was wont to stick instead to the mud.

"Bak! Mitt Bey. Bak!"

"Look, Mr Mitt," they would shout, and pointing to the earth would show the perfect paint of the moulding, *tromp d'oeil* and all, preserved on the ground, while in their hand would be the plain plaster coving, sans paint. The colour had stuck to the earth, not the moulding.

"Will you stop doing that?!" Mitt would shout at the top of his voice. And the whole process would halt, only to be repeated five minutes later.

It was a respite when a cigarette break was called, and the diggers emerged into the sunlight where they could do no damage.

But the cigarette breaks for me were memorable for the dancing which inevitably took place. One man would start to sing and clap, leaning on his shovel, and the others would take their shirts off and arms outstretched begin to tread out the measure – Hüseyn the Arab, his yellow kaffir wrapped around his crown, Cemal the donkey man in his natty trilby hat, football shorts and plastic flip-flops, and Süleyman with his milk-white skin and pantaloons, kicking up the dust with his bare feet. They were remembering old village songs, with fluid movements that they had learnt from their fathers and mothers when they were children. Shaking their chests and gyrating their hips provocatively at one another, they would emulate both the male and female parts of the dance. The others would enthusiastically clap their hands in time. It was sexual, it was sensual, but above all it was part of their very real past. Their extemporaneous entertainment defined their culture and although for some of the staff it was a tedious waste of time, I for one was always captivated by it. I can remember it to this very day.

CHAPTER TWELVE

VILLAGE OF DESTINY

'Tis all a Chequer-board of Nights and Days
Where Destiny with men for pieces plays:
Hither and thither moves, and mates, and slays,
And one by one back in the closet lays.

Rubaiyat of Omar Khayyam XLIX

Like an elongated, bony finger, the Reşadiye Peninsula extends for eighty rugged kilometres west from Marmaris. Rising and falling in a dramatic switchback of sharp ridges, it finally points down into the sea at Knidos. At its narrowest, at Bencik, the finger is less than two thousand metres wide, and at its broadest, where the Boz Dağı, the Grey Mountains, climb to almost 3500 feet straight out of the Aegean it is only ten kilometres from north to south. The jagged profile is the result of a series of aggressive geological phenomena in the earth's distant past. Evidence of ancient crustal violence some eighty million years ago shapes the eastern spine of the peninsula with the dull greenish-grey rocks near Aramutalan, the Place of Pears. They represent an example of an ophiolite sequence, where continental plates once collided, the African plate ramming into the Eurasian land mass and slowly being subducted beneath it, turning the crust upside down. The resulting rock formations were properly understood only one hundred years ago by the Alpine geologist, Gustav Steinmann, the grey-green rocks being part of the famous Steinmann Trinity – radiolarian cherts, basalts and serpentines, the last full of toxic, heavy minerals. The shape of the landscape and the paucity and impoverished nature of the soil has meant that from the village of Yuvaçık, near Marmaris, to Aktur near Datça, more than half the peninsula is actually not really fit for agriculture. It has remained untamed, the impenetrable vegetation and unforgiving ruggedness effectively cutting off the western end of the peninsula, by road at least, to all but the most intrepid.

More than half way along this scenically striking rocky promontory, for a brief distance of less than ten kilometres just to the east of Datça, the landscape changes into a flat plain and somewhere here must lie the remains of the pre-Classical city of Knidos, a city which will no doubt contain evidence going back to the beginning of the First Millennium BC or even earlier, to the age of the heroes of the Bronze Age. There has always been a heated if futile scholarly debate about exactly where Old Knidos was, based on written evidence. But geographically the only reasonable answer would have to be a low mound very close to Datça itself. It's on the edge of the sea, facing south, the protected side of the peninsula, with the remains of a small harbour. Geometric pottery from the 7th and 6th century BC has been found there. Despite all the cavilling and academic spleen that has characterised the problem, geologically and locationally, Ancient Knidos cannot really be anywhere else. It would have been a small agricultural settlement whose extent must have been limited to the flat sea lands, since to the west and east of the plain, the contours are too craggy to allow anything more than tiny hamlets.

Immediately to the west of Datça massive folds of Neogene limestone, ferociously thrust up from the floor of the Mediterranean, have created an even more rugged tip to the peninsula than its stem, panoramically beautiful but economically gruelling. Today, behind the unyielding cliffs and sharp escarpments, hidden among the mountainous folds and the fault sheers, lies the village of Yazıköy, modern gateway to classical Knidos. Here, at the very terminus of the Peninsula, the finger points out into the Aegean, towards the Greek island of Kos, famed island haunt of Hippocrates, of 'oath' fame', to the volcano of Nisyros, rising over two thousand feet straight out of the sea, and to the narrow rocky island of Tilos. In times past, from their propinquity and isolation, the villages here probably had more in common with these islands of the Dodecanese than with the Anatolian mainland

Yazıköy is the largest of three villages set close together, the other two being Belenköy, the Village in the Pass, and Çeşmeköy, the Village with a

Spring. Both these latter two have uncomplicated, locational names. But the name Yazıköy seems to have a more complex origin. '*Yazı*' means 'writing', something written, the 'Village of Writing'. Maybe it refers to the occurrence of ancient inscriptions close to classical Knidos. But '*yazı*' also has an occult connotation - 'So is it written!', or as in the Rubaiyat of Omar Khayam, 'The moving finger writes and having writ moves on', the oriental belief in the finger of fate. Here is the more appealing meaning of Yazıköy, Place of Fortune, of Luck, of 'Kısmet', and maybe the best translation of Yazıköy would be 'Village of Destiny'. For me that would be entirely appropriate. Yazıköy was my Village of Destiny, for Destiny it was that brought me to this remarkable place, so that's how I will understand it.

* * * *

Between Yazıköy, Village of Destiny, and the eastern gate of Knidos, lies the Knidian Necropolis, the ancient City of the Dead. Larger by far in area than the one-time city of the living, it was nevertheless the manifest destiny of all its inhabitants. Terrace walls, sacred enclosures, pillared porticoes, graves, sepulchres, funerary vaults and tombs are festooned on the hillsides either side of the stony cart track that winds down from Yazıköy towards the ancient site and the sea. The once prominent monumental mausolea have all long since been destroyed, robbed probably in great antiquity. All that is left of them are broken burial chambers and once majestic masonry, fallen now and shrouded among the undergrowth. The grave goods too have long ago been scattered, melted down, reused and lost and the bones of their revered occupants decayed and vanished. It seems these opulent memorials were too conspicuous by far. Ironically, vaunting their riches in death, the remains of the wealthy of Knidos have through time became utterly impoverished, while many of the humbler graves whose identity and location were soon forgotten at the time have remained intact more than two thousand years later, perhaps denoting a belated recompense for the modesty of their occupants.

It was a few of these poorer graves that wanted excavating. Well, the Management didn't really want to excavate them at all. There wasn't much prestige in digging up bones and pottery. But a farmer planting new olive trees had accidentally stumbled into one and the expedition was forced to rescue the remains.

So it was that a survey team, consisting of me, was instructed to draw plans of the burials, and since I was now the plane table expert, it fell to me to fall in. And fall in I did. Armed with my invincible Wild RKI Self-Reducing Tacheometric Telescopic Alidade, replete with cumbersome tripod and even more awkward plane table, I fell out of the jeep and fell into the shaft of the first burial to be excavated. Not yet being ready to put one foot in the grave, I extricated myself and found that I was standing in the midst of the olive grove. It was apparent that the graves being exposed were shaft and chamber burials and so I climbed down and crawled into one to take a proper look. The bones of the departed lay to one side of the chamber, while on the other had been placed the accoutrements which were to accompany them into the afterlife, an assortment of dark grey, undecorated but intact pottery vessels - a plate, a jug, a bowl and a rather ornately spouted oil lamp. Speaking of lamps, I would need some form of lighting to begin my task, and I was given a battery-powered fluorescent torch with sufficient power that the minimal sunlight shining down the shaft was not necessary for the planning of the grave's interior.

During those days in the Necropolis, working on the graves near the Village, we were all very much left to our own devices. The digging, planning, recording and back-filling of these shaft tombs didn't require much supervision. With that in mind, the diggers could misbehave themselves more than usual, taking more and longer cigarette breaks, or sloping off to the village for a quick coffee. Meanwhile, in the underworld of the dank and earthy semi-darkness, I found myself up close and personal with the last mortal remains of one or another Hellenistic peasant whom I had to presume had long since been enrolled into the eternal choirs of the bright seraphim, or with whomsoever he or she believed they would meet beyond the final curtain.

Being in the fields so close to the Village, the women would bring food and fruit for their men folk, of which I was counted an honorary member. Bunches of grapes and various meat and cheese pastries would be handed down the shaft into my eager hands, and I was left then to share my thoughts on these acceptable offerings with the ossified remains of the dear departed.

Despite the paraphernalia of death and the close proximity of a number of the one-time inhabitants of Hellenistic Knidos, for me those days in the Necropolis were idyllic, away from the quibbling of the excavations in the city and meanwhile becoming better acquainted with the living population of Yazıköy. On one occasion, I heard dull gun shots from above ground and wondered what new catastrophe had occurred. Half an hour later, a voice called at the shaft entrance and a leg of fresh-roasted partridge was passed down to me.

But working in the necropolis was not without its anxieties. On one occasion two tombs had been opened very close together and while one shaft was being newly excavated, the other was being back-filled with the same debris. I was so absorbed plotting the positions of the grave goods at the rear of my chamber that I failed to notice that to the tomb I was mapping belonged the shaft into which the men were shovelling earth. Only at the last moment, when a tiny chink of natural light was all that was left of the outside world, did I become aware of my own unintended interment, and calling through the tiny gap, was exhumed by welcoming hands from a premature burial in what otherwise might have recalled a scene from a short story by Edgar Allan Poe.

* * * *

But for me Yazıköy was more than just another village on the Peninsula. It became my alternate Knidian universe. As fascinating as the excavations were, the introverted social interaction among the diggers could often be oppressive. My own release from this hot house was to go up to the village at the weekend. It wasn't for everyone, but the road to Yazıköy led me through a gateway into another world, of Turkey and more especially of its people.

The summer brought a rash of weddings to the village and being popular with the men I was in the front line when it came to invitations. The first Sunday I went was quite magical. I had cadged a lift on a horse and trailer for some of the way, and we rattled and bounced past the olive-shaded stonework of long-ruined tombs, fragments of carved marble architraves glimpsed through the scrub - a whitening bull's head altar decorated with swags among the rocks and broom, a fallen fluted pillar lying half covered by the mud of the roadside. Each vignette held its own allure, made more romantic by copses of myrtle and twining creepers causing a dappled light and shade to play among the remains of an ancient civilisation long since re-consigned to nature. In a cerulean blue sky, the air was heavily scented with wild thyme and pine resin, and cicadas noisily punctuated the stillness of that Carian morning. It was enchanting.

We walked the last kilometre or so, Ali Karadeniz, Mesut, Musafer and me, along a stony track between low, dry-stone walls, the desiccated stems of white asphodels breaking the dry terra cotta earth. We strolled among olive trees, their bulbous, gnarled trunks speaking of great age, and I noticed their tiny green fruits starting to swell. We turned into a grove of apricot trees and Ali picked a handful and gave them to me. They were fresh and moist with flavour, like Apricot preserve. Back along the road we passed beneath deep-shaded fig trees and Musafer reached up and pulled a couple of the first fruits down - plump, the skin light green. He burst one open. The flesh was full of deep-russet filaments and a sweet taste I shall never forget. We continued through more orchards, along narrow rock-strewn paths, the limestone cobbles smoothed with age, sandaled feet, and the hooves of donkeys. I was reminded of scenes from the Bible, of Jesus and his disciples walking through the hills of Judea, but then of course it was the same setting, the same olives and figs, and the same limestone.

I had only seen the Village in darkness before, on the night I first arrived in Turkey. There were no street lamps then, and the only light to illuminate the Village had come from open doorways and windows. Returning now, I saw Yazıköy in full sunlight and shadow. I suppose for anyone familiar with rural Anatolia it would have looked just like any other Turkish village, but for me it was completely captivating, as the uneven dirt road wound around and merged into the cobbled main street, flanked by whitewashed garden walls, some made of mud-brick capped with dry twigs and plaster. Hidden behind these walls were the old, stone houses of the village, roofed with bold, burnt-umber pan-tiles. The paint on the narrow, double wooden doors leading into the gardens had long since flaked off the ancient timber, itself decorated with intricate antique carvings now bleached white with the sun. Narrow streets led off crookedly right and left to more houses, some with walled courtyards at the back. There were wooden-trellised balconies, askew with age, protected by overhanging lean-to tiled coverings from which were strung necklaces of dark red dried peppers. The occasional donkey nodded its lazy way, ears flopping, along the cobbles, piled with cement bags, green fodder, or firewood being gathered for the winter.

In the centre of the village was an ancient stone water trough and pump, set on ashlar marble blocks which had once probably been part of some nearby tomb. Women and young girls were filling plastic bowls and used olive oil cans with water, which they then wheeled away in barrows. The square cans had the end cut away, with a simple wooden dowel nailed across to act as a handle. A herd of fat-tailed sheep came waddling along the street, heads down, marshalled by a small black dog. They stopped to drink from the soak-away at the base of the trough. Here the women gathered. The jet-black haired young girls were striking, dressed in broad flower-patterned trousers, faces placid and rosy-cheeked with bucolic health; the older women looked stooped and care-worn in their plastic sandals, wearing head scarves against the sun.

Beyond the pump the veranda of the local tea house extended under a deep-shadowed pergola. Small homemade tables and chairs fashioned from thin planking were placed around the vine-shaded terrace. The men were sitting smoking and drinking tea from small, gold-trimmed, waisted glasses on plastic saucers. Some were playing back gammon, the tiny dice flicked with thumb and forefinger at lightening speed as the pieces were deftly clicking around the board. Some men, the older ones with lined leathery faces, just sat musing. They wore broad worsted trousers, collarless shirts, old waistcoats and flat hats, flipping their amber worry beads and watching the world pass slowly up the street, and their women folk pass slowly down the street wheeling barrows of water containers. Hens pecked at the ground, followed by strutting cockerels. The whole ensemble must have represented the epitome of rural Turkey here in the Village of Destiny on that sleepy Sunday morning before the wedding began.

* * * *

A Turkish wedding is an event which can last anything up to a week, the culmination of even longer and protracted negotiations involving complex social etiquette. Long before the day of the main ceremony, there will have been parties where the relatives of the bride and groom met one another; they probably knew each other anyway. They usually belonged to families from adjacent villages, or even from the same village. Arranged marriages were still the norm in the sixties, and betrothal may have taken place years before, with a series of formally conducted meetings organised for the intended couple. The local Imam would have been involved in this protracted rite of passage from the beginning. So, one might think that the actual day of the wedding was expected to be a foregone conclusion, but it wasn't that simple. Local rivalries ran deep and previous village feuds had not been forgotten.

Unaware of any forthcoming drama, we made our way up behind the main street, passed the bride's house and onto a boulder-terraced olive grove slightly overlooking the village. Someone motioned to us and we sat down on one of the groups of aged slatted chairs which had been set out on the dry grass. Young girls brought plates of nuts - dark skinned peanuts, dry, powdery chick peas and fresh almonds. A glass of rakı was thrust into my hand, thin, milky white, with the slightly smoky taste of aniseed.

"*Şerefe! Deyvit.*" "To you honour!"

"*Şerefinize! Ali.*"

Glasses were clinked all around. It was eleven o'clock in the morning. This was going to be a long day.

Wooden tables had been placed on the other side of the grove, covered with sheets of white paper and laden with food: various *börek* - thick pastries filled with yellow cheese and herbs, spicy sausage and *pastermak* (dried spiced beef); thin *sigara börek* – rolled filo pastry with crumbled feta cheese and parsley. A variety of bean dishes appeared – *kuru fasulye* (white kidney beans in a rich tomato sauce), *taze fasulye* (green beans cooked in olive oil and garlic), *piyaz* (white beans with fresh onion), and *bakla* (dried broad beans mashed into a thick paste and dressed with sumac and dusted with chilli pepper). There were cauldrons of *düğün çorbası* 'wedding soup', a thick white potage made from fatty lamb breasts, vegetables, flour and eggs, ladled into small dishes and handed round with spoons and accompanied by plastic bins of cut bread.

119

A *sürahi*, a glass carafe, appeared in front of us. Another plug of rakı was poured and topped up with water. More clinking. More nuts. Yes, this was indeed going to be a long day.

For an hour, maybe two, food and drink kept being handed round, but other than that there was no apparent sign of any formal reception - no bride or groom. This prolonged adjournment prompted me to become philosophical about rakı. Did I know, I asked myself, that in early Mesopotamia they had made an alcoholic drink flavoured with aniseed almost four thousand years ago? I cast myself as part of a millennia-transcending tradition in this part of the world, which in one bound enabled me to bypass my teetotal Presbyterian upbringing and allow our rakı-brimmed noon-time to be more culturally acceptable. Were we not part of a continuum of an illustrious and ancient past? Well, if that was the case, then *Şerefe* indeed!

The day wore on into the early afternoon and the cicadas noisily stepped up their high voltage, pulsing, telegraphic whine from the branches of the over-arching olives. The thick, misshapen boles of these archaic trees must have witnessed many a wedding party over the centuries in the Village of Destiny, I mused. But there my reverie was abruptly ended. Suddenly, there was a flurry of excitement beyond the terrace wall. We crowded forward to peer down into the street. A knocker banged and the door of a whitewashed stone house in the cobbled street below opened. In the dimness of the threshold stood the bride, an apparition of Levantine beauty, her raven hair piled high and falling back in curled tresses over her shoulders, her large, dark eyes looking out above high cheek bones, her lips bright vermillion against her pallid, powdered face. Her white wedding dress was pulled tightly around her waist accentuating her young breasts before radiating outwards in a series of cascading, stiffened scallops, ending just high enough to allow a glimpse of her dainty feet in satin shoes. She was immobile, doll-like. In the street outside, the bridegroom's family had come to claim her for their own clan and to take her to their mother's house, bringing with them their chosen representative, the groom, dressed in an over-sized shiny black suit and stark white shirt and dark tie. By comparison to his hulking brothers he looked all of sixteen. Nervously, he took his bride's hand and leading her outside, they began to walk down the street, surrounded by their supporters.

At that moment, the younger brother of the bride, who apparently had been indulging in the spirituous liquors since breakfast time, began wailing and beating his head against the door jamb, shouting, as far as I could make out, that it was a terrible travesty that his sister should be led away by total strangers (the bridegroom lived in the next street) and that unspeakable miseries were sure to befall the family as a result. Far from restraining him, his mother joined in. Then, from the top of the wall opposite came signs of a separate altercation. An old woman in a head scarf, her toothless, foreshortened face creased with age, was gesticulating wildly at the couple, pointing and screaming in a cracked guttural voice. By her tone, she was in even greater distress than the bride's family. To emphasise her case, she was simultaneously hurling stones, invective and clods of earth at the wedding party in the street below, beating her breast and demanding that someone help her. Apparently she was the mother of an alternative suitor who had failed to influence the marriage covenant and win the hand of the bride. The old hag was urging anyone who would listen to intervene on her son's behalf. She cursed the bride, the bride's family, the groom's family, and the rest of the village, calling on Allah to be her witness. Her cries became more insistent as the party moved slowly out of range. I don't know if she was invited to the wedding, but knowing Yazıköy she probably was.

Whether it was her unruly entreaties or the brother of the bride's head-banging which triggered the next event was by no means clear, but a scuffle broke out in the tightly packed alley. Fists flew among the young bloods around the periphery of the wedding party, and in that dense throng the discord quickly spread.

121

The nervous couple were urgently hustled away, the bride teetering unsteadily on the uneven cobbles. They disappeared around the corner to reappear up the steps into the nave of the olive grove. Behind them they left an evolving mayhem, as opposing groups, maybe they were rival village gangs, were attempting to knock each other senseless with clenched but misdirected knuckles. It was a bizarre scene, a no-holds-barred street brawl with all the contestants dressed in ironed white shirts and brillianteened hair. I wondered whether this pugilism was really related at all to the present nuptials, or whether weddings were a well-orchestrated opportunity to settle old grievances and redress past insults. Whatever the *casus belli*, there would be a fair number of thick lips, black eyes and gratuitous ortho-dentistry by the end of the day. Not for nothing is the Turkish word for a teenager '*deli kanlı*', 'wild blooded'. But apparently, as I later learnt, no village wedding was worthy of the name without an energetic punch-up on the side, an accepted component of local rural life.

The focus of public attention soon moved away from the continuing fisticuffs and towards the centre of the olive grove. Words were spoken by the imam, hands were shaken heartily and the newly weds made to sit awkwardly in a place of honour among the assembled guests. With that, the music began. After a series of preliminary and palpable booming thumps on the *davul*, the sharp *zurna* struck up a piercing reedy tune. The *davul* is a large double headed drum, the upper side of which produces a thunderous bass note, while the underside is played with thin sticks to produce a treble percussive counterpoint. Meanwhile, the European equivalent of a *zurna* is the Mediaeval shawm, which in the right hands emits an intensely shrill, almost wailing sound. Played together they create the familiar cacophony which accompanies all Balkan and Anatolian celebrations.

Soon the dancing and singing began, the men facing each other, leaning forward and balancing unsteadily on one leg, arms outstretched like wings, before springing cossak-like into a squatting position, then rising to a crouch and spinning slowly on the spot, timing a fully upright stance and a pace forward to coincide with the end of each drawn out musical phrase. You can imagine elements of the whirling dervishes in these acrobatic movements, though for the dervishes it is a matter of godliness. Apparently, in the Village, the more rakı the participants have consumed, the more fluid the dance. I retired to the further shadows of the olive grove, nursing my own rakı, in case some solicitous digger tried to inveigle me into joining the gyrating guests. I was never very good at gymnastics at school, I remembered, and here it would not have been helped by untold glasses of four thousand year old lion's milk.

And so the wedding party continued into the sunset. At the end, in a haze of aniseed, reedy shawms, honey-flavoured sweet-meats, baklava and thick Turkish coffee we somehow managed to withdraw into the warm darkness of the Carian night and find our way down the sinuous track through the Necropolis back to the ancient city. I still don't know to this day who married who, but I wish them well, and as I discovered the next morning, we had certainly done more than our fair share of celebrating their marriage vows.

✳ ✳ ✳ ✳

Ali Karadeniz the Bekçi was my particular friend at Knidos. Despite his surname - 'Kara deniz' 'black sea' - he wasn't from the Black Sea at all, but decisively from Yazıköy. He was a short, wiry man with a keen sense of humour. He nick-named me *domuz*, 'the wild boar'. I wore different sleeve-length shirts while working, which resulted in a banded tan along my arms hence the name, an evocation of the boar's brindled coat. There were many 'domuz' in the mountains around the Village.

The most noticeable aspect of Ali's physique was that although he had delicate facial features but few teeth, he had coal black skin. He used to joke with me that although I was becoming browner in the Mediterranean sun,

I could never achieve the same dark colour as he. There was absolutely no stigma attached to his colour, in fact, no one in the Village thought it at all different. Musing on this later, I conjectured that the origin of Ali's dark pigmentation probably lay centuries in the past, from the ethnic fusion which arose during the four hundred years of the Ottoman Empire. The Turkish Sultanate held sway over most of North Africa, which of course had cultural links to peoples of the Equator; either that or there was a connection via the Middle Eastern provinces which were contiguous with the Arabian Gulf and the East African trade with Zanzibar and beyond. Whatever his distant ancestry, he was firmly a man from the Village of Destiny.

We used to meet every day and exchange views on the dig and about the various characters we knew. But he was always scathing about gossip.

"Yani, Deyvit, çok dedikodu var ama hiç kimse anlamiyor."

"Really, David, there's a lot of gossip, but no-one understands anything."

Then, one Monday, he invited me to the Village the following weekend. I was very pleased to accept, but I had understood that he and his wife had only one son, Osman, and he was not yet in his teens. I asked what the occasion was, and he said, "Osman'un sünnet düğünü, Deyvit."

'Düğün' – 'wedding feast.' I made this out to be Osman's wedding party, and just thought I misheard the middle word. But then thinking on, I wondered how this could be, given that the lad turned out to be only eight years of age.

On the Tuesday and the Wednesday, I asked Ali again, and got the same answer. Only on the Thursday did I admit I didn't quite understand. Ali replied:

"Osman'un sünnet düğünü, biliyorsunuz," he said. Using his hands to add emphasis, his left index finger pointing upwards, his right two forefingers made the gesture of a pair of scissors cutting the top. A few seconds passed and then the deeper meaning dawned on me. This was to be Osman's circumcision party, the day on which Osman was painfully to be enrolled into the adult world.

I was both honoured and filled with trepidation by turns, not knowing what such a ceremony would hold. I need not have worried. It was to be very similar to a wedding feast, with all the customary paraphernalia – the music, the dance, the eating, the drinking. The only difference was that it would be as joyous for the guests as it was going to be excruciating for young Osman.

The day began with a memorable ride to Yazıköy, Village of Destiny. It transpired that many of the workers at Knidos had been invited to Osman Karadeniz's circumcision party, including Mehmet the Fenerci. Mehmet possessed an old CJ-3B Willys Jeep powered by a 2.2 litre Hurricane Engine and painted in a fashionable pass-water green colour, and in this he intended to turn up at the Village. It became apparent on the morning in question that all the other guests had arrived at the same idea so that as Mehmet slowly drove out of Knidos with me in the passenger seat, a whole troupe of villagers followed behind in a scene reminiscent of the Pied Piper of Hamelin. When we were out of sight of the Jandarma Mehmet stopped the Jeep, which was the signal for everyone to climb aboard. I'm not sure how many people constitute a record for this vehicle, but we had men crammed into the interior, sitting on the bonnet, standing backwards on the front bumper, standing forwards on the back bumper, hanging off the front wheel arches, crouched on the running boards, clinging to the uprights and even lying on the canvas canopy on top – it felt like a score or more passengers. Just as well the CJ-3B Willys had only a three speed gearbox. It would have been impossible to change into any more. And in this manner, men festooned all over the Jeep, we arrived at the outskirts of the Village. At a quiet command from Mehmet, everyone fell off – more Jandarma ahead – and he and I drove bumpily in solitary splendour into the meydan, the Village square near the tea house and the village pump.

We walked up to Ali's house, where a large crowd had already gathered. A glass of rakı was thrust into my hand, the familiar white liquid with the slightly smoky taste of aniseed.

"*Şerefe Deyvit!*" "To you honour!"

"*Şerefinize Arkadaşlar!*" "Cheers, friends!"

And here we went again. It was eleven o'clock in the morning. This was going to be another long day.

After a considerable while, more lion's milk surreptitiously being topped up in shaded doorways, we heard the *davul* and the *zurna* raucously heralding the arrival of the star of the show, young Osman Karadeniz with his proud Dad and extended family. Like the wedding ceremony, preparations for Osman's circumcision would have begun early. A few days before his circumcision, Osman would have visited his relatives and neighbours and kissed everyone's hands and then touched them to his forehead in a mark of respect. Every person whose hand he kissed in this way would have given him a gift of money to celebrate his coming of age. In the old days, a boy being circumcised was supposed to have memorised the whole of the Koran, repeating it aloud like a sort of catechism, but in the Village in the 1960's that was not considered necessary.

Anyway, following the orchestral accompaniment came Osman himself, riding on a horse and dressed in his specially-made circumcision outfit. This elaborate confection was composed of a white satin suit and waistcoat, a long satin cape fringed with gold frogging and epaulettes, and a white sash embroidered with the single word *Maşallah*, 'Wonderful'. Quite how 'Maşallah' Osman felt could be read in his bewildered and fearful expression. He wore an ornate képi hat topped with a white ostrich plume which swayed along with the horse. I felt that there was probably a literary allusion to a

Persian prince on his magic charger here, à la 1001 Nights, except that in this case the charger in question was not some sleek Arabian steed but a flea-ridden nag that might well have been on it's way to the knackers yard had not this procession fortuitously needed an equestrian centre-piece at that very moment. Lucky horse!

The procession stopped at the Circumcision Hall, in this case Ali's front room, and the main participants and witnesses went inside for the climax of the occasion. They were followed by the village barber who was to administer the *coup de grâce*, if that's the appropriate terminology, with his cutting edge technology, a cut throat razor. I was assured that the barber, one Alâeddin by name (which happily continued the 1001 Nights allegory), was a snipper of repute, his second profession having been handed down to him from his father, and his father's father, and so for that reason one could be assured that Osman's vital organ was in good hands.

For the more general members of the cast, like me, Mesut and the rest, we were treated to a wail of a time in the street outside – uninterrupted *davul* thumping and *zurna* cadenzas. We were ushered to slatted chairs placed alongside the house walls, and intermittently indulged with a whole array of Turkish dishes, from cheese and olives to steaming lamb kebabs and *lahmacun*, a Turkish mini-pizza, followed by an array of pre-made al fresco dining experiences. Along with the barrage of comestibles came the inevitable flow of rakı, its pale, milky innocence belying a delayed but mighty hammer blow. Whatever one's thoughts were about what was going on inside the Hall of Circumcision, they were ameliorated by the exceptional hospitality going on outside in the street.

Just when the consumption of Lion's milk was extending to riverine proportions, we were brought up with a jolt and told we may now greet the newly transmuted young man in the natural surrounds of his Dad's front room. The barber had accomplished his singular coiffure. Forming a suitable, if unsteady, queue we filed over Ali's threshold, and there, in a hushed reverence, lay Osman tucked up in a huge bed, still in his special Arabian Nights hat and cloak. He was covered to his chest with a white sheet, in the centre of which was a conspicuous bulge intended to keep the bedclothes off the offended member. We were relieved to see that Osman was in rude health, so long as he didn't laugh, cough, stand up, sit down or generally move a muscle. One by one we shook his hand and welcomed him into the questionable new world of male puberty.

"It won't be long now," I said, feeling sympathy for the lad's discomfort.

Everyone had bought Osman a gift, something I had alas forgotten to do. I later sent him a diving mask, which Ali afterwards told me had done the trick and had made Osman feel like a man. The last I heard of Osman Karadeniz was that he went from the Village to secondary school in Datça and thence to University in Ankara. He became a very successful teacher of English somewhere in Eastern Anatolia, no doubt using the 'Shorter English Dictionary', and reading 'Paradise Lost' and 'Great Expectations' to his pupils, having probably long since forgotten the unkindest cut of all.

CHAPTER THIRTEEN

VISITING MARINERS

We could not pass up the chance to stop in Cnidus, where there is so much to be seen, notably the temple of Aphrodite which encloses the statue by Praxiteles, so admired for its beauty. We made a gentle landfall amid a splendid calm, as if the goddess herself had propelled our vessel.

Lucian of Samosata, 2nd Century AD

Lucian's aesthetically-inspired enthusiasm to sail at Knidos may well have been infectious in antiquity, influencing many other ancient travellers to call at the city, but visitors to our 20th Century excavations remained few and far between. Certainly, hardly any braved the land route along the Peninsula. The road from Marmaris, bad enough at its eastern end, was well nigh impassable from Datça westwards without a four wheel drive vehicle, and these were virtually unobtainable. Only the Jandarma, The High Command and other essential personnel such as Mehmet the Lighthouse Keeper had one. The few people who did come to see us generally came by sea. But there were no local charter boats plying the Turkish coast in those days, difficult as it may be to imagine that situation today. The small number of yachts that did navigate around Cape Crio and between the two ancient moles into the Commercial Harbour of Knidos were privately owned by people who knew we were there and had come for a purpose, and usually their yachts had been chartered from Cannes or St Tropez or somewhere a long way away. They usually turned out to belong to friends of The High Command's or somebody else in the High Command who had navigated all this way to pay their respects and to find out about the latest discoveries. I suppose the Bornhardts would be considered one such party.

I was surveying high up on the mountain the afternoon they arrived so I didn't notice their opulent craft glide into the harbour. It was only when she dropped her anchor and the chain was run out that I looked up from my plotting table and saw this elegant yacht manoeuvring near the dig house. As I continued to watch through my hastily refocused alidade, I saw some of the crew in smart white sailor suits wind down a tender from the davits, into which they jumped and trailing a stern warp they struck out for the shore where they swiftly tied the rope to a fallen ancient terrace block and made the yacht fast. As far as I was concerned, there for the moment the matter rested. Sometime later, with the working day ending, I walked down to our Drawing Office and found Sonny and a few of the other lower ranks in a state of considerable excitement. Harriet, our own English Rose, was speaking.

"Ooo, isn't this fun! It's the Bornhardts. They've come to visit. I haven't seen their eldest daughter Marielle since, goodness, it must be at least three years ago in Zermatt. How super!"

"I thought they were friends of someone in the High Command?"

"No, no, no, no, no! Daddy knows Dr. Bornhardt very well. They spent a lot of time together years ago in Geneva, on some world antiquities committee or some such. He's now very big, rather gargantuan actually. He's in the diplomatic corps or something. They are lovely people. You'll all like them."

I ventured to enquire by what happenstance we were likely to meet these illustrious visitors. After all, they were on their boat, and we were stuck on terra firma. Short of going for a dip in the harbour and behaving like Busby Barclay's synchronised swimmers, I couldn't really see how we would attract their attention, what with the sun already sinking over Kos.

"Oh, but it's all been arranged. We've all been invited out to their yacht for drinks this evening. Ooo, is that the time? We're due there in three quarters of an hour and I haven't changed yet."

Well, that was a revelation. Far be it from me to oppose an opportunity to spend a happy time on someone's yacht, especially when it looked incredibly expensive to such an impoverished eye as mine. Not wishing to rock the boat, so to speak, I duly changed into my best shorts and a relatively clean shirt to await the ensuing embarkation. But maybe the High Command was going to have none of it. If these were the wealthy of Zurich, or some other Swiss tax haven, they may well have wanted to have a personal tête à tête with the owner of any associated numbered account to see if they could prise some francs out of them for the Expedition – I suppose you could say at least that was altruistic thinking. The last thing they would want was a horde of the stinking proletariat queering their pitch. Hey ho, I thought, it's the Çayhane again for me.

But in the after-glow of sunset, the fragrant Marielle arrived in person with the tender on the beach to greet her old friend and to shepherd us to the festivities, all of us. With a somewhat truculent air, we scrambled into the tender and were ferried out to the yacht and motioned to climb up the sea ladder. Reaching the deck, I saw this immaculate-looking vessel for what it really was – immaculate! There wasn't a thing out of place. From binnacle to barnacle it was like a new pin, chrome highly polished, teak decking scrubbed white, and mahogany panelling finished in such a high gloss varnish, it looked like glass. We were shown to the capacious al fresco dining area in the back, sorry, stern, and it was suggested that we sat around the broad railings, which we did.

The Bornhardts were there, as far as I remember, but my attention was at once transfixed by a steward in white flannels and crisp white shirt, handing out gin and tonics from a silver tray to anyone who reached out for one. I reached out for one. It was quite delicious, a broad, thick-bottomed, cut-glass tumbler with frosted condensation on the outside, and the wondrous juniper-flavoured spirit and quinine water on the inside, replete with bobbing cylindrical ice and slices of fresh lemon. I took another swig. Quite divine! I suppose it's good to have a Swiss bank account, but it can be just as good to know someone else who has one, I thought.

But it didn't end there. Along came Heime, or Hans, or Heinrich – well, some Helvetic 'H' or another - this time with a large tray of canapés, and he was passing them round to the indigent workers sitting on the railings, of which I, of course, was one. Have you ever seen pictures of baboons trying to pick up more maize cobs than they can possibly carry? Well, we were like that – fistfuls of Parma ham and goat's cheese, salami on crackers, anchovies on toast, devils on horseback. We were like pigs in … in … the trough, that's what we were. To my further amazement, my new friend Heinrich came round and politely asked if I would like another drink, a small refresher perhaps. Ja bitte! But what about a large refresher, I eyeballed him. It duly arrived. So did more canapés.

This performance went on for some time, thanks largely to the Management, who were so distracted by their own troop of baboons sitting on the railings stuffing themselves that they were slow to get round to the main topic of the evening and so we just continued – gin, canapés, canapés, gin. It was glorious. Only the arrival of slices of *Schokoladenkuchen* and thimble-full's of Viennese coffee signalled that the extravaganza was coming to an end. The time had come to go home.

With heavy hearts and light heads we said our farewells to the Bornhardts and climbing unsteadily down the sea ladder into the tender we were taken back to the beach. Marielle came with us to say goodbye. In case we had not been sufficiently appreciative, I shook her hand and said, "Marielle, we must thank you so much for such a wonderful time. Do come and see us again very soon. I think we are free tomorrow evening if that would suit."

I was hustled away. No promise of *Goldschläger Schnapps* and *Schweizer Rolle* for me then!

✳ ✳ ✳ ✳

Our next nautical visitors to the site arrived when I was involved with planning the excavations of the villa at Terrace East. Terrace East, you may recall, was a long way from the dig house, the Çayhane or any of the other parts of the site that people would normally come to visit, so that Mitt and his workers were very much left alone, if not down-right neglected. That didn't bother Mitt, who could be pretty anti-social anyway, at least towards the management and associated acquaintances.

It was also the time of the famous wall plaster episode. You will remember when the workers were uncovering the magnificently moulded and painted plaster which had fallen into the forward cellars of the villa and in their enthusiasm they were tending to pull up the moulding and leave the beautiful paint separated in the mud. As a result, the air was blue with remonstrations and recriminations and some choice, if disembodied, epithets could be heard emerging from the deep trench at the front of the villa, most of them relating to rather terse descriptions of the human reproductive system and its associated organs.

Anyway, on one of those mornings at Terrace East, during a cigarette break, cries of *"Vapur gelior"* echoed around the site and the dance which had accompanied the brief interlude broke off abruptly. *"Vapur gelior, Vapur gelior!"* "A boat is coming."

Around the point of the island came a beautiful hand-built schooner registered in Marseille and flying a conspicuously large Tricolore from the jack-staff. It wasn't strictly speaking a *'vapeur'*, a 'steam ship', at all, rather, a three-masted schooner with its sails reefed ready to anchor. But as far as the villagers were concerned, *'vapur'* was a catch-all for anything larger than a rowing boat, the biggest size boat they commonly saw at Knidos. We watched her as she passed gracefully between the two outer moles of the harbour, turning with a curling bow wave in front of the Island. With great panache she dropped anchor and went astern. Someone had come to call, maybe. The cigarette break ended, the men went back to work and the anatomical epithets resumed. That part of the show was over.

It was some two hours later that a couple arrived at Terrace East, toiling up the stepped street in the mid-day heat and looking over the walls at the excavation. I had set up my plane table in the middle of the atrium and was on my own, plotting the block-work in what was left of the reception rooms. All the workers were invisible, down deep holes in either the front or rear of the villa. I looked at the two new-comers and smiled. I noted that they were most elegantly dressed. The man wore a beige safari suit and lightweight Panama hat, while his wife, at least I assumed it was his wife, wore a drill skirt, light blouse and a head scarf. She was immaculately coiffured. They both exuded sophistication … and wealth. The man spoke softly, in perfect if lightly accented English:

"Excuse me, but may we come and see what you are doing?"

"Unfortunately I am not in charge of the site," I replied, "but if you like I will go and ask the site supervisor and he can show you around."

I climbed across the broken walls of the Atrium and the impluvium and reached the terrace, above which Mitt was still trying to retrieve the fragments of wall plaster.

Mitt's angry voice wafted up and across the site.

"Will you fucking-well leave that alone. Stop playing with it. Just stop!"

"Excuse me Mitt, there's a couple here who would like you to show them round the site. What shall I tell them?"

"Tell them to fuck off!" he shouted at the top of his voice. "Fucking tourists," he muttered. "Who the fuck do they think they are anyway?"

He went back to his wall plaster. I went back to the atrium.

"I'm most awfully sorry," I apologised. "The site supervisor is a bit tied up at the moment." Then, somewhat unrealistically, I continued, "perhaps you'd like to come back tomorrow?"

"That's alright," interjected the husband, "we quite understand."

And with that they continued up the stepped street, climbed over the wall at the top and disappeared up the mountain. Another hour went by and it was lunch time. I had already taken all my equipment back to the drawing office and, ambling over to the dig house, I found all the High Command in a highly emotional state.

"We've lost them," they were screaming. "We've lost them. They're lost on the mountain. Somebody do something."

"Who have we lost?" I asked, innocently. "Who's lost?"

"It's the Rothschilds. We've lost the Rothschilds. We're hoping they'll give a major grant to the excavations. Did you see them on the site?"

"Yes, we saw them."

"And did you look after them? Did you tell them where to go?"

"Oh yes, of course, we certainly did that! We told them where to go alright!"

This must have been the present Baron Nathaniel de Rothschild and his lovely wife Serena, and as far as I can tell, they heeded Mitt's advice and left. As far I know they never did contribute to the excavations of ancient Knidos.

* * * *

The ship that came into the harbour one afternoon really was what you would call a 'gentleman's yacht', an imposing cream-painted barque set with three decks and an eye-catching raked-back red funnel. Built in the 1930's when someone really did have the money, the 'Donna Vincenza' even now still represented a conspicuous display of wealth. She lay in the Commercial Harbour, tiny sparkling wavelets setting up a dappled reflection on her considerable beam. Through the binoculars you could make out the dark cherry-wood doors and the brass rails and light fittings of her super-structure and a crew who were constantly at work polishing the already polished. 'Donna Vincenza III, Genoa', it read on the amply rounded stern.

We contemplated who it might belong to, this fabulous motor yacht, this toy for the uber-rich. Apart from the crew, there seemed no sign of life on board. Perhaps she was relocating and had just stopped off at Knidos for a short respite and buff up. That would be too boring. Seeing the Italian flag draped at the stern, we fantasized about the life-style of the guests on board. They were a group of Italian financial cognoscenti from Roma maybe, with their young, lithesome wives, or better still, with a gaggle of stunning haute couture models. Perhaps the guests were all below decks taking a well-earned siesta after their extensive lunch of pasta e pesto, washed down with a glass or three of robust red Barolo, 'the wine of kings, and king of wines', made from Nebbiolo grapes lovingly gathered from ancient vines in the Monferrato Hills of the Piedmont overlooking the Ligurian Sea. Or perhaps being lunch time they would have preferred a more delicate bottle of Orvieto Classico, a golden wine to tempt the palates of the papal prelates of the Vatican, from grapes grown among the mountain folds of Umbria.

The truth, when it finally emerged, was very different in some ways and uncannily similar in others. We shall never know how many guests were actually on board, other than the single one whom we met. We were listlessly lolling about the dig house at the end of the afternoon waiting to see what festivities were abroad, namely the delights of the Çayhane and a few swifties of the Lion's Milk. The sun was already low in the western sky, turning the creamy flanks of the Donna Vincenza a tasteful candy-floss pink. On board, the crew were still polishing their maritime charge when quite unexpectedly a tender from this marine Palazzo Italiano was rowed to the seashore near the Çayhane and a single passenger, a woman, got out. Maybe she was a clandestine friend of Cengis – highly unlikely, I know, but we were in fantasy mode. We watched as Cengis pointed down towards the dig house, and like an animated robot the lady set out purposefully in our direction. We were about to receive a visitor from the Donna Vincenza III.

She was a diminutive figure, striding jerkily down the beach towards us, brandishing a walking cane in one hand and gesticulating forwards with the other and screaming at the empty air in a somewhat cracked but commanding bass voice:

"Darlink! Cara Mia, where are you? Darlink! Darlink!"

She turned out to be a formidable woman, Anna Maria Pasqualucci, for that was who our orthopaedic visitor turned out to be. She was, I was reliably informed, heiress to the Pasqualucci millions. Her husband Enzio Pasqualucci had made a fortune from construction companies outside Milano. We never did find out if the eponymous Enzio was aboard the Pasqualucci Personal Paquebot, the Donna Vincenza III, at the time, but she, the aging Anna Maria, was *da solo* this evening, except for her retainer who was waiting patiently at the tender up the beach. She wore her grey hair drawn off her face in a severe bun which accentuated her powerful jaw and remarkable visage, for firmly screwed into her left eye Anna Maria wore

137

a monocle. Not only that, she had lost an eye in a hunting accident in her teens, some unpleasantness with a cross bow I was later told, and wore a replacement glass one, but also in the left eye, or so it seemed to me, such that the monocle magnified the prosthetic pupil and gave her a fearsome if somewhat Cyclopean appearance.

She clearly was a fairly fearsome character, as she fired question after question in a heavily accented English. Everyone was somewhat defensive, as well we might be, and said very little.

"And you, what do you do?" she persisted, pointing with a powerful, bony finger at one of the cataloguing staff. "And you? And you?"

She span round on her game leg and jabbing at me, she asked loudly, "And you, young man, what do you do?"

I mumbled something about the Wild RK1 tacheometric telescopic alidade and the planning of the trenches.

She turned back to the Inner Circle.

"These young people need a drink. Are you going to give them one, or do I have to do it?"

Without waiting for a reply she stomped to the edge of the dig house and hallooed loudly to Fabio over by the tender and shouted some instruction in Italian. Obediently Fabio leapt into the boat and rowed post haste to the side of the Donna Vincenza III. A few words were exchanged over the gunwale, and shortly a cardboard box was handed down into the tender which Fabio rowed back to the beach. He walked down to the dig house carrying the box, which exuded a promising clinking sound, and put it on the table next to Anna Maria Pasqualucci. To my absolute surprise she turned to me and said:

"Come along, young man. Get these bottles open. And bring some glasses."

There in the box were six bottles of Orvieto Classico, the golden wine from the Umbrian Mountains. Eager hands fetched tumblers and a cork screw and a feeding, or rather, a wine-drinking frenzy began. It was good stuff, this Italian white wine. We toasted each other and helped ourselves to more. Anna Maria was by now in quieter, more confidential conversation with the High Command. I noticed however that no-one had thought to offer her a drink. I rummaged about and found a clean glass, and lifting a newly opened bottle from the box I went over to her.

"Senora Pasqualucci," I began, "may I perhaps offer you a glass of white wine?"

She turned to face me in an attitude of ferocious surprise which made the monocled eye of Polyphemus even more prominent, and giving me a withering, staccato repost she barked out:

"Young man, I never, ever drink!"

And with that, she stood up, turned abruptly on her heel, said her peremptory farewells to the excavational ensemble and stamped up the sand to the waiting tender to be rowed back to the Donna Vincenza. It seemed a shame to leave the remainder of the Orvieto Classico, so we continued drinking, toasting the health of the munificent Anna Maria, until we had finished it all off.

When we arose the next morning, the Donna Vincenza III had gone, having weighed anchor in the night, and the Commercial Harbour was empty except for the returning fishing boats.

I mean, how was I to know she didn't drink? Shame really though, I thought, with a boat-load of such excellent vino. Well, *è la vita*, I suppose.

139

* * * *

There was a very similar incident to the last one some weeks later. Another yacht, another lady, but this time English, or rather, I should say, Scottish. I am not at all familiar with the obscure primogeniture of the clans north of the Border, but it turns out that there are these Scottish lairds manqué, the sort who own half of Perthshire and half a dozen castles near Auchtermuchty or wherever, mad keen on the haggis, Hogmanay, heather and Highland reels, but they actually live in Belgravia and speak like the Queen. Apparently it was something to do with Highland clearances and absentee landlords a couple of centuries or so ago. Anyway, this new arrival was one of those.

Mind you, there was one compelling reason why even I would be prepared to support her claim to being Scottish through and through, even if she did sound as though she'd spent her whole life at Roedean and had views about hairy highlanders which were to the north of the Emperor Hadrian. It seems she possessed a whisky distillery. To me, that has to be an impeccable credential of Caledonian ethnicity. I mean, she owned the whole thing – malting floor, mash tun, pot stills - the whole fermenting lot. It seems she was the sole proprietor of the Speyside McThynge Glenmuchty, or whatever improbable Gallic moniker her single malt was titled. Today 'The Glenmuchty' would be heralded as a 'boutique family enterprise' because amazingly this lady was the McThynge of McThynge. After five hundred years of claymores, Bonnie Price Charlie and general clan-ridden 'mirdher maest foul', she was the last McThynge left standing.

Anyway, I digress. Once again, she'd come to visit the excavations and like her monopthalmic maritime predecessor she was familiar with various members of the Expedition, and she too had come in her private yacht, M/Y Pride of McThynge or whatever, which for all I noticed probably sported a tartan flag on the stern. Anyhow, once again, towards the end of her visit, she took pity on the lower orders in the dig house – 'such dedicated folk, you know' – who had been lurching listlessly in the background in the hope of a dram, or even a wee sensation of the aptly named Uisge Beatha – water of life. Fat chance, I thought.

However, at the end of her second day with us, when we had all showed her our discoveries and developments, some of us several times over, she expressed her thanks for our patience and enthusiasm by sending her gillie to the yacht for something with which to make an appreciative libation to Knidos, Aphrodite and the team of dedicated archaeologists who were putting Cape Crio on the map (if it's anything to do with maps, by the way, that'll be me and Sonny to the fore!).

The Young Lochinvar arrived back at the dig house with an encouraging-looking carton under his arm, and lo, inside were several bottles of the Speyside McThynge Glenmuchty. Of course, there was some confusion about to whom the elixir may belong. But after due consultation, the entire contents of the carton, the McThynge of McThynge decreed, were to be bequeathed to us all in perpetuity. A tasting was quickly arranged and the health of the McThynge was drunk with gusto in tumblers-full of her personalized pale-golden potion.

It was such a generous gift to us, the Thirsty of Knidos, that I should have liked to have thanked the lady in person when I got back to Britain, perhaps at her baronial 'Dunromin' in Scotland, or at her mansion in Mayfair or wherever. Unfortunately, however long I perused the endless shelves of single malt whiskies in the various Knightsbridge emporia where they are on display, I couldn't for the life of me remember the exact name on the bottles at Knidos, McThynge or otherwise. The stupor that their contents nightly induced always resulted the next day in a fit of Gaelic amnesia.

Still, they do say that some alcoholic beverages don't really travel. Let's say this was one of them and leave it at that.

141

✳ ✳ ✳ ✳

One evening I remember a small and rather inconspicuous yacht came into the Commercial Harbour and moored quite close to the dig house. It was flying a German flag and was registered in Bremen. I didn't take much notice of it, but several of the High Command began to show considerable signs of agitation by its presence. Apparently there had been incendiary talk about a party of Germans illegally lifting amphora from the sea bed to transport back to Europe, something which was absolutely and totally verboten under Turkish law. There was some discussion that because this yacht was German and was anchored so near to where we were living that we might in some way be involved with it by association, and with any half-inching of antiquities, putting our excavating license in jeopardy.

Urgent meetings were held with the Commissar, Hakkı Bey and the Jardarma were fetched from their evening tea-fest at the Çayhane. Fingers were pointed at the site, the yacht, the dig house and the sea in general. But nothing seemed to resolve itself. After a while, in ones and twos we all traipsed off to bed. There the matter appeared to have ended.

However, when we woke the next morning there had been dramatic maritime developments. Moored within a couple of metres of the German yacht, in what was otherwise a wide and empty harbour, and dwarfing it by its size, was a very conspicuous Turkish gun boat flying a very conspicuous blood red Turkish flag. It was a vessel belonging to the Sahil Güvenlik, the coastal security service which had come all the way from Fethiye way down the coast during the night, summoned no doubt by the Jardarma, and now it was sitting idly at anchor very close to the suspect party, the sun glinting off its grey upper-works. To emphasize its purpose, two naval ratings in white uniforms were resolutely polishing the brass fittings of a large cannon mounted on the foredeck of this menacing Anatolian 'Schnellboot'. Within a few minutes, from total inactivity the German yacht up-anchored and took off into the blue, never to be seen again. No more was heard about the illicit traffic in antiquities after that.

142

CHAPTER FOURTEEN

BEWARE OF THE DOG

Canis timidus vehementius latrat quam mordet - A timid dog barks more violently than it bites.

Curtius Rufus

Someone had brought to Knidos an ill-humoured lap-dog, a miniature pooch called Carlino, whose very name became odious among us, the plebeians below the salt. I have to say I am not a great starter on dogs at the best of times, especially these disagreeable and unattractive yapping little canines. Anyway, this particular rendition truly was the bane of our dig house lives. It poked its repellent, elongated snout into everything, and snapped at everyone except its owner. It was omni-present at meal times, when it was wont to nip our toes under the table. But we felt powerless to fight back until one day a series of apparently unrelated events was to lead to Carlino's nemesis.

We had been living for many days on the usual frugal diet of beans and tomatoes, alternating with tomatoes and beans, and, though not yet contracting rickets, scurvy or some other debilitating dietary disorder, we had all become pretty fed up with our victuals. Sitting disconsolately under the matting sunshade of the dig house after yet another lack-lustre lunch, our interest was mildly aroused by a small cloud of dust advancing down the rocky road from Yazıköy, which, when it finally emerged from its swirling cocoon, turned out to be a jeep of unknown provenance. Whatever else might befall, it was certainly something new and different. The jeep had rocked its way slowly and unsteadily past the tombs of the necropolis, past the eastern gate and the theatre before it finally stopped abruptly outside Cengis's Çayhane. The two occupants alighted and were seen to engage in vigorous manually assisted converse with Cengis's subordinate Cemal. Whilst thus gesticulating in a manner of mutual incomprehension, they were joined by Muzafer the *Bekçi*, asserting his somewhat superfluous authority over the proceedings by way of his jauntily-worn, tattered peak cap, his faded grey uniform-style jacket with frayed yellow frogging, his baggy trousers and tan plastic shoes. However, after a few lira notes had changed hands comprehension evidently improved and they set off, Muzafer and the strangers, up the mountain. For the moment, there the story rested.

Sometime later, after he had returned from accompanying the visit to the ancient site with his guests, we saw Muzafer gesticulating meaningfully towards our dig house following which the two strangers came loping down the beach. Ducking under the shade of the tamarisk trees, they approached our veranda where we were lounging about in a postprandial torpor. When they had introduced themselves, the couple turned out to be none other than the writer Eric Williams and his wife. For readers unfamiliar with this celebrated author, he had written a book called 'The Tunnel Escape', an account of his break-out from Stalag Luft III in 1943 while a German prisoner of war. As Flight Lieutenant Eric Williams, he had dug under the wire from a vaulting horse. The wooden vaulting horse was carried out to the same spot each day about thirty metres from the wire. As the other prisoners vigorously vaulted over the top, he and two accomplices dug from a trap door hidden in the ground underneath. After 114 days burrowing in the dark, they finally escaped. All three reached Sweden and were repatriated back to Britain. In 1950, the book was made into a film, 'The Wooden Horse'. And by 1969, the author of the said book had finally burrowed his way as far as Knidos.

The Brits among us suddenly perked up, naturally enamoured to meet this home-grown war-time hero and we made quite a fuss of him and his wife, ending up by inviting them to supper, such as it was. After liberal helpings of raki at Cengis' hostelry, meant to disguise our meagre mealtime, we trudged over to the dining table. The inevitable tomatoes and beans appeared. There was a noticeable period of silence after we had eaten.

"Is this all you stalwart diggers get to eat?" he enquired. Well, he'd know about diggers wouldn't he?

"Don't you ever get any meat?"

We mumbled somewhat ungratefully that the food was worse than a prison camp – an appropriate image in the circumstances, we thought.

"Well," he said, "when I get back to civilisation I'll send you some."

We forbore to tell him that technically speaking we were at the centre of civilisation here at Knidos, albeit in the wrong millennium.

Time passed. The summer days wore on. Eric, his horse and his viandes were forgotten. However, one afternoon some weeks later, Mehmet the Fenerci, returning from Yazıköy with the mail, handed out our various letters and a large brown paper package from Marmaris marked 'from one digger to another, Eric'. Inside were two large tins of *Soslu böbrek*, kidneys in gravy. The promised meat had arrived. None of us cared even if we weren't too keen on offal, with or without gravy. It was meat.

That evening, after substantial libations of Cengis' rakı, we sat down to our new experience of tomatoes, beans and meat. The first two arrived on cue, but of the kidneys in gravy we saw no sign. No-one thought to query it at this stage, nor yet at lunch time the next day, but on the second evening, when still no kidneys turned up, Halil the cook was button-holed by a restive bunch of students, starved of protein, and asked to explain himself. Halil scuttled inside to his pots and pans, but was winkled out again and brow-beaten into telling us the sad story of the kidneys in gravy.

"You see", he began timidly, "the kidneys, they were for whole camp, yes?"

"No, Halil, they were not!" opined our beefiest volunteer Rudy, threateningly. "They were a present to us, the under-fed and over-worked. So where are they?"

"You see," wheedled a more cowed Halil in a higher pitched voice, "someone told me, no?"

"They told you what, Halil? What did they tell you?"

"You see," he continued defensively, "someone say yesterday was special birthday, and I must open kidneys."

"Whose birthday, Halil? Who had a birthday yesterday? None of us did, did we? So who was so special?"

"Rudy, I tell you, OK? Please, Rudy, I tell you right now." Halil moved to put the table between himself and his interrogator.

In a grovelling and tearful way, Halil whispered the name.

"Was Carlino, Rudy. Someone tell me to give kidneys to Carlino. It was birthday party for dog, Rudy. Is not me, please. Is Carlino."

After a few moments of stunned silence, the rest of us erupted in an angry hubbub.

With a controlled but menacing grimace, Frank asked his final, if somewhat superfluous, question before sentence was to be passed.

"And what exactly did Carlino do with the kidneys, Halil? He stuck his nasty nose in them, right?"

"No Frank, please, you understand me, no? He piss on them, that's what he do. He piss on them … on open tins. Piss, piss, piss, he go, then he run away."

Collective mortification saved Halil from a more excruciating fate. We were all so dumb-struck that Halil was able to make his escape into the sanctuary of his kitchen to fight another day. But the next day, as Carlino began his lunch-time biting foray under the dining table, pent-up aggression erupted, and Management or no, Carlino was kicked from one end of the table to the other, and back again, until he flew from under our feet and scampered off whining pitifully. From that day on, he never bothered us again. Even those dog-lovers among us felt vindicated. We had struck a blow against canine interference and, indirectly, against the system.

* * * *

How many times did I tell that story over the years that followed, of how we had triumphed over this wretched hound? But more than twenty years later I learnt that all was not what it had seemed those years before. Strolling along the marina in Datça in the 1990's who should I meet but Halil the cook. Somehow his native cunning with a German yacht owner a few years before had resulted in him owning his own yacht, where I now found him pottering about among some ropes. Typically, he'd called the yacht 'Bu da Kısmet' – 'That's my luck!' Halil hailed from Datça and in company with all Datça men, he had spent his intervening life in an alcoholic haze, drinking his fill of the very worst Turkish red wine – 'Evin'. Datça males were collectively known as 'diesel drinkers' and twenty five years of fuelling up in the bars of Datça had made Halil portly and somewhat querulous.

After a fond-enough greeting he suggested we repair to his favourite bar, where the red wine was brought without asking. We toasted the past, remembering stories of old Knidos. We retold the tales of Cengis' Çayhane, of 'Rushan's restoran', of Hakkı Bey the commissar and of Mark and Rudy. Well into the second bottle I retold the story of Carlino and how we had kicked him into oblivion around the dinner table.

"See," I said, "in the end we showed that dog who's the boss!"

Halil was immediately dismissive.

"You?" he said, confrontationally, screwing up his face and waving the back of his hand towards us. "Pah!"

"You all dog lovers! How you do this? You do nothing. It was I, Halil, I fix that dog."

"But how did you do that, Halil?"

"You think I like this dog? I spit on you, dog. No, I fix him real good."

I asked about his version of events, and he told us his tale, the sequel to our own story.

"You see, when I give dog kidneys, he bite my hand. He bite my hand, two times. I say him, 'You fuck dog! Why you bite my hand? I fix you good.' You know outboard motor? Next day I take benzene from outboard and squirt it up his backside. Whoosh, like that! Whoosh! Ho! Ho! How his backside burn! How he run away, so fast! Is village trick you understand? We use for mules who don't want to work. Whoosh! You see?"

"So what happened?" I asked, astounded and slightly horrified.

"This dog, is so funny, he run straight into the sea and rub his backside on the sand."

Halil stood up and, stooping slightly, wiggled his rear end at us in some rapid, dancing emulation of 'The Twist'.

"Up and down the sea he go. Everyone they come just then and is call, 'Carlino, Carlino, where are you?' But dog not interested! Dog is now like surf board in sea. Up and down; up and down!"

Halil's wiggling became more frenetic as he remembered his moment of triumph, and he grinned gleefully.

"Then they see dog. 'Oh my God!' they say. 'What happen to Carlino. Poor baby.' They try catch dog, but dog not interested. 'Halil', they say, 'we must take him to vet in Datça."

"Next day I start Land Rover and we catch dog and take to vet in Datça. When he examine dog, no more benzene, you see. All gone! Poof! Finish! 'This dog', he say, 'she OK! Nothing wrong.' Now you understand, Deyvit, this dog want no more to be with people. This now special dog, like jet plane!"

And seemingly no one was ever any the wiser, except of course Carlino who gave every one of us a very wide berth. No wonder, after his high octane adventure.

We quaffed our Evin and sank into a contemplative silence about the efficacy of rural remedies.

CHAPTER FIFTEEN

BEAUX GENDARMES

We're public guardians bold yet wary
And of ourselves we take good care
To risk our precious lives we're chary
When danger threatens we're not there
But when we see a helpless woman
Or little boys who do no harm...
We run them in, we run them in
We run them in, we run them in
To show them we're the beaux gendarmes

Offenbach - Gendarmes Duet

Had you driven to Knidos in 1969, then indeed an adventure, upon your arrival after a gruelling journey you would have been quickly aware, in addition to the reed- screened Çayhane, of only three other modern buildings around the harbour, each built of stone. One was the store room and our drawing office combined, with a small veranda in front and a few fragments of statuary in the garden. The second, on the island across the isthmus, was our dig house, which had been built by Mehmet Bora the Lighthouse keeper and was now leased by The High Command, and the third, set back by the sea on the edge of the Trireme Harbour was a small house which served as the headquarters of the Jandarma, the local militia. If you weren't looking for it, you might miss it, except that it had a conspicuous flag pole outside, and a few white-washed stones around a rudimentary vegetable patch. The Jandarma post was undoubtedly why the road you had just driven down, if it can in any way be called a road, existed at all.

In Turkey, which it should be noted is the breadth of the whole of Western Europe, law and order is maintained in the towns and cities by the local Polis, just like anywhere else. But in the countryside, and that includes the vast majority of rural Anatolia from the Aegean Sea to the borders of

Azerbaijan and Iran, it falls to the Jandarma to keep the peace, if there is anyone there to disturb it in the first place, parts of Turkey being so impassably mountainous.

The Jandarma falls under the jurisdiction of the army, which from Atatürk's time onwards has been the great sacred cow of the *Türkiye Cumhuryeti*, the Turkish Republic. As such, the Jandarma also has the ancillary role of maintaining homeland security. For example, in the case of Knidos, this means staving off any potential invasion from the Hellenic hordes. To this end, there was a significant detachment of Jandarma stationed at their forward base beside the Trireme Harbour at Knidos. The total military complement comprised two nineteen year old National Servicemen, Erhan and Erol, whom we shall call the two Ees. They were certainly not local; they both came from the east of Turkey. It was common in those days to send soldiers on their two year National Service stint to opposite ends of the country so they could appreciate its size and also they would be able to identify with the different components of this rich and diverse culture.

Subsequent events tell us that during their posting at Knidos Erhan and Erol, the two Ees, had little difficulty withstanding any offensive phalanx of Greek hoplites, ancient or modern. There were probably other reasons too for the two Ees' military success than any simmering aggression they may have counteracted. One undoubtedly was that the Greek government, then under the malevolent Regime of the Colonels, was too busy concentrating its military fire power upon its not inconsiderable own home-grown protesters in Syntagma Square in the centre of Athens to be much concerned about external matters, let alone Knidos, the potential soft underbelly of the Turkish Republic. Either that, or George Papadopoulos, head of the Junta, had already taken the strategic decision that eighty kilometres of isolated and execrably rugged cart track was not the right way to begin any kind of serious military operation; after all, he did have his own experience of how to launch a coup. Anyway, the net result was that within reason, the two

Ees, both being of a placid nature, enjoyed an outstandingly undemanding if sometimes remote posting at Knidos.

Full of his tales of derring-do in the Mediterranean, you can just envisage the contents of Erhan's weekly letter home to his Mum in Doğubayazit, living as she did in the shadow of Mount Ararat on the fractious Turkish border with Iran and Soviet Armenia,

"Kinidos Jandarma Istasiyonu. Hafta 63. Sevgili Annem, Hergün karpuz iyiyorum. Babama çok selamlar veriyorsun. Erhan."

"Knidos Army Outpost. Week 63. Dear Mum, I am eating watermelon every day. Give my love to Dad. Erhan."

Or...

"Sevgili Annem, Şimdiye Yunan yok! Lutfen bana başka mayo lazım. Erol."

"Dear Mum, No Greeks yet! I need another pair of swimming trunks. Erol."

From this brief if somewhat imaginary correspondence it may be seen that life was not at all taxing for the two young men, army-wise at least. There was only one day I remember that our two stalwart militia were ever really put to the military test, and that was from their own ranks, or rather, their own officer class. They had been acting a little strangely for some days, painting and re-painting the stones around the melon patch outside their small house, and sweeping the ever-blowing dust away from their front door. We had put it down to a slightly guilty feeling of too much fraternisation and not enough army activity. But it turned out that this bustle was a preliminary to an impending visit by their High Command, or at least, some generalissimo or another from Marmaris who had nothing better to do than to find out how the two Ees were getting on repelling the Hellenic menace at Knidos.

In the middle of the morning of the day in question, an army jeep drove down the road in which were three very smartly dressed military police in white helmets and armed with rifles, and an august-looking older man in a pressed military uniform with loads of scrambled egg decoration, a broad belt with pistol, lines of pips everywhere and an impressive peaked cap with badge. They alighted at the Jandarmarie as the two Ees stood stiffly to attention and saluted. The whole party very formally then went inside, presumable to look at whatever paperwork they needed to examine. They emerged after about twenty minutes with the two Ees grovelling around and the generalissimo by now in a less formal, more relaxed mode swaggering about with his thumbs in his belt. Militarily all must have been in order. He pointed to the Çayhane and they all wandered over and sat outside to be served tea by a somewhat cowed Cengis and assistant. The two Ees stood there trying to look as though they had never been in the Çayhane before. The great man made expansive arm-waving gestures across the harbour and towards the dig-house, presumably making some abstruse connection between them.

Then quite suddenly, tea finished, he stood up, the three military police leapt to attention, they all clambered back into the jeep and in a cloud of dust set off back up the road towards Yazıköy leaving the two bewildered Ees behind. They got as far as the theatre before they stopped abruptly and the generalissimo got out to change places with one of the two in the front and they roared off again. Within a hundred metres they stopped again, reversing to the last place they had halted, and the three police got out and began searching on the ground. After a second or two, they jumped back in the jeep and finally disappeared. This last part of the performance, we later learned, was because the great man had inadvertently dropped his pistol on the ground when they changed places and they had come back to retrieve it. The visitation was over and the two Ees could relax once more.

* * * *

By and large, though the two Ees notionally constituted the neighbourhood peace- keeping force, in the interests of good governance they were very willing to socialize with the locals, foreigners included, in the Çayhane – strictly with tea and soft drinks of course, and the occasional fried egg. The more significant bilateral fraternisation went in the other direction, at least from my point of view. As Erhan had alluded in his letter, the two Ees had a seemingly endless supply of water melons, and of course our drawing office was within pip-spitting distance of the Jandarmarie. A refreshingly cool slice of *karpuz* was very welcome on a hot July morning, in exchange for a cup of our otherwise virtually unobtainable kahve.

But it was not the cool elements of this NATO cooperation in which I was interested, but the warm ones; the Jandarma post had a boiler heated with a wood fire. Whereas the prols of the excavation, me included, were normally accorded only a cold shower, I found that by plying the Ees with coffee I was able to slip into the Jandarmarie, surreptitiously of course, and enjoy a luxuriating hot shower most evenings. Overall, then, from the point of view of public order, all was well.

Alas, I should have guessed that this state of affairs was not going to continue indefinitely. By early September a larger than usual dispute had arisen between The High Command and the villagers in relation to the division of the artefacts excavated at the site – statuary, wall plaster, oil lamps, amphorae, pennanular bronze rings, and other generalised archaeological bric-a-brac. The rule was that at the end of the digging season, all this material would be sent to the Museum at Bodrum, having already been neatly catalogued, numbered and, where necessary, conserved. However, some unidentified village rabble-rouser supported by a corps of other pastoral malcontents got it into their minds that the artefacts should by rights remain at Knidos, for example in a newly-to-be constructed museum. If such were to be the case, they suggested, this would ensure a steady flow of yachts into the harbour, hence streams of foreign visitors and thus undreamed-of tourist bounty which could be shared by the locals to supplement their income. A substantial head of steam had built up in this regard, such that on the night before the artefact haul was to be taken from Knidos, the workers, emboldened by an informal public meeting in the Çayhane and fuelled with liberal applications of Lion's Milk, were by ten o'clock in a state of palpable insurrection against person or persons unspecified.

Bearing in mind that the main function of the Jandarma was not really to provide watermelon and hot showers to mendicant surveyors but actually to keep the peace, an altercation between the two Ees and what by now could be perceived to be an unruly and milling rabble was inevitable. Erhan and Erol, with no previous experience of public relations and without the benefit of confrontational counselling, and being charged with maintaining law and order, must have felt that the only way to fulfil their duty was to lay about the villagers with batons, which they duly did. Striding manfully into the melee they proceeded to knock ten bells out of everyone and anyone who was within truncheon-wielding distance. The result was untrammelled pandemonium, as sundry villagers were indiscriminately whacked about heads, shoulders, arms and legs. I don't know how long the imbroglio lasted, but at the end of it several prominent workers had to be carted off to the clinic in Datça, and one, the eleven year old son of my tripod bearer Mümtaz, was admitted to the Government hospital at Marmaris where he remained for a week. Quite how he had got involved remained an unresolved mystery, but it certainly heightened the immediate tension.

Not unnaturally, cries of *Jandarma fena,* "the Jandarma are bad," dominated the conversation in the Çayhane for some days after this incident, and by association I was reduced to cold showers for a week. I had missed the height of the brouhaha, being warned by my good friend Hakkı Bey the Commissar to stay away from the vicinity of the Çayhane that evening. But I could see from the bandaged heads and various splints next day that the score for the previous evening's fixture was something like Jandarma F.C. 7, Yazıköy Wanderers 0.

155

Nevertheless, after a suitable length of time had elapsed, and the evidence of the fracas had been removed, and the artefacts had duly been sent to Bodrum, normal service was resumed in Knidos. The two Ees rejoined the Çayhane as though nothing had happened. None the worse for their unaccustomed belligerence, they were welcomed back into the body of the kirk, while thankfully one plane table surveyor was able to return to his more comfortable evening ablutions.

CHAPTER SIXTEEN

STICK TO IT!

Talent without discipline is like an octopus on roller skates. There's plenty of movement, but you never know if it's going to be forward, backwards, or sideways.

H. Jackson Brown

From time to time, when the wind was in the right direction, when there were no labour disputes stalking the terraces, when the Commissar was away for a few days and when there was something they wanted to celebrate, the High Command would invite the lower orders, we the rodentia, for a soiree at the dig house after dinner. The programme usually involved two main elements – listening to a one-sided 'hurrah' about how well they'd done, coupled with a free booze allowance. You may surmise which of the two interested us most. So, on such a night we would traipse over to the dig-house again after the evening meal and wait, tongues out, for the complimentary vinho de casa to be broached.

It was on one such night, having through something of an oversight imbibed rather too liberally of the red infuriator, that I felt an urge to go to the loo. Now it should be pointed out that those of us below the salt had a long drop loo across the isthmus, but the High Command, being in charge of the whole ensemble, had their own flush toilet adjacent to the dig house, officers for the use of, or lower ranks too if they happened to be attending the soiree. It wasn't a very successful loo, it must be said. It comprised a standard toilet bowl and seat with a flushing mechanism that had some time ago ceased to function. The way it was now flushed was by means of taking a bucket of sea water from the harbour's edge, emptying half the contents into the bowl, doing whatever was necessary, then flushing the rest of the bucketful down the loo and returning it to its shallow rock pool in the sea. That much was straight forward.

On the night in question, I excused myself from what passed for the celebratory *palais de danse* and grabbing a torch and making my way to the rock pool, took up the full bucket and tottered along the path to the loo. In the inky blackness of the shed, I slopped the requisite amount into the bowl and sat down to relieve myself. As I sat there, elbows on knees and head in hands, I mused on the imprudence of life, whereby, savaged by the grape, I would have to rise the next day at 5.00 am and do a full morning's work in the intense glare of the ever climbing sun, mouth no doubt presenting a passable imitation of the bottom of a budgerigar's cage. Would I never learn?

I sat there immobile and pensive for a while, I remember, listening to the festivities afar off, when I gradually became aware that all was not well down in my industrial area. The first hint of something amiss was a sort of involuntary flexing of the gluteal muscles, the muscles of my bum, like a stationary horse twitching its flanks without otherwise moving. I was considering what such spasms might portend when a supplementary sensation aroused my anxiety further. It felt as though someone was trying silently to seal up my nether regions in swathes of parcel tape. In my current state such an unfamiliar phenomenon took a little time to comprehend, but it finally dawned on me that if I let it continue unabated, it might result in my arse being permanently put out of commission by virtue of the cheeks being irrevocably welded together.

With growing alarm, I jumped up and shone the torch behind me, and there, to my utter astonishment, was an octopus, four of its tentacles firmly grasping the porcelain and the other four writhing sinuously around my buttocks, trying to get a purchase in order to lever itself out of the slough of despond into which it had been unexpectedly pitched. As I stood up, the octopus became suspended there, between heaven and hell, I suppose you could suggest. The poor creature had come into the shallow water at the edge of the harbour to find a convenient hole in which to hide in during the hours of darkness, and that nice hole was of course the bucket, which was to lead of course to its present unfortunate predicament. With some difficulty I managed to prise the distressed cephalopod from the toilet bowl and from myself, and putting it back in the bucket returned it to the sea, trusting it would be none the worse for wear after its fundamental experience.

But you know something, ever since then I have always been a sucker for octopus.

CHAPTER SEVENTEEN

CHURCH FATE

Of that Byzantine Empire, the universal verdict of history is that it constitutes, without a single exception, the most thoroughly base and despicable form that civilisation has yet assumed. The history is a monotonous story of the intrigues of priests, eunuchs and women, of poisonings, of conspiracies, of uniform ingratitude.
W. E. H. Lecky 'History of European Morals' 1869

According to John Julius Norwich in his masterly trilogy about Byzantium, it was Edward Gibbon, he of Declining and Falling fame, who was the first influential voice raised against educating the youth of Britain in what he considered to be the corrupting influences of the Byzantine world. Somewhat obscurely, Gibbon blamed the loss of the Roman Empire's political and military virility on the later rise of Christianity. He accused the Byzantine emperors of abandoning the Church to the bishops, the State to the eunuchs, and the Provinces to the Barbarians, and he talked of 'the sacred indolence of the monks being devoutly embraced by a servile and effeminate age.' Although he went on to write his way through what he saw as the whole historical catastrophe, Gibbon clearly wasn't keen to pass on this perceived depravity, theologically or otherwise, to the impressionable unformed minds of the younger generation.

Gibbon was writing in the 18th century. By Victorian times, his successors had really taken this negativity to heart. Even if it could be styled notionally Christian, or perhaps because of its somewhat oriental mien, they dismissed the Byzantine Empire as debauched, a mysterious, malicious and suspiciously eastern confection, disagreeable and vindictive, quite unworthy of enquiry. So it came to be that Byzantine history never entered the educational curriculum of Victoria's Britain, a state of affairs which persisted long after the Queen Empress herself had passed into the Eternal Courts of her Heavenly Opposite Number. It was all well and good studying the colonial history of the Romans and their Empire, however grossly overbearing they might have been, with their militaristic compulsion and skilled and clean, if lethal, gladiatorial combat. 'We who are about to die salute you,' and all that. There was apparently something noble to commend them. But the Byzantines, well, they were simply beyond the pale.

As far as the Romans were concerned, to the Edwardian educator, reassuring resemblances could be drawn between the story of Rome's conquests abroad and political brawling at home with the rise of the British Empire. India could be visualised as the contemporary Imperial ambition and, at a stretch, and if you squinted a little, Cecil Rhodes' forward policy among the 'barbarians' in Africa could be paralleled with Julius Caesar bringing order and civilisation to the peoples of Gaul, whether they wanted it or not. So, *Gallia est omnis divisa in partes tres* was as familiar and didactic to a Twentieth Century schoolboy from Surbiton or Sunderland as the Lord's Prayer. Caesar was part of the warp and weft of our island's history, part of the very fabric of European society. But mention Belesarius, general to the Byzantine Emperor Justinian and one of the finest military leaders of all time, and we would probably all be mute on the subject. By the way, for those latter-day students to whom the above stirring lines of Latin have no resonance, they are the opening lines of Caesar's Gallic Wars. They were part of the stock in trade of even the most linguistically challenged grammar school pupil until right up to the end of the 1950's.

But back to Asia Minor. In the hallowed British Educational system, which was incidentally also exported throughout the red areas in your then school atlas – most of the world in fact – the folklore was perpetuated that Byzantine history was completely unfit for impressionable young minds. In an era when even the sun's rays were considered potentially deleterious, such human endeavour as studying the life and times of Constantine, Constantius or Constans was thought to be similarly unwholesome. There was a suggestion that it carried with it a tendency to corrupt.

What an omission! The Byzantine Empire, which had lasted for 1123 years, more than a whole millennium in fact, from 330 to 1453 AD, was to be dismissed without a second glance. The Byzantine Empire, by far the longest the world has ever experienced; the Byzantine Empire, the only bridge between the Classical World and the Renaissance, was consigned to the curricular dustbin as too degenerate to learn about.

Even more significantly in its favour, Byzantium had acted as the bastion of Christianity against the darkening Middle Ages, and it was Byzantium which withstood and acted as a buffer against the otherwise unstoppable march of Islam. Moslem armies had even clamoured at the Gates of Vienna. Worse! Umayyad forces had pushed north from Moorish Spain even as far as Bordeaux. My God! If it weren't for the Byzantines, we might all now be tee-total. Surely that frightening prospect makes them worthy of some consideration?

Anyway, by the time I appeared within the erstwhile borders of ancient Byzantium, modern day Turkey, this collective chasm of western European ignorance meant that I personally knew categorically nothing about Byzantine history, its extent, its theology, its rise or its fall. And if I knew nothing about that, I knew an even smaller amount about its architecture and archaeology – absolutely zero about Zeno and even less about Leo.

But Byzantium represented almost exactly one third of the total life of the city of Knidos. After its foundation in Hellenistic times, and its continuation and rebuilding during the Roman period, Knidos went on to enjoy a Byzantine revival, the third incarnation of its people, the third reconstruction of its streets and houses, and the third reconstitution of its religious buildings, indeed especially its religious buildings, for Knidos became peppered with churches. The veneration of Christ arrived at Knidos in bricks and mortar. So, how did that whole thing happen?

$* \quad * \quad * \quad *$

In 325 AD the Roman Emperor Constantine convened a Council at Nicea on the Asiatic side of the Sea of Marmara in northern Turkey. Attending the Council were all the bishops and clerics of Christendom and its ostensible purpose was to regularise the tenets of the Christian faith, healing the differences and schisms which had developed, and leading to the issuing of the Nicene Creed, the one still used in Christian services today, though I'm sure that few people in the pews of Macclesfield or Manchester know where it originally comes from. Anyway, at an appropriate moment during the Synod, Constantine, we are told, made a ceremonial entrance in raiment which glittered with rays of light, a reflection of the glowing radiance of his purple robes adorned with the brilliant splendour of gold and precious stones. In such a wise he announced like some heavenly messenger that as Emperor of the New Rome he was also God's vice-regent on Earth, and thus their spiritual and temporal head. Clever eh?

Constantine had appreciated the power of the Cross some years earlier when, at the Battle of the Milvian Bridge outside Rome in 312, he had seen a sign in the sky and the message, 'In this Sign, Conquer!' The sign was 'XP', the Greek Chi Rho of the word 'Christos' and one of the talismanic symbols of Christianity. Now he was set to espouse Christianity as the main religion of the Empire, and to establish a new capital at the old Greek trading post of Byzantium, to be renamed Constantinople, the City of Constantine, in his honour.

Actually, the Christianising process had already begun with Constantine's mother, the Empress Helena, wife of the one time Roman general Constantius Chlorus. Unfortunately for Helena and her first born son Constantine, the chloritic Constantius had abandoned them both, divorcing Helena to marry some other more politically connected floozy. Though Constantine thrived, Helena was left out in the cold, the jilted wife. Incidentally, there is a tradition, probably spurious, that Helena was originally the daughter of a British Chieftain named Coel, as in Colchester, of Old King Cole fame, and that as such she was an Essex girl, which may help to explain what happened next. She took herself off to the Holy Land in search of the meaning of life, or at least, the meaning of Christianity, and while in Jerusalem she was shown the location of Calvary where Our Lord had been crucified. In a personally supervised excavation of the site, she discovered not one but three crosses which she interpreted as those of Jesus and of the two malefactors. She took fragments of the authentic Cross, along with some nails, a couple of thorns from Christ's crown and one or two other bits of crucifixion bric-a-brac, back to Rome where the rediscovered relics are still housed in the Basilica of Santa Croce in Gerusalemme. The Pope has since authenticated them so they must be genuine mustn't they?

Anyway, back to her son. Constantine's city, Constantinople, became the *omphalos,* the navel, of the Empire, and despite protestations from a string of popes in Rome, the Byzantine rulers for the next one thousand years styled themselves '*Autokrator hoi Romanaioi*', Emperor of the Romans - curious really, as the title is in Greek. The legitimising of Christianity led to the frenetic building of churches and monastic complexes throughout Asia Minor and most of the cities of ancient Caria thus persisted into the early Byzantine period, including Knidos. Some became bishoprics, others religious centres for the worship of one or other of the early saints and martyrs of the Church.

Under the Emperor Theodosius 1 (392 - 395), orthodox Christianity became the sole religion of the Empire. The old Roman order was disintegrating, and just after the end of Theodosius' reign the west had collapsed, overrun by the Goths. Incidentally, to many historians, the Middle Ages began in AD 410. But Byzantium, the Empire of the east, continued for another millennium, surviving the onslaught of a hydra of enemies – Goths, Huns, Vandals, Persians, Bulgars, Avars, Magyars, Pechenegs, Seljuks, Serbs,

Saracens and droves of others. During the reign of Justinian (527-565) the Byzantine Empire reached its furthest extent. The Imperial armies, under the leadership of that most able general, Belesarius, retook Italy and even campaigned in North Africa. For Caria, Justinian's reign was the highest point of the Byzantine period. The wealth of Empire transformed what had by now become the moribund Classical cities of the Hellenistic and Roman era and at the same time promoted ecclesiastical settlements along the coast of south-west Asia Minor. The Byzantine Empire was here to stay, at least for a bit, but how was it architecturally expressed?

* * * *

After the finely-tuned harmony of the Doric and Ionic orders, where every chiselled nuance is charged with meaning, every angle mathematically calculated and where proportional design was, even at the time, a matter of passionate scholarly debate, after the ubiquity of Hellenistic masonry, with its studiously rusticated yet bubble-accurate horizontal coursing and wide vocabulary of form, and after the bravura of Roman grandeur - gigantic barrel vaulting, lavish marble-clad bath-houses and grandiose theatres - one might be forgiven for overlooking the remains of Byzantine buildings altogether. Their relics retreat into the undergrowth of a ruined city like undistinguished piles of misshapen rubble, because that in essence is what they are; that's how they were built. To the architectural eye, with its search for symmetry and analogue, looking for the horizontal and the perpendicular to materialize from the wild creepers and among the spiny shrubs, the chunks of this low-grade manufacture merge with the very hillsides from which they were once raised, rendering them if not actually then subconsciously invisible to all but the keenest observer.

At provincial sites along the coast of Asia Minor, these long-abandoned Byzantine ruins can be an abomination to the architectural purist and the Graeco-Roman archaeologist alike. Rumours abound about diggers unceremoniously and hurriedly shovelling off Byzantine remains at the surface to reveal the all-important Classical buildings below, a practice no doubt exacerbated by restrictions of funding and constraints of time. In such cases, presumably, no dimensions are recorded; no notes are made; no artefacts kept. After all, who would care about this lacklustre refuse from 'Late Antiquity', often indistinguishable in form and manufacture from a recently ruined goat pen or livestock enclosure? At first sight, that is what it looks like – amorphous rubble and mortar of no apparent significance. Knidos is littered with it.

But walk into Justinian's Church of Holy Wisdom in Constantinople, the Hagia Sophia, Patriarchal focus of Byzantine worship at the *omphalos* of Empire, and you step into a brilliant new world, an architectural panegyric without its parallel on earth. The vast dome of the central basilica appears suspended in a misty space, the mantle of Heaven, a boundless sky above the marble-floored earth. It hangs there, thrust upwards into the ethereal cosmos and held floating by a particularly Byzantine invention - pendentives. These concavely triangular vaults span the cuspate surfaces between the right-angularly set load-bearing arches upon which the whole structure is raised. In so doing they transfer the downward weight from the circular ring of the cupola evenly outwards to the ground. Not even the Romans had worked that one out. It appears as though the dome has no visible means of support. In the Hagia Sophia it's astounding, and so is the rest of the building, with its galleries and mosaics, its carvings and red porphyry columns brought from Egypt and its green marble from Thessaly. When Justinian entered the church as it was being completed, he gazed up at the cupola and was heard to say, 'O Solomon, I have thee outdone!' And he was most probably right.

No such airy grandeur can be discerned rising from the dusty goat paths of ancient Knidos. Among the wind-swept ruins at Cape Crio no archbishop or acolyte, presbyter or priest has left any trace of once high-minded theology translated into high-vaulted stonework, above ground at least. Today, on a warm spring morning, the colourful arrays of spring flowers obliterate the ancient world as though it barely existed. Clouds of tall, yellow and white ox-eye daisies, meadows of vivid red poppies and carpets of trailing purple morning glory speak only of the naturally chromatic present. Even the humble field walls are overgrown with stunted holly oaks, mastic trees and white-flowering Daphne. Wild nature has wrested back its preserve from the unnatural offensive of ancient human enterprise and the peninsula is at peace with itself once more. Here and there a rare, broken, ill-formed arch protrudes above the foliage, cobbled together with rubble and mortar, the remains of a vaulted Byzantine cistern. Elsewhere formless outcrops of similar debris indicate the collapsed walls of houses and streets. There is nothing monumental or romantically Classical about these disjointed heaps. Their very presence accentuates the blight which struck the great city in its terminal decline more than a millennium ago. The lowly method of building seems to reflect its people's decaying culture. For the citizens of Knidos the rise of Byzantium could be seen as inauguration of the decline of their own polity, the beginning of the end.

However, scratch the surface and this dismal picture is not substantiated. Knidos did endure for more than three hundred years in early Byzantine times. The city was rebuilt and must have achieved a revivified excitement, albeit with a new way of life, a new style of architecture. As marble and limestone had been to the Graeco-Roman world, so bricks, rubble and mortar were to the master masons of Byzantium, especially here in the provinces. With mortar and shuttering and damaged masonry borrowed from earlier buildings, and with roof trusses and pan-tiles, a new city arose phoenix-like from the ashes of the late Roman period. This was the new way to build, and if it looked a little substandard by comparison to its forebears, the imperfections could easily all be straightened out, literally, with a liberal application of rendering. The innovative way was to beg, to borrow, to steal and then to plaster. Getting used to the shock of the new, one can come to love it in its flexibility and simplicity.

One reason for the revolution in building technique was geologically initiated. Had the Hellenistic town planners all those centuries before been aware of Plate Tectonics, of the sutures, lineaments and rifts along which our planet's land masses periodically convulse, they would have known that Cape Crio was the very last place they should ever have chosen to build a long-lasting major conurbation. It is clear now even to the unpractised eye that Knidos sits astride two, if not three, major and vigorous faults, part of a whole web of parallel and sub-parallel fractures with which the Anatolian continental plate is shot through. They are so obvious and geologically active that they can plainly be seen on the surface – one downthrown to the east of the lighthouse, another on the eastern end of the island above the mole of the Commercial Harbour. Suspending belief for a moment, there is even a suggestion that far from avoiding them, the original Hellenistic planners were actually aware of these potential earthquake zones and that in a mulish sort of way they allowed and encouraged construction here. Note for example the building of the Temenos of Demeter right on top of an active fracture, because in a piece of convoluted logic they felt they would be closer to the creative forces of the underworld. How were they to know, as we have only recently discovered, that the opening of the Red Sea is currently pushing the Arabian Plateau northwards into the Taurus, causing the whole of Turkey to pivot and shudder with frequent and periodic violence along the North Anatolian Fault and the ancillary faults along the Aegean coast to jerk uncontrollably in a sub-crustal continental St Vitus' Dance.

Whatever the thinking behind it, the city certainly must have shaken itself to pieces, partially or totally, on a number of occasions. The evidence is everywhere to be seen in the excavations. In the agora near the harbour isthmus, the pillars have fallen as if felled. Street steps are dislocated, masonry smashed, and as if proving the point, the front foundations of one of the temples have been ripped asunder seemingly by giant hands. We can only guess at when these incidents might have taken place, but certainly by Byzantine times most of the magnificent temple facades and porticos that had graced the city Strabo had written about around the time of Christ, or gave Knidos its elegance when Hadrian visited in 129 AD, had been shivered to the ground. It was left to the Byzantine builders to re-use the broken blocks and decorative fragments of the wrecked city and to mend, mortar and make-do.

In the empire of the New Rome, the strict canons of the Hellenistic street plan of Knidos were abandoned. The middle of the city above the harbour, where once the civic buildings had been, was reconstructed with rubble and mortar houses, courtyards, well-heads and cobbled alleyways. The surfaces of stepped streets and road-ways still in use were patched up with pieces of fallen Classical masonry – Hellenistic marble architraves and door jambs, abandoned basalt mill stones, a lintel here, a column base there. At the main street junction where the street from the harbour led to a high terrace on which a temple had once stood, a Byzantine villa was erected overlooking the junction, but right across the road-way, thus denying any access to the upper continuation of the street. From now on, the steps of the erstwhile street led not in upward expectation to the fragrant gardens of temple's bower, but straight through to the front door of the villa into its atrium. This re-statement must also have been intended to prevent physically or spiritually any apostasy, any back-sliding into polytheism and the re-adoration of any of the ancient deities once worshipped here.

And so the life of the city continued, not as in the panache of its Classical heyday perhaps nor yet with its former elegance, but the people survived until the next major earth shattering event. We do know that a Syrian lawyer and historian, one Evagrius Scholasticus writing in the 6th century AD, describes an earthquake in 459 AD as so treacherous, 'so severe that Cnidus and Cos were completely destroyed.' Once more, the citizens of Knidos set to and re-established their city and life continued, as we can see by the churches that were faithfully re-built by the faithful.

* * * *

For me there is something profoundly moving about standing in a long-abandoned Christian basilica, roofless, without windows or doors and concealed among olive and myrtle, pine and arbutus. The dappled light reveals a floor piled irregularly with moss-covered debris, offering a glimpse of a broken piece of marble altar screen or in-post capital. But despite its ruinous state this once-roofed space communicates a certain sanctity, an echo of chanting and hush of prayerfulness. Despite its total neglect, it stands as a memorial to the thousands upon thousands of men and women who through the centuries had once congregated within its precincts in penitence and watchfulness, to hear the sacred scriptures being read and to bear witness to the glory of God. Perhaps it's the notion of the endurance of faith through adversity that gives it its reverence, that the persistence of spiritual and sacred devotion which once drew people to its halls is still being maintained today, if not here then elsewhere, one shared and collective belief. Anyway, when it comes to ruined basilicas, Knidos has its fair share.

So it was that one Monday morning a team of workmen armed with the usual assortment of picks, long handled shovels, axes and wheel barrows began to attack the foliage on the terrace just below the ruined Doric Portico as a preamble to uncovering a major monument of ancient Knidos, the large Byzantine Church.

Interestingly the Turkish word for 'Church' is *Kilise*, which originates from the Greek, '*Ekklesia*', from which we also derive the English word 'ecclesiastical', pertaining to the congregation. Hailing from the steppes of Central Asia in the 11th Century the Turks would have been unfamiliar with the Christian world. But for the next few hundred years they lived cheek by jowl with the churches of Byzantium, hence the loan-word.

Anyway, in charge of the excavation of this church was a rather portly figure named Zvi, an Israeli whose name apparently wasn't Zvi at all, but Hans, and who wasn't actually from the Holy Land but originated from Schleswig Holstein, or Latvia or somewhere on the Baltic. He was a jovial enough sort of a chap, much given to rather obvious and heavy Teutonic humour. He being a Jew, the workforce being Moslem, and I being a Christian, all three of the world's great religions were represented, so you could say that the uncovering of the Large Byzantine Church was the most ecumenical of excavations. The High Command was careful not to expend too much manpower on the building, but a few strategically placed test trenches soon revealed the scale and extent of the church, which could in the absence of anything bigger at Knidos be interpreted as a cathedral.

The one abiding memory I have of the excavation is of an overpowering earthy smell which pervaded the trench at the eastern end of the church, a strong concoction of soil and sap more pungent than any incense that might once have been used around its altar. The mastic trees had grown broad and strong among the heaps of rubble and their roots had penetrated down to the moist ground above the marble floored nave. These pistachio bushes have a very distinctive aroma in their leaves and berries, some might say it's an unpleasant smell, and just to touch them today transports me straight back to the excavation of the sanctuary of that once beautiful building, a bouquet of pure nostalgia.

Gradually, as the excavation continued, the outline of the eastern extremity of the church became clear. In the centre was a wide apse, flanked on either side by two smaller apses. These semi-circular walls had survived only in their lower part – the once surmounting hemi-domes had gone long since. To save time and manpower, only half of the central apse was dug to floor level. And there, at the back of the apse, behind the altar whose position was indicated by the sockets for the baldachin, were three semi-circular seats, the

171

synthronon, the seating for the clergy. This had been indeed an important building in Byzantine Knidos.

More trenches were opened to reveal what must once have been an impressive basilica. Two parallel rows of columns once divided the middle part of the church into three, a wide central nave flanked by two side aisles. Arches must have sprung the length of the nave between the rows of pillar capitals so that from above these there would have been clerestory windows which could act as a longitudinal lantern allowing light to flood into the church. Now only a sad jumble of stub walls, fallen pillars and the floor remained.

Ecclesiastical architecture had been slow to develop in Christian times and when it did finally emerge it owed nothing to the Classical temples which had so dominated the cityscapes of Hellenistic and Roman Knidos. This was due in part to the secrecy with which believers surrounded themselves for fear of persecution, but also early Christian worship needed no dedicated building, no house built by human hands. Only after Constantine had made Christianity the religion of the New Rome, only then did formal buildings appear. They were made up of three elements - an atrium, or courtyard at the western entrance, which gave into a vestibule, the narthex, from which the eastward-trending plan led into the body of the church proper. The atrium and narthex were derived from the secular villa, where so much worship had up to now been held. The basilica was based on the Roman Law Courts and Corn Exchanges which had been designed to span a large interior space.

The most hallowed part of the Large Church at Knidos, the sanctuary at the eastern extremity, had been separated from the nave by an altar railing with waist high screens carved with geometric patterns, on top of which had been a pillared tracery. Beyond this had been the altar. There were slots carved into the floor where once a canopy had been raised over it. Hans alias Zvi ventured a date on the foundation of the building to 530 AD, based on a motif carved on the little marble pillars which held the altar tracery,

172

showing a cross and orb. It apparently dated to the reign of the Byzantine Emperor Justinian.

And it was on the flags of the floor of the sanctuary that the Arabic graffiti were discovered, eight or nine groups of them, though at the time no one could decipher them. It was some years later that an Arabist whom I took to Knidos was able to help me to translate some of them. They had been written in a very early form of Arabic script, the so-called Kufic script, dating to the late 7th century AD, not long after the first Hajj. Unsurprisingly there are few if any Kufic inscriptions outside Arabia, and of course there was no Arab presence in Asia Minor at the time, with the one exception of the Arab military campaigns along the coast as far as Cyprus and Rhodes by Muawiyyah, and further west into the Mediterranean by his son Yazid. And here was Yazid's name, scratched into the marble at Knidos. It can only date to that day he moored at Cape Crio on his way to the Aegean Sea in 672 AD, the day that Knidos breathed its last.

"O God Pardon Yazid ibn Sufyan."

CHAPTER EIGHTEEN

PARALLEL LIVES

We who with songs beguile your pilgrimage
And swear that Beauty lives though lilies die,
We poets of the proud old lineage
Who sing to find your hearts, we know not why.
What shall we tell you?
Tales, marvelous tales,
Of ships and stars and isles where good men rest.
James Elroy Flecker (1884-1915) 'The Golden Journey to
Samarkand'

The mention of Christian Knidos brings to mind a number of occasions when, long after the excavations had finished, I was invited to accompany pilgrimages around the coast of Turkey and, of course, I always made sure that Knidos was a focal point. Over the years various clerics – deacons, reverend fathers, deans, bishops and even one archbishop – have asked me to provide that all-important historical background to their ministries. I was always pleased to do so, if a trifle embarrassed when occasionally they want to hold religious services in the ancient site and I had to use my influence with the *bekciler*, the site guardians, to turn a blind eye in return for accepting a little *bakshish* for doing so. Anyway, if I might digress for a moment at this point to relate the tale of one such pilgrimage, it will give the flavour of such events. It all revolved around a lay couple, the Hampels, from the very English cathedral town of Ombersley.

Malcolm and Lindsay Hampel were of a religious if albeit a somewhat socially superior persuasion, the latter outwardly demonstrated by the brick-coloured chinos and Panama hat for him and the twin set and pearls for her, and I was to encounter them on a cruise to Knidos ostensibly in the Wake of Saint Paul as mentioned in Acts 27.7. If the Good Book is to be believed the peripatetic, epistle-writing Apostle had sailed along these shores no fewer than three times, haranguing the Athenians, berating

174

the Colossians and seriously upsetting the Ephesians en route. Wherever else he might have stopped on his travels, there is a problem with this particular passage in the Book of the Acts of the Apostles which leaves a distinct uncertainty as to whether Paul actually did reach Knidos at all. It revolves around how you interpret the behaviour of the winds, as described by the Blessed Luke, the author of the piece. One translation suggests that Paul was hard pressed to arrive at Knidos but implies that he did actually get there in the end, while another says that though he was trying to get there he never quite made it and being blown off course ended up in Crete instead. The sticking point is how to read the association of a single Greek preposition, ambiguous at the best of times in my experience. Knowing the frightful winds around Knidos, few of which are usually favourable, I am inclined to believe the latter interpretation, that Knidos never did receive the benefit of Paul's prickly, misogynistic preachments. But for the sake of those promoting 'In the Wake of St Paul' cruises, I suppose one should allow the possibility of the former – that he really did get to Knidos after all. Anyway, whatever the truth of the matter, that's why we were heading there on this occasion.

The Hampels were shakers and movers in their local Diocese of Ombersley and had persuaded their Bishop, the august and Very Reverend Neville Cornwallis-Fenchurch, to preach a boating pilgrimage to Turkey from the pulpit of St Nicholas and All Saints. This was on the somewhat slender theological grounds that St Paul really had messed about in boats in the Aegean which subsequently led him to write fraternal letters to several of the cities with which we are all familiar – well, some of us are familiar anyway. To add more spiritual substance to such a pilgrimage, as in this case, it is possible also to include visits to the 'Seven Churches of Asia Minor' addressed by St John the Divine in the first few verses of the last book in the Bible, the Book of Revelation. As a piece of writing, the 'Apocalypse', as it's known to the cognoscenti, is so obscure, so whimsical, and its cryptographic passages so dark that just about any explanation of its meaning can be advanced, making

175

it totally plausible to visit the remains of the 'Seven Churches' in Turkey as part of a Christian itinerary, even if in the eschatological scheme of things they were textually meant to be metaphorical. Creative marketing, I think they call that.

Anyway, here we were hymning our way down the lee of the Island of Kos sailing to Knidos, accepted on this occasion as another Pauline landfall. The Hampels had promoted the Bishop's tour with vigour resulting in them having attracted a large group now spread over no fewer than five yachts sailing in convoy – well, it was supposed to be in convoy, but the local Captains took this armada as a sign that the journey could be transformed into an All-Turkey classic wooden powerboat contest. The opportunity to race accentuated the bravado which characterises the young modern Turk even if it was only at nine knots an hour – the sub-text for which, if you were paying the bills for the tour, would be 'let's see who can use up the most diesel in a week?'

At home, if their postcode is anything to go by, the Hampels lived in some style. They owned a six bedroom mansion with stabling and manicured gardens in a chichi village on the outskirts of Ombersley. Despite their conspicuous donations to the Cathedral roof fund, frequently referred to by His Grace, or by Malcolm if the Bishop was absent on another boat, this didn't stop them from surreptitiously claiming a free trip for two in return for their efforts in filling the Turkey trip. Also, to enhance their own *soi disant* elevation among the other members of the Bishop's flock, it was made clear to everyone that Lindsay Hampel was to be known on board ship as 'Countess' Lindsay on the somewhat questionable grounds that she was a third cousin twice removed of a relative of Edward VII or some such personage. I can't remember the exact details, but 'pass the beetroot to the Countess' or 'would the Countess like a little more chicken?' became slightly comical after a while and to their credit the lower orders on board all joined in the fun.

To add to their social impedimenta the Hampels had brought with them an aged uncle of Lindsay's rejoicing in the title of Sir Arnold Truss, who, we were all told in the strictest confidence, had been involved with hush-hush operations during the War. From his appearance, this either had to have been the Great War, or possibly, because of his constant references to Africa, even the Boer War; it was difficult to tell. To extrapolate from the way he walked, legs akimbo, and by his neatly trimmed moustache, he might well have once been part of the 18th Princess of Wales's Own Hussars or some other long defunct cavalry regiment. Anyhow, continuing the Hampels' quest for public acclaim and adulation, we were told that Arnold was to be referred to by the hoi polloi at every occasion as "Sir Arnold," as in "Sir Arnold must sit next to the Bishop," or "Sir Arnold has just popped to the … you know where…" or, "I think Sir Arnold has had quite enough wine to drink tonight, don't you Edith?"

Arnold was essentially a fascinating man and in fact he talked freely about his secret work to anyone that would listen. He was slightly deaf, which meant he was wont to speak rather loudly. Also he had a minor speech defect which made him aspirate some of his consonants, so that his pronouncements became rather unclear, especially as he rarely gave any historical or geographical context to his anecdotes.

"Of coursh, I wash with Genewal Ashley Pishley, in the shide of the show, you know? Well, over the hill came theshe dashtardly sheiksh shporting shabres and shouting at ush. I shay, what a shambles! Well, there wash noshing for it. We jusht had to shit it out."

Seeking to obtain some clarification as to where we were in time and space, I ventured to ask him in what way the French might have been involved.

"The Fwensh," he shouted. "The FWENSH? Absholute looshers, the Fwensh! Do you know that the Fwensh have losht everything shincsh Waterloo? Don't talk to me about the Fwensh!"

On another tack, someone helpfully mentioned the Germans.

"The Germansh," he bawled. "The GERMANSH? Absholute looshers, the Germansh. Don't talk to me about the Germansh!"

And so on through a list of various other possible European combatants, none of whom Arnold rated as anything other than an utter catastrophe. His approach to allies and foes alike might lack a little of the milk of human kindness, given that this was a Christian pilgrimage, but I have to say that it made for some amusing meal-times.

One group of people he did have time for were the Romans. On visiting the site of Knidos, talking about the Temple of Aphrodite, I made mention of the Emperor Hadrian and his visit to Knidos in 129 AD and all the Roman copies of the statue of the Praxiteles masterpiece.

"Exshellent chapsh the Womansh. And Hadwian, well, he wash a shuper Empewor."

This I felt was a positive step, until he continued, "Yesh, Hadwian! Kept the thieving Schotsh out, thatsh who! Yesh, bwing back the Womansh any time."

One evening, after dinner on the poop, Arnold was in lively form, holding the party enthralled with stories of his early diplomatic career in Africa - at least, I think that's where he was.

"'Corsh, Algie and I didn't have the faintesht idea what we were doing. I wash working for HMG ash ADC to the GG of the EAF at the time, and the local DC shaid to me stwaight away, 'Trush, you know about banking. You short theshe buggersh out.' Well, he wash wight in a way, you shee. Family'd been in banking shinch … God knowsh when."

And gradually the story emerged that Arnold's great grandfather had been one of the founders of Twentyman Truss, whom, I soon gathered, many years before had been private bankers to the wealthy of Monte Carlo, a sunny place for shady people as some wit described it.

"My father shold the whole kit and caboodle for an absholute fortune! Yesh, absholute fortune! Shtill living off the pwosheeds, what! Ha! Ha!"

At which point a rather large penny dropped. The Hampels - Malcolm and the Countess - distantly related as they might have been to most of the crowned, if defunct, heads of Europe, had mentioned before that they were to all intents and purposes the only living relatives Sir Arnold had in the whole world, well, the only ones who really cared about him. That's why, they said, they'd brought him on the cruise, so that they could look after him in a kindly atmosphere. His younger brother and all that side of the family in Leicestershire just disowned him, cut him dead, as the Countess graciously if rather pointedly refer to on several occasions. However, this new piece of intelligence about a bank was understood by the lesser cruising mortals somewhat less charitably. They took the view that in due course, when the old warrior was recalled to join his financial forebears, the Hampels hoped to cop a large share of the Twentyman Truss residue for taking such an interest in Sir Arnold's current well being. That was provided of course that he didn't go and get married or do anything stupid in the meanwhile, an exceedingly long shot given his advancing years. Praying, for the Hampels at least, was considered to assume a different dimension as an essential part of the cruising liturgy after that.

Arnold enjoyed his time on the boat immensely. He was looked after so well by the crew, who made sure he always had the best of everything, and they certainly kept his wine and whiskey topped up. When we got back to Bodrum at the end of the cruise I watched as he had his photo taken with the crew then slip them an extra note or two as he got into the transfer bus for the airport. Maybe he'd forgotten that the tips had been collected the night before to be given communally to the Captain at breakfast time. Mind you, he'd gone out on the town on his own after dinner and hadn't come back till late, so maybe he'd missed the whip round. The Bishop said his goodbyes to us and wished us God's blessing for our next group. And the pilgrimage came to a happy end.

"Shuper twip!" as Arnold might have said.

That was the last I heard of Sir Arnold Truss KCMG, until, that is, about three years later.

$$* \; * \; * \; *$$

Lord Fauntleroy (not his real name!) was a big man of generous proportions and expansive gestures. He was on his third cruise with us when I met him and he exuded the confidence that only a sinecure in the Upper House and a well-padded seat on the boards of a number of major city companies can bring. He had been a rising luminary for a brief period in a sometime Westminster cabinet until they had been comprehensively voted out of office and his star rapidly began to wane, but not before he had managed to get himself kicked upstairs and through his title had attained a number of lucrative directorships in the Square Mile. He and his wife Charlotte were good company. She had taken a starred First in Mods and Greats at Oxford, the arcane title of the Classics degree amid the Dreaming Spires, part of which had involved Classical archaeology, so it was probably she that had persuaded the good lord to accompany her on their archaeological odysseys rather than the other way around.

I had to be a bit careful in my lectures about Knidos, Alexander, the Roman East and such like as Charlotte personally knew most of the modern scholars in the subject and more impressively knew most of the ancient authors too, from the original texts. The Odes of Horace and the poems of Catullus were meat and drink to her, but mercifully I discovered that she was a bit shy on the Hellenistic world, so I played to my strength on that one. Charlotte's husband, by comparison was also interested in meat and drink, but of the more modern and corporeal kind. His own academic achievements had long ago been left behind on the roundabout of the affairs of state. But he oozed a rather toping bonhomie, especially in the evenings.

"Oh do let's have another bottle, shall we? Kate, Hugh, you'll have another glass won't you. The night is young, as they say."

"Oh we can't just leave it at that. How about another flagon of red to round off the evening? Julian, you've been a bit quiet tonight. Go on, have another glass, why don't you?"

This was the Fauntleroy style; the studied largesse of the well-born host, the well-kept board of the well-heeled peer. He would reach across the table and slightly ostentatiously fill up the glasses of his fellow travellers; and geeing them up with hearty good humour he would raise his own glass and make a toast 'to travel', 'to good companionship', 'to Knidos', or to anything that took his fancy really, a kind of oenophile version of 'I spy'. His rather impromptu, 'hang-the-expense' approach was of course popular with the other guests, as they weren't paying for the wine he was ordering, but it did lead to a slight private unpleasantness when he was presented with the bill at the end of the week. In a hectoring tone he bickered, "Oh but Charlotte and I only ever drink one bottle between us of an evening. I mean, how can this possibly be? It says here, 'Cabin 6, Fauntleroy, 16 bottles of red and five of white.' Well, there you have it. I never, ever drink white, well, only on holiday. So you see, it must be wrong, mustn't it? Take it away and bring me the correct one."

In the end I had to pay half his bill to allow the matter to rest, and if I could tell you who he really was, I would gladly do so. Bloody politicians! But my lips are sealed, permanently. Besides, learning the sequel to the Hampel brouhaha was well worth the money, as you will hear in due course.

Some days before the unpleasantness with the drinks bill, Charlotte had asked if we should like to hear her read a poem or two of Catullus, her literary hero. She said she happened to have a slim volume of the poetic oeuvres of the Roman bard in her luggage. I said it would be a real delight for the other guests and that I knew of the ideal place on the mainland of Knidos, way over near the eastern wall. Below the eastern gate, overlooking the sea, with the Island of Tilos in the distance, there had been an excavation before my time which had exposed a small odeon, a tiny theatre where the people of Classical Knidos would have put on just such performances – where lute players, singers and poets could present their own artistic efforts. Perhaps even Catullus himself had performed here – who knows?

Anyway, after breakfast one morning we walked up the dusty road past the theatre and then headed down among the thistle-covered fields along the shore and there, in the quiet, we found the few original semi-circular seats that had survived the passage of time. There we sat in quiet contemplation with only the susurrus of the wine-dark sea for company as Charlotte read one or two of the more vulgar poems to get us in the mood. He was pretty vicious, this Catullus, I thought, and could be so crude. Then she read a poem he had written to his mistress whom he named in his poems 'Lesbia' and with whom it seems he had had a most turbulent relationship.

dulce ridentem, misero quod omnis
eripit sensus mihi: nam simul te,
Lesbia, aspexi, nihil est super mi vocis in ore,

lingua sed torpet, tenuis sub artus
flamma demanat, sonitu suopte
tintinant aures, gemina teguntur lumina nocte

182

Your sweet laughter, something which robs me miserably
of all feelings: for as soon as I look
at you, Lesbia, no voice remains
in my mouth.

But the tongue is paralyzed, a fine fire
spreads down through my limbs, the ears ring with their
very own sound, my eyes veiled
in a double darkness.
(Trans: "Catullus" *New World Encyclopedia*)

The experience was magical, and after a period of suitably contemplative silence we trooped back to the boat. The past really had come alive that morning.

Before lunch, I was talking to Charlotte about Catullus, about life and loves, and she confided to me that her own son who was apparently emotionally quite delicate was about to marry a girl from an extremely wealthy family whom he found a trifle intimidating – a bit like Catullus with Lesbia. She was worried about the disparity in their backgrounds. They owned endless market gardens in the East Midlands and their brand was a household name – even I had heard of it. But the family name was Truss, she said. I racked my brains and from the well of memory I drew up the vision of Sir Arnold, of Malcolm and Lindsay, and of the ADC to the GG of the EAF on behalf of HMG. Was he any relation, I wondered? She went quiet, and it was left to the male Fauntleroy to fill in the blanks.

"Ah yes, well, there is an Arnold in the family, but he's rather old now."

I jumped up from the table and went down to the galley. I asked the chef for the picture which I knew he kept in his locker that had been taken three years earlier, the one with the crew standing on the quay either side of a beaming Sir Arnold before he got on the bus to the airport. I showed it to Charlotte.

"Is that him?" I asked, thinking what an amazing coincidence it was that he had been on the same boat with the same crew.

"Yes, I suppose that is the man," acceded Charlotte unenthusiastically

Then the story tumbled out. The Noble Lord continued; "But he won't be at the wedding, you know. Oh no! In fact he's been banned, so I understand from my son. You see, he's somehow blotted his copy book with the family. He was on some cruise or other on a boat somewhere around here, maybe this was the one, and on his last night he took himself off to a bar or something where he became friendly with some local woman. Well, blow me down if within the month he didn't marry her. He's shacked up with her here somewhere – gone native I shouldn't wonder."

Well done Arnold, I thought – gone and found himself a dark-eyed Anatolian beauty with whom to share his declining years.

"Oh dear!" I sympathised. "But didn't he have a lot of money?"

"Oh yes, he did. Something to do with a bank, as far as I remember. But he's absconded with the lot. It really is a family scandal. And what's worse, I'm led to believe he's deliberately left it all to this local floozy so that no-one in the family will get any of it. Isn't that terrible?"

Well, it depends on your perspective, I mused to myself. The Lord giveth, the Lord taketh away; blessed be the name of the Lord! - that sort of thing. He must have thought hard, though probably not for very long, about his family in England.

"Absholute looshers the lot of them!" as he might have said. Amen to that!

CHAPTER NINETEEN

THESE LITTLE THINGS

Any intelligent fool can make things bigger, more complex, and more violent. It takes a touch of genius and a lot of courage to move in the opposite direction.

Albert Einstein

By far the least romantic of the areas that were being excavated at Knidos the year I was there related to the houses on the slope of the island, not far from the dig house. You will recall that the designers and engineers who originally conceived the plan for the new city in the fourth century BC had the idea of joining the off-shore island at Cape Crio to the mainland with an isthmus in order to develop two harbours, one on either side, the commercial harbour to the east and the trireme, or military, harbour to the west. The slope of the island that looks over these harbours faces north, right into the teeth of the 'boreas', the cold winter wind that brings the rain from the Black Sea and the freezing steppes of Southern Russia. As a result, it must have been considered a less favourable part of the city in which to live and it was here that the residences of the common people of the city had been built. Because of this, unlike the mainland part of the metropolis, the houses had not been rebuilt over and over again, obscuring their early stages by later reconstructions, so they retained their original Hellenistic design more or less intact throughout their history. No Classical temples or Hellenistic or Roman public buildings seem to have been created on the Island. No Byzantine churches or other extensive late villas were built here. As a result the excavations held rather less appeal for the High Command. Nevertheless, they were of interest to those dirt archaeologists among us.

Indeed, these original houses had been well-built. The island had been terraced, like the mainland, but the terraces, which were of polygonal masonry, formed the backs of the houses, the front facades being made of beautifully carved and orthogonally laid ashlar blocks, their outward facing faces rusticated and left with a slightly rough and pillowed finish. The same as on the mainland, the whole area had been divided into insulae, islands of habitation, by the horizontal road-ways and the stepped streets set at intervals joining them together, and in each insula there had been four houses, two entered from the front street and two from the back, via the next road-way up the slope.

But one question was always puzzling. It's hard to see from where the inhabitants of these houses on the island obtained their water. On the mainland there is a perched water table, an aquifer which follows the contour of the mountain not very far beneath the surface. For example, at Terrace East you may remember a well had been sunk only three metres deep into the hillside at the back of the villa, and amazingly when we excavated it there was still water in it. In Byzantine times, at various points in the city they had also built large underground cisterns rendered with waterproof plaster to store additional rain water. And in today's world there was still a strong spring actually on the surface just west of the theatre which was very much in use to water the donkeys and where the work force and the Çayhane got their daily ration. The water table and the springs were fed by the winter rains falling on the mountain which formed the back of the city. On the north facing side of the mountain precipitation could be quite substantial, and this rain would percolate into the limestone and thus the whole mainland city had drinking water. But the surface area of the island was very restricted, not enough I would hazard to support the people who lived there. They must have brought water from the mainland.

Speaking of which, I remember being at the island site one morning when Hasan the Sucu, the water-boy, put in his usual appearance. Incidentally, 'su' is the Turkish for 'water, and on a further linguistic note, the suffix '-cu' or '-ci' (pronounced 'ju or 'ji) in Turkish indicates a person's profession, 'kahveci' a coffee-ist, 'gemici' a ship-ist, or sailor, hence 'sucu' would be a water-ist, or water-boy. Less complementary by the way, there is also 'yağcı' (yaji), one who oils. At Knidos this particular sobriquet was applied pejoratively by the villagers to anyone who was believed to be sucking up to the Management; I suppose he would be the equivalent of a 'greaser'.

Anyway, every day between nine and ten o'clock, during the mid-morning cigarette break, Hasan the Sucu would trudge up to each site to bring refreshment from the spring near the theatre. Filling a battered aluminium cup which he had tied with string to the handle an old terra cotta amphora he carried on his shoulder, his task was to offer a drink to each of the workers in turn. Each man quaffed a mouthful of the cool water, the older ones with enthusiasm and the younger bloods with practiced distain. As the expedition water-boy, I suppose that in the order of things Hasan might be considered somewhat below the more manly 'pickists' and 'shovelists', a perception perhaps emphasised by his slightness of build.

So it was that at whichever site I was working in the whole city, whichever trench I happened to be surveying that particular day – the Pink Temple; the Byzantine Church; Terrace East or wherever – Hasan the Sucu, the water-boy, would always put in an appearance.

"Bu evler mi, Deyvit Bey?" Hasan the Sucu asked me, looking at the doorways and walls.

"Are these houses, David?"

Well, on one particular day I happened to be working again at the houses on the Island. When he had finished his round of the workers, Hasan cadged a cigarette from someone nearby and came over to my drawing board and looked with deep concentration at the pencil scrawls which were part of my emergent survey. After a time, he asked, *"Ne düşünüyorsun, Deyvit? Bugün ben çok küçüğüm, ama çok! Doğru mu?"*

"What do you think, David? I am very small today. Isn't that right?"

Every day after that, no matter where I was, he would come over and ask me the same thing, the same way more or less – variations of 'Aren't I small?'

His daily enquiry put me in an awkward position. Hasan was demonstrably slight of stature but from his questions I also assumed that he felt that he was of a lowly social position too, though I confess I couldn't quite follow his logic. Was he referring to his physical size when compared to the muscular diggers, or was this by way of a cathartic admission of some inner inadequacy? I tried to bolster his self esteem.

"*Hayır,*" I replied. "*Sen küçük değilsin. Sen çok büyük bir adamsın, çok büyük, Hasan, çok önemli bir adamsın sen ya!*"

"No, you're not small. You're a very big man Hasan, really big, a very important man!"

But each day he became more insistent.

"*Bugün ben çok küçüğum, ve yarın daha küçük olacağım.*"

"Today I am very small, and tomorrow I'll be even smaller."

Not unnaturally I could discern no physical change in Hasan from one day to the next. What was I to make of this gradual but patently illusory diminution? Maybe he felt that lugging a heavy amphora full of water hour by hour all around the mountain-side was slowly crushing the life out of him. Maybe he was afflicted by some rare South West Anatolian bone-wasting disease that I knew nothing about? Perhaps he had been put on a diet because of some life-threatening internal illness? I tried in my halting Turkish to discover more, somewhat arbitrarily bringing doctors, hospitals, clinics and medicines into the conversation in the hope that he would seize upon one of them and elaborate, though I have to say that the finer points of medical diagnosis would have been way beyond my linguistic competence. Nothing!

On one occasion with a solemn expression I frowningly asked each of the workmen at that particular trench, why is Hasan so small? One or two said it was because his dad and his mum were small, which really didn't help.

When I asked if he was sick, or psychologically disturbed, some simply said, *"Dangalak"* - "Idiot." Because I was uncertain whether this applied to Hasan or to me, I didn't pursue it. My analysis never went any further.

The weeks wore on. Hasan the Sucu continued his self miniaturisation, though even more puzzlingly without any real sense of unease.

"Bana bak, Deyvit, bugün hayatımda bu kadar küçük olmadım bugün gerçekten en küçük oldum di mi?"

"Look at me David, in my life I have never been as small as I am today, I'm the smallest I've ever been, isn't that so?"

This was trying my very limited grasp of the language to its limit, but if I had understood him correctly, I was at the point of despair. Then quite suddenly one morning, the matter came to a head. Hasan had heard that the dig was soon coming to an end and during our opaque daily exchanges he asked me if I was leaving and where I was going. I told him that I would be going back to London, to which he said, *"Eminim benim gibi küçük bir adam görmedin o kadar küçüğümki valizinin içine koyup beni seninle Londraya götürebilirsin."*

"I'm sure you have never seen such a small man, I'm so small that you could put me in your suitcase and take me with you to London!"

189

Finally I got the point of the daily descriptions. Hasan giggled merrily and all the workmen who were listening laughed uproariously until I too was forced to join in. So that was it! He never had been worried about his size at all. It had been a huge practical joke all along, and I had taken it all too seriously.

But thinking about it later, I also wondered if there wasn't a hint of truth behind Hasan's idea. Was he thinking that life in the Village, with its cloying traditions and unchanging way of life, had hemmed him in and that if only he could get out of Turkey, to London, or to anywhere, he would better himself and return in triumph? Did he feel that what I took to be an idyllic way of life in the village, a life of innocence and simplicity, was for him by comparison a never-ending and purposeless monotony, a continuous drudgery?

On the day I did eventually leave, and the truck came from Marmaris to transport us all to 'civilisation', Hasan shook my hand and turned, smiling, away. Bugger our European educational system and my attempt at social psychology, I thought. It was obvious that Hasan had never given his life another thought.

Or had he? As my large brown hold-all was being lifted into the truck, did I just imagine that I saw him eying it pensively?

CHAPTER TWENTY

DIALLING A LARGE NUMBER

Eudoxus was the greatest mathematician that ever lived. It was he who invented the method of exhaustion that Archimedes developed so successfully; it was he who enunciated the subtle principle we call the Archimedean axiom (but which Archimedes himself attributes to Eudoxus); he did extremely intricate work on the apparent motion of the planets and he founded mathematical physics with a work on dynamics.

Confessions of an Apostate Mathematician by Edward Nelson
Department of Mathematics, Princeton University

There is an unmistakable summer tang associated with Knidos, an enduring middle-of-the-year aroma emanating from the fusion of limestone and dried flora fumed into a sharp bouquet by the shimmering heat. From late spring onwards, this perfumed air pervades the whole region with an unmistakable piquancy, a particular odour that affects the whole of ancient Caria, but nowhere is it more pungent than at ancient Knidos. It's a combination of the desiccated sap of shrunken stalks of white asphodel, carpets of mallow, of the dried flower heads and stems of crown daisies and rock roses, the star clover and wood anemones, of the wild vetch and the ubiquitous poppy. Accelerated by the pronounced rain shadow of the Knidian Acropolis, this dry atmosphere always recalls for me the nostalgic essence of that time long ago.

Each year, in February and March, the ancient fluted columns of the fallen temples and the worn treads of the stepped streets are hidden waist-high amid a profusion of yellow, white and violet blooms. Convolvulus and the spade-leaved smilax twine across the ornate marble carvings of long forgotten friezes, while the shady stems of the light green spurge and giant fennel conceal bee orchids among their roots. As the months advance, the prolific wild flowers succumb to the growing intensity of the Mediterranean sun and quickly fade to form a sweet-smelling carpet. The jades and lime greens of the spring lose their colour to the manila tints of high summer. On the slopes of the ancient city the evergreen bushes of the mastic pistachio, tiny flowered daphne and dwarf oaks are the only splashes of green, as the earth, the thistles and the grasses are transformed to a uniform parched buff colour. Near the ancient harbour sea lavender and sea daffodils keep the chromatic spirit alive a few short weeks longer until they too die away into the August drought.

And then, in September, just as it seems no plant life will return until the rains, the long stems of sea squills break through the parched ground and force their way upwards from their gingery bulbs, waist high creamy flowers clustering around their heads. Among the craggy outcrops, mauve autumn crocuses peer out, harbingers of the storms to come. At sea, the waves flatten to a glassy calm as the summer winds die away. Locally this is known as 'sarı yaz', the yellow summer, before the first of the winter storms begins to lash the waves into a white spume and another year draws to its close.

* * * *

On the terrace below the Temple of Aphrodite there was once a large Byzantine church. It had clearly been built, as with so many others, directly on top of the foundations of a much earlier Greek temple, no doubt its location intended to thwart any religious apostasy or back-sliding, so that Christian monotheism might prevail over the multiplicity of gods of the Greek and Roman world. Not the least reason for this deliberate prohibition of uncertainty was of course political - the ascendency of the Byzantine emperor in Constantinople. Most of the temple had long since disappeared, its statuary vanished and it stonework reused, but the make-up of the altar outside the temple proper, which was large and square and solid, was still there. It had perhaps been too large and too square and too solid to be robbed completely. All the marble facings had been stripped off, but the carved footings which formed the kerbing surround were still there and the coarse local stone block-work to which facings had been attached was still standing and now formed a sort of disembodied platform to the east of the original building.

In the spring-time, like the rest of Knidos, the ruined altar is covered with creepers and a mass of colourful, diminutive flowers giving it a rather romantic appearance, which always put me in mind of the musings of that great 20th century Greek scholar A. W. Lawrence, in his seminal work on Greek architecture, where in an epilogue he considers the spiritual gulf that lies between the ancient and the modern world. Describing a similar altar outside such a temple, he depicts it rising 'grey and worn, with flowers in the crevices and round about, amid grass and aromatic bushes gay with butterflies and bees: here the ancient Greeks heard the bellowing of frantic cattle, watched the flies blacken the widening carpet of blood, and smelled a reek that was fouler than any slaughter-house.' All very thought provoking! But he goes on to evaluate the religious world of the ancient Hellenes, with their superstitions, their multiplicity of gods, their sprites and spirits, their unseen dangers and ominous portends, their omens and oracles, and their terrifying animation of simple, natural elements. It was, he suggests, a quite frightening and very alien world to our own today, no matter how much we might empathise academically with their philosophy and literary achievement.

I well remember A.W. Lawrence. He used to come periodically to our own Institute of Archaeology in London to consult the library on the Fifth Floor which held the collections of the Institute of Hellenic Studies. Academically he was a rather distinguished elder statesman by then, an august and revered Victorian gentleman in a wing collar and tie. He was accepted as one of the great authorities on the Classical Greek world and his superb book on its architecture has since run into many editions. As a professor at Cambridge, he was known to be rather tetchy and somewhat aloof. Less well known is the fact the he was the younger brother of T. E. Lawrence, Lawrence of Arabia, the hero of the Arab Revolt during the First World War. I once visited an exhibition about Lawrence of Arabia, and in a rather quiet corner of the exhibition, away from the well-known photos and the relevant artefacts, there was a framed copy of a letter sent by Thomas Edward to his younger brother, the said Arnold Walter, who must have been about ten years old at the time, and to my amazement it began, 'Dear Worm'!

Anyway, back to Knidos and the area below the Temple of Aphrodite. Sitting askew atop this ruined altar was a magnificently carved fragment of an architrave, a long section of pristine cream-coloured marble sculpted into three facias with a surmounting border of 'egg and dart, and bead and reel' design. Obviously it didn't belong here, but it did belong to a feature nearby, the entrance into the Temenos, the sacred area surrounding the original temple, and where the citizens of Knidos had erected a very extravagant monumental propylon, a decorative gateway leading into the complex from the street outside.

Now this was no ordinary portion of the street; it was actually on a street junction. But it was no ordinary street junction either, rather the one where the main horizontal street of the city, which stretched the whole breadth of the metropolis from the eastern gateway, from the main land gate into Knidos, met the stepped street which led up from the harbour isthmus directly to the temple of Aphrodite. It was the one junction to which every visitor to Knidos would eventually arrive. And the citizens of the city obviously wanted to make an impression, for this junction, the terminus of the horizontal street, was dominated by the graceful propylon.

It had been designed in the Ionic order, a formal gateway on the west side of the junction with a portico of four pillars facing the street, then leading through a roofed porch into the sacred area which surrounded the temple beyond. Excavations exposed parts of columns with their typical fine, deep-fluted drums littering the junction. There were one or two broken pieces of rouletted column bases too, but there were only small fragments of the voluted palmette capitals, the curlicued portions which sat atop the columns. Lying about were more lengths of the finely carved architrave which surmounted the columns and capitals, above which had been parts of a very elaborately carved frieze with floral designs. It would indeed have looked very striking.

The street junction had been modified in Roman times. A large block-built, barrel-vaulted conduit had been built beneath the paving and under the main horizontal street to drain off the water from the various buildings along its length. Terracotta pipes could be seen leading into the conduit, and the whole duct itself must have continued westwards underneath the city wall into the sea. The Romans loved the luxury of having water in their city and went to enormous lengths to provide it. Lower down the same stepped street they had built a monumental fountain to provide water for the local residents.

But that was not the end of the story of this all-important street junction. Some time in the early Byzantine period, presumably when the Temple of Aphrodite was no longer in use, at least by the end of the fourth century A.D., one of the good burgers of Knidos had built a mansion right across the northern exit of the junction, thus rendering it defunct. The first two treads of the upward staircase of the street now provided the rather elegant steps up to a door in the newly built front wall of the villa which blocked off its onward access to the Temenos of Aphrodite. In this way then, the whole history of the city with its three phases – Hellenistic, Roman and Byzantine, about one thousand years in all - is represented in the archaeology of this unpretentious street junction.

* * * *

Slightly to the east and slightly lower than this all-important junction, the Knidians had built their triple terrace which no doubt was intended to be the focus of the city. It was on top of this that the massive Doric stoa, the main market place of Knidos, had been erected, some ninety columns in length. It must have made a considerable impression on any mariner coming into the Commercial Harbour for the first time, elevated as it was on this first high terrace of the city and stretching along its entire front edge above the Temple of Dionysus. It is now totally ruined and only the foundation steps and a few fragments of columns and capitals remain scattered among the undergrowth. Newton and others believed this had been designed by the engineer Sostratus, a native of Knidos and the same man who designed the famous lighthouse at Alexandria which became one of the seven wonders of the Classical world, along with the Mausoleum of Halicarnassus and the Colossus of Rhodes, both of which by the way had been erected not very far from Knidos. Given Knidos' all-important maritime position I often wondered, since he was obviously a familiar of the city, if Sostratus might have had a first go at creating a prototype lighthouse here at Cape Crio, close to where the modern Turkish lighthouse now stands at the tip of the island, but no-one to whom I suggested it ever seemed to warm to that idea.

Behind the stoa, a little further to the north, was a small Corinthian temple. This building had been investigated by Newton. It is typically Roman in form, with engaged half-columns along the sides and a free-standing porch in the front, the eastern face, with a long monumental staircase leading up to it. Leake, the military gentleman who visited Knidos some years before Newton in the early 19th century, thought for no good reason that this might have been, as he called it, the 'Temple of Venus of Cnidus', where the famous statue of the goddess of love was displayed, but Newton discounted this idea, and as we now know, he was right to do so.

Near the temple stands a sundial carved from a large block of marble. I can't remember if we excavated it the season I was there or whether it had been found the previous century, but everyone I later took to see it was fascinated by the fact that after two millennia it still told the time, which of course it would, wouldn't it. Nevertheless, later on, whenever I stopped at the sundial with a group, I considered that this would be an appropriate point in their visit to make mention of famous sons of ancient Knidos, such as Sostratus, and, more appropriately here, the ancient astronomer and mathematician Eudoxus, another local boy who figures highly in the annals of the Hellenistic era and is said to have built an observatory at Knidos. I didn't know a lot about this worthy scientist, but I always suggested, rightly or wrongly, and to fill the story out a bit, that he was associated with the observation of the star Canopus, though in point of fact this is one of the brightest stars in the night sky and seems to have been know to everyone, including the ancient Egyptians. Anyway, it was on one such occasion I was accompanying a group of various academics from the USA around the site, showing them the standard monuments and discoveries, when we came at length to the sundial. As usual I mentioned Eudoxus, the famous ancient astronomer and mathematician and celebrated son of Knidos. Suddenly, one character at the back of the party became quite animated, waving his arms and pushing his way to the front.

"You mean THE Eudoxus?" he blurted, in a high pitched voice. "Eudoxus of Knidos? THE mathematician?"

"The very same," I replied. "Who else but he?"

"But, but … do you know who he is, mathematically, I mean?"

"Well, only that he was well known for his way with figures," I said, somewhat facetiously.

The person who had become so agitated about this piece of information about Eudoxus turned out to be himself a well-known mathematician, also a Greek as it happened, though a modern one of course. He was currently at Princeton University in New Jersey, and it so transpired that he knew all about Eudoxus, far, far more than I did, in fact.

"Do you realise that in his lifetime Eudoxus created probably about one third of modern mathematics," he continued. "He was especially known for his large number theories. We would not have modern calculus (I think he

197

said 'calculus') without him. Wow, that's truly amazing! He was here, in this very place? Wow!"

And happily, with that, he subsided and the party moved naturally on to the stoa and the lower theatre.

I contemplated this revelation about Eudoxus many times since that seminal afternoon with the Greek professor from Princeton, and of course I went on to incorporate his story into my tales of old Knidos. Whenever we came to the sundial, I brought up Eudoxus and said, now with a somewhat condescending authority, that here at Knidos he had created one third of modern mathematics, though I have to say I didn't really understand one iota of what that might mean. I was guessing that no-one else did either.

Some years later I was accompanying a group of British diplomats around the site and of course I showed them, amongst other things, the sundial and told them the story of the Greek professor, linking it as usual to the mathematical importance of Eudoxus, local boy made good, and his large number theories. Then we carried on with the visit as usual. At the end of the trip, the leader of the group, a distinguished knight of the realm who had been 'Our Man' in a variety of senior postings around the world, was thanking me profusely for my lectures and site explanations, and of course he said how much they had all enjoyed and been absorbed by my presentations at Knidos, the highlight of their trip, he said. However, as he was finishing off his thanks, he happened to mention rather ungraciously that he felt his bar bill was rather high and what could be done about it?

"Ah!" I said quickly in response. "Then you have truly enjoyed your stay and what is more you have been admitted to the mysteries of ancient Knidos, in particular, to Eudoxus, the Knidian mathematician."

"How do you mean?" he asked.

"Well, with your bar bill you too have now discovered the theory of large numbers!"

CHAPTER TWENTY ONE

BEING SOMEWHERE

A good traveller has no fixedplans and is not intent on arriving.

Lao Tzu

There was a moment in the middle of the 1969 season when some of the High Command felt the need for someone to go on a shopping expedition. We were apparently running short of vital supplies that only the large centres of population could provide. Someone from the team would have to be deputed to be sent along the peninsula to carry out this life-saving mission, and the one chosen to do it turned out after much discussion to be me. This was on the grounds that I knew how to negotiate the route, having first arrived this way, and more importantly that having no trench to supervise I could be spared for a day or two without upsetting the careful balance of the workers. Furthermore there was a jeep leaving from Knidos for Marmaris the following day; I could easily travel with that. So without knowing exactly what I was meant to do, it was all organised for me. To my delight I learned that Cengis was to accompany me on this expedition and next morning the jeep was waiting near the Çayhane for the journey to begin. I walked over to the dig house to get my instructions. I was handed a list and an envelope of dollar notes. I was then handed a second pile of money "for the crossing."

"What crossing?" I asked. I had understood I was going to Marmaris.

"Why, the crossing to Rhodes!" I was told. "That's where you'll get the things we need."

I didn't know that's what was meant by the trip I was about to take. I hadn't even got my passport ready.

"You'll be fine!" they encouraged. "And you can enjoy the Grecian flesh pots while you're there!" said somewhat enviously I thought.

So, I obediently took the cash and the list, I repacked my bag, got my passport ready and went over to the jeep.

"Hazirsun Deyvit?" asked Cengis. "Are you ready?"

And off we went, rattling up the track past the theatre and the Eastern gate, pitching through the romantic ruins of the Necropolis and the olive and almond groves to Yazıköy, Village of Destiny. There we stopped. It was tea time again. But this time, as we sat idly drinking tea, large round tins were being lifted into the back of the jeep until the pay load space seemed full.

"Bal, Deyvit," waved Cengis. It was honey. These tins represented the annual produce of honey from the village co-operative's hives and Cengis was going to Marmaris to negotiate the sale of it. So, that was why he was making the journey. He beckoned to me to get back in the jeep, and we swayed forwards up the street.

After about a couple of hundred yards we stopped again. A gaggle of women stood in the road looking glumly at the jeep. One or two of them were crying. After a minute or so from this throng emerged a youth carrying a bundle with him; he looked about seventeen years old. It seems he was the son of one of the wailing ladies and he was setting off to report for his compulsory military service. He had barely been outside the Village before, and now he was going to be sent to join the Jardarma, the militia, in some far flung province in Eastern Anatolia for two whole years, to be among strangers in a strange part of the country. His mum hugged him longingly but was too emotionally overcome to say good bye. The boy got into the back of the jeep with the honey, as did his dad who was also waiting in the wings, and the jeep rolled away leaving the women waving their sad farewells.

We turned a corner and headed out of the Village. At the end of the cobbled street where the dirt track began again, the jeep stopped one last time and the son and father disembarked. They stood for some time looking at each other, before the son embraced his father and said, *"Allahaısmarladık Babam!"* "Goodbye my Father," the equivalent of sort of "May God stay with you."

And the father looked at him intensely, his eyes filled with tears, and uttered the moving reply, *"Oğulum, Güle, güle!"* "Go smilingly my son."

It was most touching, the private farewell to his son. He didn't know if he would ever see him or even hear from him again, a son who was being sent to what the people of Yazıköy must have thought of as a foreign land, and who, whatever may befall, would surely never be the same again.

"Go smilingly!"

Full of emotion the boy got back in the jeep and we took off. He waved until we turned out of sight and then he looked morosely at the honey tins and cried. It took him quite a few miles to recover.

Beyond Datça we drove through the mountains. Cengis asked where I was going and I explained about the need for vital supplies for the Expedition. It was then that I pulled out the list to show him. When I opened it and read the list my eyes came out on stalks.

2 cases best quality Madeira
1 case Lemoncello
3 boxes of red hot pepper cocktail sardines
 And so on and so on through a host of trivial items

This was totally insane. What was I doing travelling all this way for such ephemera? Still, I thought, it got me away from the hothouse of the dig and I had a free ride to Rhodes in the meanwhile.

With no stops en route, by comparison to the last time I had travelled this road the time passed quickly and we were in the Maydan at Marmaris, the centre of the village, in time for a late lunch, Cengis said. Knowing where I was trying to get to, he first went to the customs shed and enquired about boats going to Rhodes. There was a private one leaving in the middle of the afternoon. I was in luck. We walked over to the 'Maydan Lokantası,' the Town Square Restaurant, which in those days was the only place you could eat in Marmaris, and we had fresh fish and chips before I was taken to the quayside to meet the boat.

The boat, a small, locally-made wooden vessel, had been chartered by a German couple who wanted to take their little car with them to Rhodes and somehow it had been driven on board, I assume with the assistance of planks. Anyway, when we were all aboard the captain started the engine and we put-putted out of the harbour towards the open sea. I sat in the stern with the captain, making what conversation I could, while the Germans sat in haughty separation in the prow. I must say that I felt very superior, being now apparently a part of the indigenous life of the place. And how many times had I done this particular journey...well, once actually, in the opposite direction. The sea was a bit sportif that afternoon, with a strong Meltem, the summer wind, blowing across the straits, and I could see the Germans looking anxiously at their cherished auto wondering if it would be pitched into the briny at any moment. But there were no mishaps and we finally reached Rhodes harbour at the end of the afternoon. I had already established that the captain was taking his boat back to Marmaris next morning and we had made an arrangement for me to travel with him, free of charge no less. We were becoming great mates.

I found a room in the same hotel in Kolokotroni Street I had stayed at the last time I had been there and after a clean up I went into the old town to find my acquaintances in the bottle shop. They greeted me like a long lost friend and when I handed over my list they said they would take care of all the purchases and would I like an ouzo? Well, yes was the obvious answer. It was like being at a home from home, not a stranger in a strange land at all. They even took the boxes of booze and the other items down to the harbour in their three wheeler truck and put them aboard the boat for the morning. I really felt like one of the locals. I paid all the bills and went back to the hotel and to sleep.

Next day we left the harbour, just the captain and me, and headed back to Turkey, sailing in a fresh morning breeze. It was only as we came into the narrows in front of Marmaris that I began to worry about the Customs. I was bringing about five cases of alcohol with me and a horde of other 'luxury' items. Surely this shouldn't be allowed? When we had moored and gone into the customs house, the police stamped my passport again and asked if I had anything to declare. I pointed to the boxes and told them about the Madeira and the other booze I was carrying.

"But it's not allowed to bring that into Turkey," was the response. I looked blankly at the officer concerned; I had no idea how I would get around the problem.

"So let's just say that you haven't, OK? Good morning to you!"

And with that I was ushered out of the customs house with a trolley-full of the illicit goods and I made my way to the minibus stand. The person in charge also remembered me from some weeks before and said, *"Knidosa?"* "To Knidos?"

"Evet, lutfen." "Yes please," I replied, as strong hands lifted all the boxes onto the roof rack and ushered me into the front seat. What service! Within a few minutes we were off again up the dirt road over the mountains. I felt like I had done this all my life.

It's a strange thing but if you've made a difficult journey once, the second and third time you do it, it seems so much easier…and quicker. In what seemed like no time, but actually the same four hours, we reached Datça and stopped for tea. I was told that the same minibus could take me further this time, and after a few more glasses we continued all the way to Yazıköy, arriving there while it was still daylight. I got out of the mini-bus and watched the cases being piled up by the side of the local çayhane. After a couple of teas, the mini-bus departed back to Datça, and I was left in the çayhane still some distance from my final destination. Selahattin, who ran the local tea house and whom I knew from his visits to Cengis, told me that a jeep would be along shortly to take me to Knidos. I just had to relax, sit down and wait. I sat down and I waited.

An hour went by, and then another. The daylight faded and the dark night approached, and here I was miles from anywhere. I became visibly agitated. I asked over and over again when the jeep would arrive.

"Is it coming? Is it coming soon? When will it be here?"

Finally Selahattin placed a large glass of rakı and a bottle of cold water in front of me and waving his arms about said:

"*Bak Dayvit, rakı var, yemek var ve bir yatak var! Ne düşüniyorsun?*"

"Look David, there's rakı, there's food and there's a bed! What are you worried about?"

Suddenly, in that moment, it was as though a huge load was lifted from my shoulders. It's absolutely true, I thought. I have everything I want; I'm among friends and I don't need to be anywhere in particular. I am already somewhere! It was one of the greatest moments of my time in Turkey. I had everything I needed. Why be anxious about anything? It was a totally different but equally correct way of looking at life than worrying about it. But it was not just a philosophic debate of the here and now I had won. For me it went far, far deeper than that.

Since I was five years old, or even younger perhaps, I had been beset in my imagination with a dreadful defect. It was called by some 'home-sickness,' one of the most awful feelings one can experience, a deep melancholia with no cure but to return home, a profound feeling of physical insecurity which dominated every part of my existence. It was non-specific, in that it wasn't especially the exact place of home that I was longing for, but the familiarity of people who made my life secure and the consequent fear of the unknown. It had threatened my time all the way through school, when some individuals suggested I should see a psychiatrist about it. It threatened my time at University, when I personally suggested I should see a psychiatrist about it. And here in my mid-twenties, my mid-twenties no less, it threatened my very career. Only the previous year I had turned around with the same affliction on my way to a very prestigious excavation in the Middle East and returned to London. People who knew what had happened gossiped about it, saying that I was washed up, no good, not reliable. And they were right. I had cared too much for the exact circumstances of my every day welfare. It was markedly affecting what I could and could not do. And incidentally it was always noticeably worse as darkness approached. I desperately missed the comforting presence of my familiar surroundings. I had already felt incapacitating twinges of it at Knidos.

Now, for the first time in my life, at the age of twenty five years old, I found myself in a relatively strange place, in the growing dark, among many people I actually didn't know very well, with no means of running back to familiarity, and I abruptly discovered that I didn't care. I really, genuinely didn't care. It was the first time ever I enjoyed not knowing what was going to happen next, the first time I could relax and drink in the experience, not to mention the Lion's milk, of being totally free of anxiety. And here was the crux of my Pauline conversion at Knidos. This was the different planet on which I had landed. For the first time I was free from the cloying melancholia that had haunted me all my young and adolescent life.

And you know the most remarkable thing about that conversion in the tea house in Yazıköy? It has been permanent. I have been travelling ever since with not a trace of apprehension. I have travelled to some of the remotest parts of the globe. I have been to the islands of the Antarctic Peninsula, and slept on the ground of the spinning earth in the middle of the Kalahari Desert, and nothing of that debilitating neurosis has ever returned. Knidos for me was the baptism into a new life in more ways than one.

I seem to remember that the jeep did eventually arrive and we did get to Knidos that night, with all the ephemera which I had bought, but I didn't care any more. I was not the same person who had left Knidos the day before. I had that evening been reborn.

Bismillaharrahmanirrahim! – (Travelling) in the name of God, the merciful and compassionate!

CHAPTER TWENTY TWO

SONNY AND THE MAGIC EYE

This is the precious present, regardless of what yesterday was like, regardless of what tomorrow may bring. When your inner eyes open, you can find immense beauty hidden within the inconsequential details of daily life.

Timothy Ray Miller.

You will remember my companion in survey, Sonny, the man from Brooklyn. When I met him he was on his second season at Knidos, but none of the glamour and excitement of the site had diminished for him. Knidos had been his first ever stay outside the US. Here he was, a boy from the dismal streets of New York City, suddenly propelled into the sapphire seas and warm sun of the Mediterranean, cast up on the beautiful shores of Turkey, the most exotic of locations, and at Knidos, one of the most romantic sites in the whole Classical world. For Sonny, as he perpetually reminded everyone, Knidos had more history in just one of its old stones than the whole of the USA put together. Its theatres were two thousand years old, a veritable aeon of time older than anything on Broadway. Its streets had been abandoned almost a millennium before the New World had even been discovered. For Sonny, the whole encounter was, and continued to be, totally astounding. And I should add that his infectious romanticism and his boundless enthusiasm, combined with his delicate, sallow features and dark eyes, made him very attractive to women.

By this his second season he had grown in confidence. He had surveyed the streets and terraces, the walls and gateways, the harbours and breakwaters of the whole city. The site supervisors looked up to him and the workmen greeted his familiar figure with unalloyed enthusiasm as he clambered about the ancient ruins with his theodolite, measuring the landscape. But the one difference between his first and second season was Coral, a newly arrived helper from the top echelons of privileged Washingtonian society. Coral was top drawer, in some ways the diametric cultural opposite of Sonny. She was the daughter of one of the US's leading diplomats and had a CV to match - private schools through her teens; a year studying art in Paris, another in Florence, and now she was on her way to that most exclusive US women's institution, Radcliffe College. She was signed up to become a 'Cliffie' when at Knidos, right in her line of sight, intervened the singing Sonny, with the full orchestral accompaniment of the Old World allure and the ancient walls of Knidos, City of Aphrodite, Goddess of Love!

Ask anyone in the archaeological world and they will tell you that all excavations, especially ones in strange and outlandish locations, are emotionally guaranteed to have the effect on the participants of an over-productive, sexually-charged hot house. This is particularly true of, but certainly not confined to, young and impressionable staff members. It frequently acts in the same way upon older and supposedly wiser staff members too, often with disastrous consequences, as I have periodically observed. It's a well known phenomenon, brought on by the almost total isolation, the intimate social and physical proximity, the romance of ruins, the unusual day-to-day routine, the sexual repression, the drink, and, in the case of Knidos, the added mix of the azure Aegean and the soft moonlight reflecting on a wine-dark sea. This heady mixture has certainly fertilised more than its fair crop of extraordinary seedlings over the years. At Knidos, relationships grew rapidly, like sinuous climbers in a time lapse movie, clinging together and spiralling ever upwards. Sometimes the limbs of these leggie plants would de-couple only to recombine with another upward stem, twining and re-twining as the season wore on. One such coupling, the most celebrated the season I was there, was Sonny and Coral.

Despite having had no previous experience of excavating, Coral had arrived with the intention of becoming a serious-minded site supervisor. Her presence at Knidos seems to have been the result of some winter assignation that had been made in one of the East Coast soirees with the great and the good, the rich and the famous, and the politically and diplomatically connected. In an unguarded moment, one of them had been inveigled into taking Coral to Knidos by her proud parents, who were in New York on their way to their new senior posting to the US Embassy in Ankara. Coral was to have an educational and entertaining summer. Just how educational and entertaining would unfold later. Shyly at first, almost imperceptibly in this gold-fish bowl existence, Sonny made his move. Coral asked Sonny all sorts of pertinent questions about the site that he, with his previous season and his survey work, was ideally placed to answer. They enjoyed a shared and significant knitting of brows about subjects as diverse as Roman history, the chemical composition of mortar, and how you could tell as you excavated if one wall was bonded into another.

"Sonny, do you think this bonds into that?" was a familiar question about Coral's trench. As the days rolled on, Sonny seemed to spend more and more time adjusting his trigonometric points near where Coral was working and thus reinforcing his own notion of bonding.

Anyway, one question led to another. Sonny and Coral would walk deep in thought to her trench, way over on the eastern side of the city. Gallantly, Sonny would carry Coral's site bag as well as his own theodolite. Coral would ask technical questions and listen attentively to Sonny's answers. They ate breakfast together. They ate lunch together. They went swimming together. And they sat in the evenings in Cengis's Çayhane, holding hands in the semi darkness and sipping one glass of raki between them. Amid all the mêlée of the daily round of excavations, and all the frustrations and unrequited passions of the rest of the group, Sonny and Coral's relationship seemed to stand out as a beacon of optimism for us all – a sort of pastiche of what passed for normal in those abnormal circumstances. Their obvious devotion acted as a kind of totem, a mutual warmth to be enjoyed and an unpretentious enthusiasm to be admired by the rest of us, the otherwise disgruntled and rakı-imbibing lower caste. Like watching a sea squill grow skywards into a beautiful tall flower out of the dry, unyielding earth of a Carian September, we observed and were fascinated by this socially unlikely but, for us, totally comprehensible liaison, for we too were part of the hot-house, detached from the actuality of the world outside.

The excavations continued inexorably onwards. The parabola of our own digging season had arched upwards, climbing shining to its apogee, but now it was turning slowly down, imperceptibly at first then noticeably falling more and more precipitately towards its inescapable close. From time to time in those later weeks, sharp gusts of a threatening reality rustled our leaves. We tried to ignore the tell-tale signs – the checking of air tickets; the mention of brothers, sisters, lovers, parents; the talking about money or bus schedules. But in the end, as the last days careered by, we had to admit the inevitable. We were all going to have to formulate a re-entry, both actually and metaphorically, into the forthcoming autumn and winter of real life. We all had to go home. And what was to become of us? More especially, for this part of the story, what would become of Sonny and Coral.

Now it so happened that on the Knidos expedition that year was a youngish Turkish archaeologist by the name of Özcan (pronounced Erzjan). Özcan had been wished on the excavation as part of a worthily conceived localisation programme to involve Turkish trainees and others in Classical archaeology, to encourage more Turks to put themselves forward and become involved in the fabulous heritage of their magnificent country. We lower echelons had not ourselves had much to do with Özcan for most of the season. He had been trying, somewhat unsuccessfully, to ingratiate himself with the Management. However, now, at this eleventh hour, he changed sides and joined us in our evening symposia with the workmen. There was a slight element of discomfort in his arrival, he clearly being from a well-to-do Turkish family and we very much siding with the impoverished workers. But he did his best to fit in, and along with the rest of us paid court to Sonny and

Coral, so that when the question of what would happen next arose, Özcan made a remarkable proposition.

We had learnt that one idea was that we were all to be transported by truck to Bodrum like so many cattle. Should this be the case, then Bodrum was to be the final point of dispersal, just ten days or so hence. Naturally enough, it became the overwhelming topic of our last few evenings together. It was then, in full hearing of our team, that Özcan told us that his mother lived in Bodrum and that if Sonny and Coral would like to, they could stay at her house, instead of the dormitory pension where the rest of us were destined to spend our last night together, hugger mugger. He was sure his mother wouldn't mind, and in any case there was a spare bedroom they could use. We were all filled with a rosy glow at the suggestion of such intimacy, something which was hardly accorded to any of us during the tented accommodation of the excavation itself. We tried not to think what might happen after that – the inevitable parting of the ways as they resumed their very different lives; the estrangement; the tearful letters before the final end of their dreams, and with them perhaps of our own.

One night, the huge truck came and took us all in its deep pay load, lurching through the peninsula villages in the dark as though transporting us clandestinely away. We reached Bodrum early the next morning in an afterglow of emotion and thus we once again entered into the unfamiliar reality of the real world. As we had never wished to imagine but as we might have more sensibly predicted, we all lost touch with each other almost at once as actual life resumed its inexorable path. The story of Sonny and Coral became a legend wrapped in a dream which alas too faded with time.

* * * *

It was many years later that, to my surprise, I caught up with Sonny, or rather, he caught up with me. Despite our close friendship at Knidos, Sonny swiftly disappeared out of my life. He was, after all, a surveyor, not an archaeologist, so there was no reason why we would have kept in touch. For me, I began to mature in my own chosen profession and, as an archaeologist, I had moved on to other parts of the world. However, following some important discoveries in prehistory with which I was involved, it came to be that I was giving a series of lectures around the United States for the Archaeological Institute of America, part didactic, part fund-raising, and one of the venues where I was to speak was City College, New York. That night, there was an audience of over four hundred people who had come to listen to me expatiate about the newest evidence for early man in Africa. The lecture was well received and after it had finished, a small crowd of admirers gathered around me on the stage. Through that crowd pushed Sonny.

"I saw the advertisements for your lecture in the AIA bulletin. I thought, there can't be two of you with the same name can there? So I came along to see you."

I was dumbstruck. I excused myself from my hosts, and Sonny and I left to find an Italian restaurant nearby. We sat down and after some self-conscious chitchat we began to reminisce. Unhurriedly, we summoned up the djinns of old Knidos, the ghosts of the excavations those years before. We enquired about this or that person. We exchanged a few stories and indulged in a little gossip. At an appropriate moment, I naturally asked if he was married, which he said he was. I tentatively mentioned Coral.

"Oh hell no, David!" he said emphatically. "After Bodrum, I never saw her again. Don't know where she might be now."

"But we were all so excited for you, you and Coral, about the house in Bodrum and everything, the night of passion, you know?"

And it was then Sonny related to me the extraordinary account of The Wizard of Öz, the Ottoman Mansion and the Magic Eye. After pouring us two more glasses of wine, very quietly Sonny began to talk about the eschatology of his relationship with Coral. I got the impression he had never told a soul about it until now. Maybe it had been the most sacred moment in his life for him. Who knows? Anyway, he began his tale.

They had met Öz, as Sonny called him, at a pre-arranged leather shop in the old market in Bodrum. Öz had handed Sonny an impressively large iron key.

"My mother's away at the moment, visiting her relatives in Izmir, and she wants me to join her there, so the house is quite empty," he had said. "Here is the key. It's the ancient-looking house with the blue door in that narrow street beyond the Castle, the one opposite the sponge seller's shop. You can't miss it. My mother has left everything ready for you. When you have finished with the house, just leave the key with Harun here. One day I hope we'll see each other again."

And saying his goodbye's he had strode off leaving Sonny and Coral to the ardour of the night.

"Man, that was some kind of a place," resumed Sonny.

"After we'd had eaten a kebab or two, we found the house, just where Öz had told us."

Sonny described opening the huge panelled door, engraved with archaic Turkish ciphers – crescent moons, scalloped rope patterns and floral designs. They entered the dark recess of the hallway decorated with antique camel bags and wall hangings. Sonny felt that it was like something from an ancient *Kervanserai* on the Silk Road. He led Coral up the creaking stairs and found the bedroom just as Öz had described it to them. Against the back wall was a truly massive French bed, maybe 18th century Sonny thought, set on ancient polished pine floor-boards, with a wardrobe to match. On the far wall was a window with a wrought-iron balcony which opened onto the harbour and the sea.

"It was like a scene from the movies, you know? Just fantastic! It was sure a long way away from the sleeping bags and tents at Knidos."

And so it was, in that 'Arabian Nights' setting, that Sonny and Coral spent their last night together. There was a harvest moon that night, he remembered. They didn't switch on the arcane electric light in case it spoilt the romance of the moment. They left the drapes open so that a flooding luminosity gently accentuated the shading of their bodies with a soft aura. They kissed each other and made love so tenderly before laying naked in each other's arms, holding each other with a heart-rending obsession, trying to blot out the uncertainty of what tomorrow might bring. For Sonny, the boy from New York City, this was his ultimate oriental idyll, as he lay there with Coral beside him, his very own princess, his own Scheherazade. He was almost afraid to sleep, in case he should be shaken from his dream.

Entwined together, they woke to the sound of waves softly brushing the shingle beneath their room, as the first rays of the sun rose above the Black Island opposite. Sonny went over and stood by the balcony, peering out at the Crusader Castle, its ancient walls and towers reflected in the still water of the harbour.

"You know something, that castle was built by the Crusader Knights in fourteen hundred and something, think of that, and it stands on the site of the old palace, the Zephyrion, built by Mausolus over 2300 years ago. Just imagine that! There's more history outside this window than we have in the whole of America."

They made love again, this time more urgently as they felt the last hours slip away.

"Coral, just check out this very room – it's old, old, old, you know. Man, look at these bedroom walls; they must have seen hundreds of years of history. Just look at those ancient beams and the ceiling boards, made so wide. I'll bet you can't get trees like that today."

The mention of 'today,' the here and now, brought about it's own rueful silence, as they lay on their backs, straining their eyes to look up at the smooth, hand-sawn pine boards from the ancient forests of Caria, veritably knotted with age. And as they peered upwards at the knots in the planking, they noticed that directly above them one knot was missing. There was a hole where the knot should have been, and through that hole glinted an eye. It was the eye of Özcan who had been watching them…all night long.

CHAPTER TWENTY THREE

'ROUND ONE'

Aphrodite stands in her temple in such a way that she is equally admirable from every angle.

Pliny the Elder

And so we come to the climax of the piece, the search for the real nucleus of Knidian fame. You will recall that around 350 BC the good citizens of Knidos decided to move their city to its new location at Cape Crio. It was at that time also that they felt the need to commemorate their urban upheaval by selecting a new patron deity. They were looking for something a little more modern, a little more *avant-garde* perhaps, to celebrate their entry into the brave new world of Hellenism. They were searching for something with a more Greek essence, to replace, or at least to meld with the somewhat wilder Anatolian deities of their archaic and oriental past. So they chose Aphrodite, Goddess of Love, and appropriately named her Aphrodite Euploea, Aphrodite of Fair Navigation.

It was a natural choice for their new harbour city. Aphrodite is reported to have strong marine connections, or so her biographers suggest. According to Hesiod, and who am I to contradict such a hagiographer, Kronos, youngest of the Titans, was directed by his mother Gaia to castrate his own father Ouranos with a flint sickle which, it is reported, he succeeded in doing, hurling the newly-reaped genitalia somewhat randomly over his shoulder. The story goes that the disembodied organ hurtled through the air and finally fell into the sea where, some time later, a spume began to form and from this foaming mass a girl emerged who turned out to be none other than that loveliest of goddesses, Aphrodite. After wandering in the ocean for an unspecified length of time, the froth-born goddess finally materialized from the briny at Paphos, in Cyprus. So it was that Aphrodite became the deity associated, amongst other things, with the sea, and more especially in the case of Knidos, with seafaring. All perfectly reasonable, I think you will agree.

In that the Knidians had chosen the remote tip of the peninsula, the precise point where the Aegean Sea and the East Mediterranean meet, in order to take advantage of the new maritime trade that had recently sprung up, what better symbol could they have adopted. With this in mind, they had sent a delegation to Athens for a suitable emblem to support their new civic resolution. There they eventually found what they were looking for in the studios of the famous contemporary sculptor Praxiteles. It seems that the great artiste had just created two statues of Aphrodite, one suitably attired with a drape around her midriff, and the other who was as naked as the day she was formed, or perhaps that should be 'foamed'. The nature of the haggling that must have ensued has not been vouchsafed to us, but the end result was that the Knidians bought the nude version and the Koans, from the Island of Kos across the straits, bought the other. The Knidian statue, so Pliny tells us, became one of the most renowned pieces of sculpture of all time, whilst the Koan one disappeared into the maw of ancient history, never to be heard of again.

Praxiteles had modelled the Aphrodite statues on his own mistress (and it seems lots of other people's as well), a well-known Athenian hetaira (aka sex worker) called Phryne. She was supposedly the most beautiful woman of the age. Actually, her name wasn't really Phryne, it was Mnesarete, and she didn't come from Athens either, she came from Thespiae, but I suppose few things are what they seem at this remove. Phryne was her nick-name. It means 'the Toad', on account, we are told, of her yellowish complexion, or perhaps, maybe more honestly, because that was the name the other less lovely ladies of the night gave her out of pure feminine malice.

During her lifetime, if the stories which adhere to her are in any way to be believed, the Toad achieved considerable notoriety even before her petrified form became so celebrated. It is said that she was once arrested in Athens for

217

lewd behaviour, profaning the Eleusinian Mysteries by flashing her frontal accoutrements at people in the street. She was dragged before the courts and charged with conduct likely to deprave. In the Areopagus – the Athenian court– she was vigorously defended by a most loquacious orator, one Hypereides, but even he found he was losing to the forces of prejudice and prudery. In a final bid to clear Phryne's name, they say that during his summing up he ripped off the bodice from her shoulders in front of the court thus exposing her full pneumatic beauty which had an immediate and arresting effect on the jurors to the extent that they immediately acquitted her, on artistic and quasi-theological grounds so they quickly maintained. As a result, it led to such a distressing bout of post-trial recrimination it was decreed that in future no accused person could remain in the court during the summing up lest such titillating inducements should distract the jurors from returning the correct verdict.

Another rather delightful story tells of how, in later life, she had made so much money 'on the game' that she said she would pay for the rebuilding of the defensive walls of Thebes, down the road from Athens, which had been destroyed by Alexander. She offered to do this on condition that they wrote in large letters – 'Knocked down by Alexander the Great; re-erected by Phryne the Tart!' or something to that effect. The Thebans coyly seem to have declined her offer.

But getting involved with women had it's moments for Praxiteles too. Phryne wrote him a letter in which she says a little ruefully,

"You have set up a statue of your own mistress in the sacred precinct. But do not begrudge me this honour. For, when they have gazed at me, it is Praxiteles that people will praise."

Meanwhile, Aphrodite herself, after having studied the statue, was heard to say, at least according to one Platonic epigram, words to the effect that, "Well, where did Praxiteles ever see me naked?"

Having returned to Cape Krio with their purchase, the Knidians installed the statue of Aphrodite, which, we are told, was larger than life (perhaps 1.2 : 1 life size), somewhere in their new city. At first the statue was treated with assiduous and sacred reverence by the inhabitants of the city, but within a couple of hundred years she had become inordinately famous for her innocently erotic likeness as well. Over the following centuries crowds of people came to visit Knidos to see this amazing statue and gaze upon the face, and no doubt the other attributes, of the Toad, lithologically transubstantiated into Aphrodite Euploea. The best known story is by the celebrated Lucian, who arrived at Knidos with two of his friends, one a homosexual and the other a heterosexual. They had been arguing about the relative merits of the male or the female form. Lucian wrote:

> We could not pass up the chance to stop in Cnidus, where there is so much to be seen, notably the temple of Aphrodite which encloses the statue by Praxiteles, so admired for its beauty. I took the two experts on love by the arm and we went round Cnidus, delighting in the erotic terra cottas, worthy of a town dedicated to Aphrodite.

> As soon as we reached the confines of the temple we felt as if caressed by the very breath of the goddess. Heavy clusters of grapes hang from the gnarled vines: indeed, Aphrodite is only more attractive when united with Bacchus; their pleasures are sweeter for being mixed together. When we had exhausted the charms of these places we pressed on into the temple itself

> The goddess stands in the centre; her statue made of Parian marble. Her lips are slightly parted by a haughty smile. Nothing hides her beauty, which is entirely exposed, other than a furtive hand veiling her modesty. The art of the sculptor has succeeded so well that it seems the marble has shed its hardness to mould the grace of her limbs.

Apparently Lucian's straight friend swooned at the full frontal view. But there was more.

> The temple has a second entrance for those who wish to contemplate the goddess from behind, for none of her parts should escape admiration. It is easy in that fashion to gaze upon her hind beauty. Wanting to see the goddess entire we approached this gate. Upon being let in by the woman who kept the keys, we were overwhelmed by her abundant beauty.

This time it was the gay friend's turn to swoon:

> By Hercules, what a harmonious back! What rounded thighs, begging to be caressed with both hands! How well the lines of her cheeks flow, neither too skinny, showing the bones, nor so voluminous as to droop! How inexpressible the tenderness of that smile pressed into her dimpled loins!

His tactile desire for the Toad's posterior was no doubt encouraged by the fact that Greek sculptors tended to make their ladies a trifle boyish in rear view, or so I am told.

Speaking of her appearance, we know quite a lot about the way the statue must have looked, complete with furtive hand, the so called 'pudica' gesture which slightly occluded her equipment. This is not only from the many writings like Lucian, but also from all the sculptural copies that have been made of the statue of the Aphrodite of Knidos, known to art historians as 'the Knidia'. There are so many of them, though nearly all are Roman, much thicker in the beam I'm told, with more fleshly delights than the slender Greek original. The Knidia, say the art historians, is shown rising innocently, as though unobserved, from her toilet - her bath, that is - pudica at the ready. There are several copies in the British Museum, there's one in Munich, and are no less than two in the Vatican Museum, at least one wrapped in a tin skirt for modesty's sake. Quite what the Pope wants with these is a point to ponder.

But the one attribute among all others which these copies of the naked Aphrodite exhibit, the one defining physical feature which marks every copy out, for me at least, to be unmistakably Phryne, is the nose. The line of her nasal profile flows from the base of her forehead straight down the outline to the tip - no bridge, no hook, no curve, no terminal bobble, no Semitic bulb, and no trace of an up-turned ski-jump – just straight. Recently, there was an exhibition at the Louvre in Paris dedicated to 'Praxitèle,' with a collection of his own sculptures from all over the world, and including a number of later copies of the Knidian Aphrodite. Being there was an extraordinary affair, like walking into a 'Phryne Look-alike Convention.' And there was 'the nose,' here, there, everywhere. The Toad would have been proud.

* * * *

But I digress - back to the dig. Over the centuries, sundry people have tried to find the statue at Knidos, or at least the location of the temple dedicated to the Knidian Aphrodite – Beaufort, Graves, Newton and others. Newton discovered the Temenos of Demeter, replete with statuary, but he found no trace of the Goddess of Love, or the shrine in which she had been housed. Like others before us, the Expedition was determined to have another stab at finding the temple, if not the statue. So it was that one lunch time in that summer of 1969, whilst we were all seated around the table after our customary blow out of beans and tomatoes with an accompaniment of tomatoes and beans, our attention was drawn to a covert mêlée among the High Command. Voices were raised, fingers were pointed, and 'Aphrodite' punctuated the conversation. One of the Top Brass had been walking the site that morning and said he had stumbled across the outside edge of a single curved marble block of a monumental building. That was what had ignited the flames of interest. It wasn't the statue of the Knidia, it wasn't yet even an in situ building, but it was felt that it may be a tiny straw in the Knidian wind.

Curvilinear buildings are not common in the Classical World. The tholos at Delphi, the Pantheon in Rome and a few others spring to mind, but they are rarities. With this thought to the fore, a posse of the Management strode purposefully up the mountain that lunch time, past the Temple of Dionysus next to the theatre, past the 'Pink Temple' and higher still to a barren outcrop of rock high in the western city. Just below the ridge, on a narrow ledge and covered with the accumulated debris of centuries, was the newly discovered curved block. Eager hands swept the earth away, tracing the edge of the block around until, under grass tussocks and the roots of spiny bushes, that edge led on to another edge, describing the same circle, and then another. They appeared to be in an unbroken arc. Could this arc be a lead to Aphrodite? Personally, I was not really *au fait* with the thinking here, but the discovery led to conspicuous junketing that evening at the dig house. We were all allowed free rations of vinho de casa, and who was I to say 'nay'?

Next morning, I was asked to lay out a trench, two meters wide, from the back of the newly discovered terrace across the middle of the heap of debris, and the excavation of what was to become the 'Round Temple' began. It turned out to be a circular shrine, or nearly so. I say nearly so because before the footings of the building were fully exposed all the way around, by surveying only the parts of the curve that were being excavated I could only come up with an ellipse. It turned out that the front portion of the podium on which the shrine stood had cracked and fallen forward in some earlier earthquake. It had originally been a perfectly circular marble dias supporting an eighteen-pillar round colonnade, probably of the Doric order. But had it been a gazebo, its sides open to the elements, or a walled shrine surrounded by a ring of exterior columns? At any event the columns had been topped by capitals and an austere architrave, atop which there would have been a conical, tiled roof.

This round building, I was eagerly told, was the missing Temple of the Aphrodite of Knidos, and so for me it will always remain. Subsequent excavators, specifically Turkish, have comprehensively repudiated the Aphrodite idea, pointing out that there is inappropriate late Roman rubble of the Corinthian order nearby; or that there is a fragmentary inscription to another deity, Athena, found near the temple; or that the attribution of the building to the Knidia was wishful thinking. As I have said, the methods and conclusions of the High Command have often been ridiculed by later scholars, keen to show off their own questionable superiority. There is certainly an element of resentment in their criticism, or in some cases undoubtedly an unadulterated academic ill will. They maintain that the whole attribution of the temple to the Praxiteles masterpiece was too far-fetched and lacked any archaeological rigour, however one might have displayed such a thing.

But I have always thought that the attribution to Aphrodite was correct. Just look at the location of the temple, set on its high terrace directly above the most important street junction of the whole city, the one where the main stepped street coming up from the Harbour crosses the main east-west horizontal street from the Eastern gateway. There is no stepped street more important than this, the one which leads upwards from the isthmus where the landing stages were, and terminating at the high terrace on which the Round Temple sits. Surely this is the street up which Lucian (assuming it was indeed he that wrote the piece) and his friends had reached the Temple precinct that day?

The Temple may be said to have the best view in the city. Overlooking as it does the two harbours, it commands a view west across the Aegean to Kos and east over the Mediterranean towards Rhodes. It can see and be seen by mariners a long way out at sea, for part of the time in profile. What more natural position for the Temple of Aphrodite Euploea, she of Fair Navigation, than the one with the most prominent seascapes? And there, on top of the ruins of the temple podium, we found a statue base which once held a statue slightly more than life size … the Knidia was 1.2: 1 life size.

But the argument which for me clinches the identification absolutely, short of resurrecting an ancient inhabitant of the city who would point to it and say that this was indeed the Temple of Aphrodite, is an intriguing but a very specific one. It has to do with the Roman Emperor Hadrian, he of 'Wall' fame. In 129 AD Hadrian made a passage through his Eastern Empire, ostensibly to press the flesh and make sure his subjects in Syria and Asia were in good heart. In fact, the trip was intended to reorganise the grain traffic so that his armies in the west didn't revolt for want of a crust or two. At any event, the great man appeared here and there with his entourage and many cities somewhat sycophantically erected monumental arches, temples or granaries to commemorate his visit.

Now, we learn that Hadrian was a man of great discernment and among his back-up team were counted botanists, zoologists and architects, studying their various disciplines in the colonies. Hadrian had an eye for buildings and whenever he came across one which he liked, he commanded his architects to make the relevant notes so that when they returned to Rome, they could erect exact copies of each building there for his own amusement. One such replica was the temple of the Knidian Aphrodite. In the gardens of Hadrian's Villa at Tivoli, just outside the Eternal City, still stands a Temple to the Venus of Cnidus. It's a circular temple of the Doric order, and of the same exact dimensions as the Knidian Round Temple on that high terrace at Knidos looking out to sea. But then, it would be the same, wouldn't it? The Knidian Round Temple is where the measurements came from in the first place!

And me, well, I was the first person to survey the Round Temple, so maybe I have a vested interest in its affinity with Aphrodite too. I have been involved, in my own researches anyway, with many much more important academic discoveries after my time at Knidos, but when it comes to 'great moments in archaeology,' this is the one which for me takes pride of place. So to Los Amerikanos, and to Praxiteles, much thanks.

* * * *

Ah, but what happened to the statue, I hear you cry? Whatever happened to Praxiteles' masterpiece? What befell the likeness of Aphrodite aka Phryne which had gained Knidos such world notoriety? Well, we certainly didn't come across her in the excavations. For us, she was no longer to be found at Knidos. There are accounts by later Byzantine historians that the Knidia eventually wound up in Constantinople, exhibited in the Palace of Lausus. Lausus, somewhat ironically given the erotic nature of the statue, was a eunuch in the court of the ultra-religious emperor Theodosius II in the early 5th Century AD and who rose through the ranks to become his imperial chamberlain. Having arrived at such an elevated position he went on to build his own palace in the centre of Imperial Constantinople, located on the other side of the Hippodrome from his master's, where he was said to have housed a considerable collection of the confiscated statues of Classical deities which he had amassed from eastern temples when they were being sacked during the reign of his zealous imperial master, and amongst these was our own lovely Aphrodite. Here, the chroniclers say, is where she finally came to rest, and they go on to maintain that alas the statue was burnt with all the rest in a conflagration which destroyed Lausus' palace in 475 AD. If indeed such was the case, then she had survived just over 830 years in the mortal world, but the fire of 475 AD it seems is when her earthly story ends.

Or maybe it doesn't, not quite, at least. Some years ago, in a small town in West Sussex, I felt a twitch on the cords that for ever bind me to Knidos. It was at Petworth House on the South Downs, near Chichester. Once part of the Leconfield estates, the house is now run by the National Trust. In the late 18th century, an august ancestor of the one time owners, Lord

Egremont, strove to emulate the Grand Tour by accumulating Classical fragments and memorabilia to enhance his country residence and thus his standing in the community. Among his collection was a disembodied head of Aphrodite. I am not an art historian, but some among their number have labelled the Leconfield head a true and original Praxiteles sculpture. On discovering this, I hurried to Petworth House, paid my entrance fee and went to view the Egremont collection. Turning a corner in a rather ill-lit corridor, there, on a wooden pedestal, in a forgotten alcove, was Phryne, aka Aphrodite, a little larger than life size. There was the unmistakable nose. It was a stunning experience, to see that nose, which had come all the way from the sunny Mediterranean to the gloom of rural England. There I stood, transfixed, gazing into the cold marble eyes of Phryne, but she disdainfully looked beyond me into the middle distance. Did she always do that to her admirers, I wondered? With her unmistakable nose and contemptuous stare, was this indeed a true Praxiteles? And if so, could it once have been part of one of the two statues that had been in his studio in Athens in the 4th century BC when the burgers of Knidos came to call? And if it was, could this have actually come from Aphrodite Euploea, she of fair navigation, who had once so famously been installed at Knidos, here somehow saved from incineration and sold to Rome, and then, much later on, to Britain?

So enwrapped was I that morning in Sussex, looking for a long time into Phryne's unresponsive and stony soul, that one of the attendants came over and asked what it was that so interested me. I explained *con brio* my connection with Knidos, and so interested was she that she called the curator of the collections from his office upstairs. Down came the young man, a callow youth who had clearly been disturbed from his elevenses. I related the story of my experiences at Knidos, with four part harmony and full orchestral accompaniment – the curved blocks, the excavation, the connection with the Tivoli Gardens, etcetera. He too began to be enthusiastic. He asked more questions and I carried on with all the descants, *fortissimos* and *rallentandos* I could muster. He was fascinated. As we parted, I asked if I might take a photograph of the lovely Phryne for my records.

"Oh," he said huffily, "I'm afraid we can't allow that. The head is very fragile you see, and your flash light may damage the delicate marble."

Exasperated, I explained to him that the rest of the statue had probably been unceremoniously incinerated in Istanbul, so what would it matter. He was unmoved. The head must remain, like the rest of us, in the dark, so I left without my tribute to Aphrodite. Imagine my chagrin therefore a year later when, on glancing at the in-house National Trust magazine, which sports the natty title of 'The National Trust Magazine,' what should stare out at me but a photograph of the same head, with an article, written by the same callow youth, including everything I had told him in orchestrated detail. Perhaps this was Phryne's revenge against me for having disturbed her sacred and ancient slumber?

* * * *

If it wasn't possible to take pictures in Sussex, then at least the ruins of Aphrodite's city in Turkey are still there for all to see and to photograph. Today, on that windswept terrace, high above the Trireme Harbour, are still to be found the remains of the uncovered circular podium, just as we left it almost half a century ago. And in the centre can still be seen the deep trench which we sank at the end of that season in order to assess the date of the temple from the sherds of pottery in the filling. Another reason for the deep sounding was that it was felt, with a certain logic, that maybe after some earthquake or other disaster, the inhabitants of Knidos had buried the original, or even a copy, of their treasured statue under the floor of the building to hide her from marauders or predatory tourists and that there was still a chance of finding her on the site. But though we dug down all the way to bedrock, no trace of any statue was discovered. Alas, for the Top Brass, or any of us for that matter, there was to be no Toad in the hole!

Some years ago my brother chose to escort a group of aged British ladies around Knidos. Until they arrived at the Round Temple, all had gone well. He had entertained them with various 'tales of old Knidos' borrowed from my extensive repertoire, and having arrived at the apogee of the tour, he explained about the discovery of the temple, about the statue, and about the deep sounding that was still very much in evidence, including the large spoil heap that had come from the diggings. He was in the process of suggesting that this was his own brother's finest hour, when one of the ladies, of dowager proportions and restricted intellect, declaimed in her hoity-toity Home Counties voice: "Did your brother leave all this mess behind?"

God preserve us all!

✳ ✳ ✳ ✳

Here is one final and rather sad anecdote about the Temple of Aphrodite and the wondrous statue. It was told by the guardian of the Temple to Lucian and his friends sometime in the late Roman period, in response to a comment which he or one of his fellow travellers had made about a blemish they observed in the marble, what looked like a stain on the inside of one of the thighs of the otherwise flawless sculpture. The guardian then related to them how a young boy of a distinguished family from Knidos had fallen in love with the statue and was wont to spend his whole day from sunrise to sunset in the temple precinct, whispering endearments to the Goddess and throwing dice made, so it was said, of the bones of a Libyan oryx – 'she loves me; she loves me not,' that sort of thing.

So overwhelming became the boy's infatuation that one night he contrived to become locked inside the temple and it was then that he released his pent-up desire and had his evil way with her. In the morning, the mark of his excesses were to be seen on her otherwise unblemished torso, the very mark that Lucian had noticed. So ashamed was the boy, the guardian said, that he disappeared that very day and threw himself into the sea, his love unrequited. He had doubtless found out that the goddess had a heart made of stone. Well, in point of fact, he must also have discovered that she had everything else made of stone as well.

Perhaps he might have enjoyed more success in his ambition if he had followed the suggestion of my old Knidian friend Ali Karadeniz:

"Deyvit Bey, ben bugün beton gibi olacağım."

'Today I shall be like concrete!'

CHAPTER TWENTY FOUR

THE DEMES OF KNIDOS

In the Vilayet* of Muğla
Where the patlacans** are cooler,
And the theatres roll gently to the sea;
Where the natives are so surly
And the work is şurle burle***
Eski**** Knidos is where I want to be!

Our dig song of 1969

* The Province; **aubergines; ***Com ci com ca; ****Ancient

As I have related, the excavations at Knidos were drawing to a close, but before they did I became involved with two mad-cap schemes which have until now somehow escaped my attention. Both had to do with small boats of one sort or another. The one concerned the investigation of a classical rumour for which there was no substantive evidence. It involved a certain amount of messing about in a dinghy and resulted in a conspicuous fiasco. The other may nearly have cost me my life.

The first was to do with the Trireme Harbour, the harbour to the west of the isthmus of Knidos, the one facing the Island of Kos. It was Strabo that had suggested in his mention of Knidos at the beginning of the first century AD that this western harbour was the military harbour. Strabo was a man from Pontus, near the Black Sea. He was educated by some of the foremost Greek savants of the day and during his lifetime he travelled extensively around the Roman Empire. His magnum opus was his seventeen volume work, 'The Geographies,' which is a sort of gazetteer of the Roman Mediterranean, its cities and peoples. In this famous work he mentions Knidos and amongst other things says that:

"It has two ports, one of which can be closed, and is intended for triremes, and it has a station for twenty ships."

This is thought to be the western harbour, which could be closed at its sea gate by a chain. The triremes he mentions were large wooden hulks rowed, it is believed, by about one hundred and seventy men, from three banks of oars each side, one man per oar. They were obviously quite deadly in sea battles and it has been claimed that they were able to travel in any direction at will at speeds of up to twelve knots. They carried a bronze 'beak' on the prow at the waterline with which they could ram and sink any other vessel they encountered. It was these triremes which won the battle of Salamis described in Aeschylus' play 'The Persae' quoted earlier.

Speaking of triremes, and if I might digress a little, twenty years after my experiences at Knidos I was very peripherally involved with some of the people who built a replica of a trireme, a huge undertaking which was constructed with all the classical references taken into account. Two scholars from Britain, a classicist and a marine engineer, combined to create what they calculated was a life-sized version of a trireme, thirty five metres long and some five metres wide, which for some curious reason when they had completed it they gave to the Greek Navy, who subsequently took all the credit for its origins, before letting it rot among the Greek Islands.

Anyway, having constructed this vast rowing boat, our two intrepid trireme builders had to assemble a group of rowing volunteers to propel their monster through the sea, which they did from among the rowers of Oxbridge. But even with a full complement of oarsmen they could never get the vessel up to its anticipated full speed because it seems they had used the wrong-sized 'cubit' as the unit of measurement in its construction. Apparently there were a variety of different cubits used in antiquity, including a 'natural cubit' and a 'Royal cubit', but they are all based upon the length of a varying number of widths of palms of the hand, or various numbers of digits – it gets very complicated. Well, in the case of the reconstructed trireme, it was truly confusing because they chose a cubit which was a couple of inches too short. The result was that the rowers in the lowest bank of oars, if they pulled really hard on their oar, banged the back of their head on a cross beam behind them, and if they leaned too far forward for the stroke, they banged their forehead on the cross beam in front. The result was that however hard they were exhorted to row they preferred to stir the water lightly rather than to knock themselves out. The overall result was thus a bit of a damp squib, but it did look amazing rowed through the water – like a giant centipede.

But let's go back to the Trireme Harbour at Knidos. Earlier in the season we had excavated some kind of a monumental building on the north side of the harbour. It turned out to be a purpose-built stoa, a small market place surrounded on four sides with inward-facing pillared porticoes. On the harbour side of this the portico doorways opened onto a marble quayside at the height of a trireme gunwale. It seems to have been designed to service the war-ships when they came into the harbour. Maybe this was the trireme station mentioned by Strabo. The gateway into the harbour was overlooked by a beautifully-made drum tower which guarded the outer approach to the sea entrance, and thus we could see that the whole ensemble had been very elegantly designed. And that is the moment when some implausible fantasist in the High Command from some source I know not where, came up with the notion that the floor of the trireme harbour, that is, the underwater bit, had in antiquity been paved with marble slabs, which, if true, would have made it one of the most elegant harbours in the ancient world. Step forward a surveyor to organise an investigation into this possible phenomenon, and that is how I was dragooned into sampling the local ordure.

The harbour was, of course, full of water, so there was no question of draining it. The winter storms had pushed hard through the entrance for the past two thousand years, sea spray regularly lashing the western mole. The debris brought in by the storms had built up a considerable deposit of mud which made the harbour quite shallow. To investigate whether or not the harbour's bottom had been covered with marble tiles, someone had the bright idea that we should drive a pipe into the ooze and take a core sample – quite how this was going to help I really don't know. Anyway, a surveyor was necessary to find the centre of the harbour, and this is where I came in. I made a measured map of the harbour edge and established a centroid where the 'core' would be made. Using the dinghy, the team weaved about in the middle of the harbour until I guided them into the centre, at which point they raised a hollow plastic drain pipe and began to knock the pipe vertically into the water with a heavy sledge hammer. This was not as easily achieved as it had been imagined, for as the cumbersome hammer descended, the force of the blow sent the dinghy backwards, causing Alf, the chap with the hammer, to lurch forward and fall over the front of the dinghy into the water. Dives and fumblings were then made to recover the hammer before the process began again, with the same result.

After a while it became obvious that no progress could be made with this enterprise without adding to the work-force in the water, one to hold the pipe and two to hold the back of the dinghy steady, and after a few false starts, the pipe began to be driven into the mud. But by then, another problem had arisen. Although the water was warm enough for a casual swim, standing chest high in it for fifteen minutes or more made the marine team extremely cold, and shivering, they had to come out for half an hour to warm up in the sunshine before we could continue.

This bizarre pantomime continued for some hours, the pipe being slowly hammered into the mud before everyone had to come out again for an extended cigarette break and a thaw out. It was during one of these breaks that a penny dropped with one of the team in the water. They noticed that on the island side of the Trireme Harbour, above the round tower, there was a small house, well, more of a hovel than a house, but a family was still living in this dwelling, and all their household effluent was being piped directly into the mouth of the Trireme Harbour, whence it was pushed by the storm surges back into the middle of the harbour itself, where it lay in the mud. What we were hammering the pipe into was not the preamble to an elegant marble installation but several generations of human effluent mixed with sand.

The expedition to ascertain whether or not the Trireme Harbour had a marble floor was brought to an abrupt close and the team began to pack up their belongings. It was only then that Alf said that it would not be right to abandon the pipe standing proud in the middle of the water – it offended his sense of the natural. So, a further half an hour was spent trying to pull the pipe out of the mud, before it finally came loose and was hauled on land. Nothing more was said.

* * * *

The second episode took place during the final days of the Expedition at a time when it was suggested that the whole expedition team should decamp to Bodrum before disbanding. The question that was in everyone's mind was how was this to be achieved? The road to Marmaris by which any landward journey would have to be made was pretty hairy, especially the first part as far as Yazıköy, and it would be very slow, but there were only tiny fishing boats tied up at the jetty in the Commercial Harbour so that travelling to Bodrum by sea was a long shot. Nevertheless, someone in the Çayhane suggested one night that he had a brother with a small cruiser at Palamut Buku, a little way down the coast, and that this could take a number of us up the Sound of Kos to Bodrum harbour. He could bring it to Knidos the day after tomorrow, he said, ready to be embarked. We were enthusiastic at the prospect of a short sea journey, rather than travelling for many hours over the dreadful road.

Duly, two days later, we waited by the Çayhane for the cruiser to arrive, imagining a largish, comfortable vessel with cabins and a powerful engine. What chugged into the harbour and tied up at the jetty was a boat scarcely bigger than a rowing boat, floating somewhat lopsidedly in the water. This craft did have a cabin of sorts, a short roof over the wheel, but it would only have been able to house one person, sleeping with their feet out in the open at the back. On the prow in uneven hand-painted letters was the name, 'Altın Yunus,' The Golden Dolphin, though this craft had absolutely none of the grace and poise of the elegant sea creature for which it had been named. It was powered by an ancient single cylinder two stroke Lister engine, which had been made in Britain by R A Lister & Company of Dursley, Gloucestershire some decades earlier – still, they do say that they're built to last.

Somewhat reluctantly, the four or five of us who had said we were prepared to travel to Bodrum in this conveyance climbed aboard and sat on the cabin cover. That was the sign for the other spectators, whose presence in the harbour that morning we had wondered about, to climb aboard as well – several of the workers dressed in their best clothes, a couple of villagers leading goats, one woman with a large basket full of fresh figs and a whole gaggle of young children – until it was packed with people. The boat rode lower in the water with each additional passenger so that eventually the water line was only just below the gunwale. Still, it was apparently a calm morning, at least in the shelter of the harbour. After a few teas had been drunk and the glasses handed back to Cengis and farewells had been said, the captain of the boat started the engine, pulled up the rope to which the anchor was attached, and we turned and set off across the bay, between the two moles, and out around the island.

As we rounded the eastern end of the island, the inevitable spin drift surrounded us and the wind, which we had been unaware of until this point, started to pick up. We thumped our way underneath the cliffs of the island, the engine exhaust echoing hollowly against the steep rocks. As we approached the far western tip of the island and turned into the Sound the full brunt of the wind funnelling down the side of the island of Kos struck us. The boat rocked outrageously and wave after wave began to break over the prow, smashing more and more heavily as we tried to ply northwards. Within minutes the people who were huddled on the front were soaked. The engine was pushed to full throttle, but the wind and waves were so strong the boat made hardly any headway. I covered myself with an old blanket on the roof and forced myself to go to sleep. If I was going to drown, I pondered, I didn't want a lot of time to think about it. When I woke up, twenty minutes or so later, everyone on board was drenched and we hadn't made any progress at all. We were still banging away in the same spot in the sea, underneath the light-house, still fighting with the wind and waves which if anything were getting stronger as the morning was advancing. Someone was bailing. It was hopeless, and a few minutes later the captain turned the boat around in a trough between the wave crests and we cruised back around the side of the island and into the commercial harbour and the jetty where we had started.

We clambered off of the boat and with thanks sat down outside the Çayhane. A bottle of rakı was opened and we toasted our good fortune at having braved the tumultuous seas and survived to tell the tale. That night, we left Knidos by road in the back of a huge truck and arrived at Bodrum in the middle of the morning of the next day after a most uncomfortable but at least safe journey. And from Bodrum I went to Istanbul and flew back to London. My Knidian adventure had come to an abrupt end. So sudden was the change that I wondered if I was I ever going to return.

* * * *

But I was to go back to Turkey time and time again for the best part of half a century. It had become engrained in me – its people, its food, its language, its landscapes and its archaeology. And at Knidos itself I was gradually to be perceived as the grand old man, known by no fewer than three generations of the local people from Yazıköy and the other villages - the families of Mehmet the Lighthouse keeper, his son Altan and his grand daughter Damla; of Birol, his brother, and his son Mehmet and family; of Ruşan and the others from the Village of Destiny. Little children I didn't know and had never seen before would come up to me in the dusty streets of Palamut Buku and say 'Hello Deyvit' to me and be proud to recognise me, as though I was a long-lost relative. Old men I barely recognised would meet me in Knidos and ask affectionately about Coral, or Eddie, or Olga as though I had seen them the week before, when in fact it may have been more than three decades since I had last been with them or even heard of them. But I had now become an *efe*, a village hero, perhaps a living memorial to the last time anything of note had happened on the Peninsula.

More importantly I was to take hundreds and hundreds of people back with me to Knidos. I've mentioned some already - groups of students, clouds of tourists, all the members of my family, fellows of the Royal Geographical Society, Diocesan pilgrims, an archbishop, media supremos, travellers from the Smithsonian Institution and from many similarly esteemed bodies. Everyone who went with me wanted to hear about the excavations all those years ago, about the dynamics of the dig, and about the discovery of the Temple of Aphrodite. And with each new group, I would enthusiastically describe what had happened and how I had been involved, bringing it all back to life, although actually it had died long ago.

Invariably we would arrive by sea. With each new party we would begin our visit in the afternoon after lunch, sitting among the Hellenistic houses on the island and looking out across the commercial harbour to the mainland. When everyone was settled, from this vantage point I would sketch out a description of the city as it might have looked two thousand years ago, picturing the terraces and stepped streets still alive with people and still with their temples and markets intact.

I would persuade them to imagine sailing up the Gulf of Doris approaching Knidos in a trading vessel from Rhodes, maybe towards the end of the first century BC. It would have felt as exciting as it would have been dramatic, the expectation mounting after a long, exhausting sea voyage. Looking intently beneath the sail's foot through the Carian haze the seemingly uninhabited mountains of the peninsula would stretch monotonously off our starboard beam, ridge after barren ridge, ever westwards, seemingly unending, until rounding the last headland the impressive dark-soaring apex of the island of the city with its vertical cliffs would come into view silhouetted against the open sea beyond. As we navigated nearer, the high ashlar walls protecting the mainland of the city would be seen off to the right, rising abruptly from the water's edge near the eastern gateway up the steep crags above, the myriad block-work defences punctuated by square towers all the way to the fortress high on the summits over the city. The walls would hem in and partly obscure the residential quarter and the civic centre of the lower part of the metropolis. But inside, the city's upper buildings would be visible above the battlements, including way in the distance the tholos of the famous circular Temple of Aphrodite Euploia whom I am sure we would all have felt had guided our bark to her bower.

Slowly the view would resolve itself as we sailed ever closer. Finally, passing between the two moles of the Commercial Harbour the breadth of the city-scape would become clear, the white-grey marble walls ascending terrace upon terrace, their rusticated, purposely rough-hewn faces mottled with the light and shade of the high-angled sun creating what might appear to be a series of almost natural parallel rocky outcrops, tier upon tier up the mountain-side.

The wharfs around the harbour would be packed with ships where stevedores would be busy unloading their cargoes. At the focus of the city, the marble-clad isthmus would be full of people of all casts walking past the statues of the great figures of Knidos' former times, each elevated on a marble plinth. To the right would be the ranked seating of the harbour theatre, and, to the west of it and slightly behind, the triple insula of the lowest terrace with its *rustica* blocks, reached on either side by stepped streets, and on top of which was the magnificent façade of Knidos' most important Stoa, a row of almost ninety solidly carved Doric columns which rose dominantly over the lower city. The Stoa, heart of Knidos' international market, had been built by the great Knidian architect Sostratus, the same that designed and built the Pharos Lighthouse at Alexandria which had become one of the seven wonders of the ancient world. At the back of the Stoa, row behind row of terraces rose up the mountainside, each crowned with a pillared temple or civic building, backwards and further up to the break in slope. Higher, off to the left, and dominating the western city was Aphrodite's sanctuary, its high temple surrounded by an arbour of sweet-smelling trees.

The friezes of each of the buildings, painted in deep blues, reds and blacks surmounted the lighter colours of the fluted columns which they adorned, and were in turn roofed with red pan tiles. These formal, vertically designed and chromatically varied constructions would appear in total contrast to the wilder, geologically natural appearance of the horizontal blocked terrace facades on which they had been erected. It was an urban scene full of aesthetic beauty and of innate magnificence, undoubtedly one of the most stunning and admired urban vistas in the whole of the Classical world.

When the group I was with that day had absorbed the whole vision, imagining the city as it once had been, we would cross the isthmus, passing under the now old and gnarled tamarisk trees next to our one-time dig house and through the fields where we had once camped. We would climb up the mainland portion of the city, up the old stepped street, pausing at the Pink Temple before continuing up past the main cross street coming from the eastern gateway and up to the Round Temple, the Temple of Aphrodite, which would be the climax of our visit. Sitting on the steps leading up to the circular podium, I would rebuild the temple in their mind's eye, reminding them of the descriptions written by Pliny and Lucian. I would recall the magnificent likeness of the uncovered form of the beautiful figure of Phryne as Aphrodite Euploia, she of fair navigation, the scale of the statue, the gesture of the hand, the stories associated with her loveliness, and of the perfumed bower which surrounded her shrine. We would end by looking out over the sea to Tilos and to Kos, wrapped in a collective silent contemplation of the past.

Then unhurriedly we would descend the narrow path past the Corinthian Temple, past Eudoxus' sundial and the ruins of the monumental Stoa and Byzantine Church, and we would finish our walk sitting together on the topmost seats of the lower theatre overlooking the commercial harbour where I would recall performances of the Classical plays and the dramas of the past. After a while, as our visit came to an end, I would begin to recount to them some of the tales of old Knidos, and how my time here almost half a century earlier had undoubtedly been my finest hour, just as I have told you now, and how I had joined in looking for Aphrodite. Slowly and gradually the sun would sink in the west, and with it the stories would come to a close, fading away into the growing Carian dark.

The expedition was over.

MUSINGS AND ACKNOWLEDGEMENTS

In retrospect, I have found that time, the fourth dimension, doesn't really behave like the other three. It seems to be neither as rigid nor as predictable, but behaves in a rather pliable, more plastic manner. In the mind it can be moulded by the vicissitudes of memory and the need for order. It can be reduced to almost nothing by a wish to forget, or it can be extended to an eternity by a longing to remember. From my own recollection, getting on for half a century ago, the brief period I have described, actually an episode of only eleven weeks in south west Turkey, stands out as perhaps one of the most protracted, one of the most intense, experiences of my entire existence. In just eighty days, from July to September 1969, my whole life turned around, rotating on a cultural pivot which amongst other things transformed the gaucheness of my late adolescence into the beginnings of maturity.

Momentously, as you know, Man first landed on the moon during those same eighty days in 1969, but for me that was as nothing. I had simultaneously landed on another planet in another universe. In some ways I've been there ever since.

In this recollection, the years didn't just roll mistily back, nor did the amnesic clouds part to reveal some opaque, indistinct vision. For me, in some respects, time still vividly hovers in that one place, a whole epoch of animation derived from just over one thousand waking hours.

But was it really like that? Well, maybe! Some of the stories I have written here I have retold so often, where they happened, that by now I sometimes wonder if I haven't just made them up, merging truth and fiction. Or maybe they did happen, but to someone else. Has time flowed inwards into my memory or outwards from my imagination? Perhaps I can no longer differentiate the one from the other.

241

As I wrote, conversations came stuttering into life, unbidden, striking my screen like the self-impelled cursor of some old-fashioned telex machine, speaking about the chronological past but animated with all of today's vitality. I know the people speaking were real because I could hear them clearly and see their faces, unchanged with age. I smelled the dried flowers and the shovelled earth, and I tasted the 'lion's milk' again. I felt the wind and the heat, and I touched the very stones. These events did happen, they really did; if not quite in one way, then certainly in another.

There was such a clamour of voices – Ali, Mesut and Musafer, Mehmet and Birol, Cengis and Ruşan, Hakkı Bey, Cumhur, Süleyman, Hasan, Huseyn, Mumtaz and Osman, as well as all the others - so many others. To them, who launched me into my new trajectory, I owe my endless gratitude.

For all the others, some of whose names I seem to have altered and whose own lives I have mercilessly distorted to fit my preconceived ideas of what I thought had happened I apologise. These were some of the most remarkable moments in my life, and I can't change them now, even if they're wrong!

And to Iris, the catalyst without whom none of this would have taken place, I must extend my heart-felt appreciation for her kindness. I was but a very small cog in her huge machine.

I have also to thank my brother, '*Yr Hen Was*,' for his invaluable suggestions and corrections.

And to Jemma, thank you for remedying my abysmal written Turkish and for laughing in all the right places.

But most of all, to Sue, and to Alice and Daves, who have travelled foot-weary with me so many times along the paths of memory, these, as you know, are the Tales of Old Knidos I promised.

Map of South-Western Turkey and
the Dodecanese Islands (© DPW 2012)

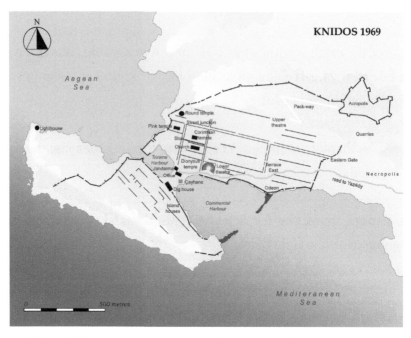

Plan of the excavations at Knidos in 1969 (© DPW 2012)

Sitting outside the Çayhane drinking rakı in 1969. Fenerci Mehmet is seated second from the left. Seated in the centre looking down is Cengis, and seated far right wearing a hat is Ali Kara Deniz. Standing behind Cengis is Mesut the Bekci, and behind Ali is Birol, Fenerci Mehmet's brother. Standing on the far right is Osman.

DPW and the Pink Temple crew, with Hasan the Sucu and Beyaz the Billygoat.

Top: The excavation of the Knidian Round Temple, 1969.
Left: Roman copy of the Praxiteles Aphrodite, British Museum.
Right: The Leconfield Head.

DPW levelling at the island site in 1969, with the mainland city in the background.

DPW surveying the Pink Temple in 1969.

Lightning Source UK Ltd.
Milton Keynes UK
UKOW07f0401050216